T0373932

QUEEN'S PARK

A HISTORY

STEVE CRABB

QUEEN'S PARK

A HISTORY

STEVE CRABB

The
History
Press

*This book is dedicated to my parents, Valerie and George Crabb,
who showed me how fascinating history can be.*

First published 2022

The History Press
97 St George's Place, Cheltenham,
Gloucestershire, GL50 3QB
www.thehistorypress.co.uk

© Steve Crabb, 2022

The right of Steve Crabb to be identified as the Author
of this work has been asserted in accordance with the
Copyright, Designs and Patents Act 1988.

All rights reserved. No part of this book may be reprinted
or reproduced or utilised in any form or by any electronic,
mechanical or other means, now known or hereafter invented,
including photocopying and recording, or in any information
storage or retrieval system, without the permission in writing
from the Publishers.

British Library Cataloguing in Publication Data.
A catalogue record for this book is available from the British Library.

ISBN 978 1 8039 9038 5

Typesetting and origination by The History Press
Printed and bound in Great Britain by TJ Books, Padstow, Cornwall.

MIX
Paper | Supporting
responsible forestry
FSC
www.fsc.org   FSC® C013056

Trees for LYfe

CONTENTS

ACKNOWLEDGEMENTS

The enthusiasm of local people for this project and their willingness to help has been wonderful. Space doesn't permit me to list all the people who were part of this, but I must thank my wife, Natasha, for her editing and endless encouragement; my children Ellie and Rhydian for their help with research; Adrian Hindle-Briscall for his amazing support, particularly on the mapping side of this project; local historians Alan Hovell, Dick Weindling and Irina Porter for their insights; Mansukhlal Hirani for giving me access to Salusbury School's archives; Lucy Parker and her colleagues at Brent Archives; Helen Durnford, Christine Maggs, Susan Rees and Anthony Molloy for the archive material they lent me, and all the local people who agreed to be interviewed for this book. Thank you all, and to everyone else who encouraged and supported me along the way. It's a privilege to live in a community that cares so much about its past, with such a collective spirit.

INTRODUCTION

Any history of Queen's Park needs to start with a definition of what we mean by 'Queen's Park' – where it is, what it is and even when it came to be.

This isn't as easy as you might think. After all, there's a tube and a rail station with the name, not to mention the eponymous park. The prosaic answer is that it's a district of London, around 4 miles from Charing Cross,[1] in north-west London in the Borough of Brent.

Search for Queen's Park on Google and you'll learn that Queen's Park is a family-friendly residential area with quiet streets of Victorian and Edwardian houses surrounding the park of the same name, home to a bandstand, flower gardens, and a playground with a paddling pool. Community hub Salusbury Road is lined with indie shops, gastropubs, cafes, and global eateries. The weekly Queen's Park Farmers' Market has organic vegetables, dairy products, and free-range meats.

Which is a pretty accurate description – even if it does leave out half the area.

In fact, the reputation of this little part of north-west London has spread to the point where the Boundary Commission was thinking about creating a new parliamentary constituency called Queen's Park and Regent's Park. Not only is Queen's Park now as famous as Regent's Park, it takes precedence![2]

But try ordering anything online using an NW6 6 address and you'll be told you either live in Kilburn or Kensal Rise. The postal system doesn't recognise the existence

---

1   Charing Cross is the spot from which all London distances are measured. When you see a motorway sign saying 'this many miles to London', it really means 'this many miles to Charing Cross', not 'this many miles to the edge of Greater London'.

2   https://boundarycommissionforengland.independent.gov.uk/wp-content/uploads/2016/08/Queens-Park-and-Regents-Park-BC.pdf

of Queen's Park as an area. The local Anglican parish is called St Anne's Brondesbury with Holy Trinity Kilburn – not a park in sight.

This isn't helped by the fact that the boundaries of Queen's Park are surprisingly fluid. According to the Queen's Park Area Residents' Association (QPARA), Queen's Park stretches from the mainline railway out of Euston in the south to the London Overground railway in the north, and from Chamberlayne Road in the west to Donaldson Road in the east. This makes sense as it matches the limits of the local government ward of Queen's Park (Brent), although in fact that has now been extended all the way to the Harrow Road, far into Kensal Green.

And very confusingly, there is another, older, Queen's Park immediately to the south, in the Borough of Westminster, with its own history and character. It's no coincidence that the two share a common name.

So Queen's Park fluctuates from being a community with a very clear definition in time and space, to one that swells and ebbs, to one that doesn't appear on some maps at all.

In one sense this is because Queen's Park is a comparatively recent concept: until the late 1950s, few people called this district Queen's Park. Most people would have said they either lived in West Kilburn (sending their sons to Kilburn Grammar, borrowing books from Kilburn Library and reporting crimes at Kilburn Police Station, all of which are squarely in what we now call Queen's Park), or that they lived in Kensal Rise. The destination on the front of the No. 36 bus used to be 'West Kilburn', not Queen's Park as it now is – even though the bus's route is exactly the same.

From the Middle Ages (as far back as the Norman Conquest), the area was split between three different manors. Until the 1960s, the streets east and west of the park had different councillors. And until the 1970s, Queen's Park was split between two Church of England parishes, with the dividing line running down Kingswood Avenue.

Far from being the unifying heart of the community, the park itself has historically served as the dividing line between two thriving communities, each centred on their own vibrant high streets, Salusbury Road and Chamberlayne Road respectively, each with its own state primary school.

'Queen's Park' has been used by some people, some of the time, to signify a community (as well as a park) for most of its recorded history. In the 1930s, a Pathé newsreel showing a fire on Salusbury Road refers to 'Queen's Park, Kilburn'. Some First World War soldiers from the area gave their address as Queen's Park, although most said they were from Kensal, Brondesbury or West Kilburn. But these references were sporadic and fairly inconsistent. Queen's Park as we know it today was largely the brainchild of local estate agents, keen to rebrand a district they thought had the potential to become more upmarket. It took decades, but it has been a spectacularly successful reinvention.

But in another sense the estate agents took the area back to its original roots. Because the park – Queen's Park – came first. Before any houses were built in the area, and when Chamberlayne Road and Salusbury Road were farm tracks and the other future roads of the area just mud and grass, Queen's Park stood alone and proud in a landscape of wheat and skylarks, surrounded by a picket fence, waiting for the people who would inevitably give it meaning.

For the purposes of this book, I will use the Queen's Park Area Residents' Association (QPARA) definition of Queen's Park – the land between the railway lines to the north and south, Chamberlayne Road to the west and Willesden Lane/Donaldson Road to the east. I will, though, meander along the way through Kilburn, Kensal Rise, Brondesbury and over the railway lines into the 'Queen's Park estate' (in the Borough of Westminster), as it is impossible to tell the story of one without the others.

Personally, I have come to the conclusion that Queen's Park should include the land between the railway lines and Kilburn Lane, and the section of Salusbury Road between the Falcon pub and Queen's Park Station. This was an intrinsic part of the area before it was sliced off by the railways. In fact, it was the only place locally where people lived from medieval times, working the farms on the north side of Kilburn Lane, or 'Flowerhills Lane' as it was known in the past. Queen's Park is incomplete without it.

The area is very obviously divided into three zones: one east of Salusbury Road, one between Salusbury Road and the park, and one west of the park. It was only when I studied the ancient manorial boundaries of this area that I realised that this division isn't a recent accident of history: it dates back over a thousand years, when the land west of Milman Road was in 'Chambers' manor, the land east of Salusbury in 'Bounds' and the bit in the middle in 'Brands'. If Queen's Park were a Tuscan hill town, we'd call these districts *contadas* and celebrate them each year with the *contadas* competing in horse racing or barrel-rolling competitions. I think we should go further and admit a fourth *contada* of 'Flowerhills'. Finally building a footbridge over the railway to make it easier for the residents of 'Flowerhills' to reach the park (a project that's been discussed for well over a century) would be another symbolic act. Queen's Park (as in the actual park) only exists today because of the campaigns mounted by people who lived south of the railway lines. The least we could do in return is make it easier for our southern neighbours to reach it.[1]

In the course of writing this book, I have discovered, and grown fond of, some fascinating characters I wasn't aware of before – Violet Doudney, the trainee teacher and dedicated Suffragette who bravely threw a metal weight wrapped in paper saying 'Votes for Women' through the window of the Home Secretary's house, knowing she'd be gaoled for it; Reginald Johns, the First World War fighter pilot ace who was

---

1   I don't think it's a coincidence that the three zones of Queen's Park match the medieval boundaries. I'll return to this later.

loved by his comrades for his infectious, absurdist sense of humour and basic decency; the 8-year-old Jewish refugee children who came on the Kindertransport and enrolled at Salusbury School. My admiration for characters I thought I knew, like Solomon Barnett, has grown and deepened the more I've learnt about them.

I've also had to reappraise others about whom I had previously made quick judgments: I had no idea that Reg Freeson, our former MP and a man I knew personally, essentially saved Queen's Park from demolition, or that Charles Pinkham, the fearsome councillor, magistrate and MP of the Edwardian era, had such a quick sense of humour. I discovered artists, writers, musicians and actors who helped shape Queen's Park as we know it today, any one of whom could fill a whole book. I hope you'll enjoy getting to know these characters as much as I did.

I've learnt more about the racism, sexism and other forms of bigotry that were an overt and ugly part of everyday lives for many people in Queen's Park for most of its history, and that continue today in (mostly) more hidden forms.

I've also seen a 'golden thread' of compassion for refugees and people fleeing persecution that has run through the history of this area since the very first days, when Jewish people fleeing racism and economic hardship helped build this area and made their home here. It continued with the welcome the area gave Belgian refugees in the First World War, the shelter Jewish children received when they arrived on the Kindertransports in the 1930s, the work that Salusbury World has done for refugee children from around the world since 1999 and at the time of writing, the fundraising that local children are doing for people in war-torn Ukraine.

I hope you'll enjoy reading about how Queen's Park came to take shape – literally and figuratively – as much as I did researching and writing it.

Steve Crabb
March 2022

SECTION 1

THE HUNDRED
ACRE WOOD

For most of recorded history, the land that is now the area of Queen's Park was a 100-acre wooded hill, gently sloping down towards the River Thames, devoid of any buildings and visited only by foraging pigs and the odd wood-gathering local. Queens and great nobles passed close by, ownership of the land was contested by important families and human development expanded in every direction, but the woodland kept itself to itself, unperturbed by the history swirling around it. Chapters 1 and 2 will therefore tell the story of Queen's Park largely through development of the villages and roads that surround it, framing the future community of this corner of north-west London.

Manor of Chambers
a Upper Hill Field
b Three Acre Field
c Twelve Acres Field
d Bean Field
e Ploughed Field

Manor of Brands
f Little Kiln Field
g Great Kiln Field
h Butchers Leaze
i Upper Brands Wood Close
j Lower Brands Wood Close
k Woodfield Close

Manor of Bounds
l Winter Leaze
m Little Rough Field
n Kilburn Meade

Mapes Lane is now Willesden Lane
Flowerhills Lane was the name given to Kilburn Lane near the present Queen's Park
Kilburn High Road was known as **Edgware Road** before Kilburn was built up.

This map, created for this book by Adrian Hindle-Briscall, shows the manor boundaries (the thicker lines), field boundaries and major roads and farm tracks as they were in 1816. The railways, Queen's Park and Paddington Cemetery have been added for context. This is drawn from multiple maps and illustrations from the nineteenth century. Adrian Hindle-Briscall

1

THE DEEP PAST

It's not easy to read London's landscape today, since so much of it is covered with buildings. Underneath all the brick, slate and concrete though, there are gently undulating hills and valleys that were shaped millions of years ago.

Queen's Park is no exception; it reveals its secrets if you look closely enough. Although much of the area may look flat, the land rises steeply south to north as it heads up to the peak of the Brondesbury Ridge at Mount Pleasant. The highest point in Queen's Park is the corner of Chevening and Salusbury Roads, just below Brondesbury Park station, at approximately 49m above sea level. The lowest point is the corner of Brondesbury Villas and Woodville Road, nearly 20m lower. Although the north–south gradient is clear and consistent, east to west is more complicated. At the top of the park, on Chevening Road, the land declines gently between Salusbury and Peploe Roads, then rises again as it approaches Chamberlayne Road. At the bottom of the park, Harvist Road looks flat enough to have been laid out by the Romans, but there's actually a 3.5m difference between the west and east ends of Harvist road. You can trace this in the rooflines of avenues like Montrose and Summerfield, which are stepped to accommodate the falling ground. There's even a small hillock on the south side of Harvist opposite the old Lych Gate entrance to the park. The number of steps up to the front doors suddenly increases, and drops off again just as quickly. The small mounds in the park itself at the bottom end and east of the bandstand are modern creations though: spoil heaps left from the excavation of land drains to prevent flooding.

This undulating landscape is topped with a thin layer of loamy soil, and underneath that is the London Clay. Next time you pass deep roadworks or a basement extension in progress, take a moment to look at the blue-grey clay, deposited in the London basin 50 million years ago at the bottom of what was then a tropical sea. The teeth of giant sharks that once swam above our heads were found in the clay in Islington. If you are lucky, you might find the fossilised remains of a palm tree. On sites between Chamberlayne and Salusbury roads, you are bound to find some of the tons of broken bricks that were poured into the liquid mud in 1879. I live in hope of one day finding a long-lost pocket watch or Victorian penny, but so far the clay has held fast to its treasures.

At its deepest, the London Clay runs to a depth of 150m (492ft), providing a secure bed for tube lines like the Bakerloo, which emerges from the darkness at Queen's Park. The clay's capacity for expanding and shrinking according to the weather is prodigious, which is why London had few skyscrapers until new building techniques were invented relatively recently.

In this part of north-west London, the clay is 330ft deep. Below that there's 12ft of sand and pebbles, and underneath that, chalk and flints.

The London Stock bricks that most of Queen's Park is built with are moulded from London Clay, probably produced at the brickworks at the top of Chamberlayne Road. Fine though the houses, shops and public buildings of Queen's Park are, we are still living in homes made of baked mud with roofs of wood and stone that would not have been entirely unfamiliar to our ancestors millennia ago.

The first humans arrived in Britain around 800,000 years ago. If they visited Queen's Park, they left no traces that have yet been discovered. For most of the period since then, humans have been playing a cat and mouse game with the environment, occupying Britain and retreating again when the weather turned foul. Half a million years ago, in the Pleistocene ice age, gigantic glaciers over a mile from top to bottom edged south as far as the M25, diverting the Thames from its old course through Hertfordshire into its current channel and carving out the valley of the River Brent. It's only in the last 10,000 years – a mere blink of the historical eye – that humans have permanently occupied this land. However, it's not too fanciful to think that prehistoric humans hunted and gathered here: flint tools from the Lower Paleolithic (from 2.5 million years ago to 200,000) were found in Dollis Hill,[1] while both Acton and Hampstead Heath are rich in Stone Age remains.

Around 4,000 BC, settled farming replaced the hunter-gatherer way of life. The first surviving written description of Britain, by the Greek traveller and explorer Pytheas of Messalia (around 320 BC), says the people were farmers who lived in thatched cottages and were ruled by kings who lived in peace with each other. David Miles (former Chief Archaeologist for English Heritage) describes how the Lower Thames Valley was intensively settled and farmed during this period, with defended enclosures dominating 'each block of intensively exploited land'.[2] It may be that the heavy clay soil of

---

1   www.brent.gov.uk/media/16403320/summary-of-archaeological-excavations.pdf
2   Miles, *The Tribes of Britain*, p.96.

Queen's Park was less attractive to prehistoric farmers than the free-draining gravel higher up the valley, but Brent Council's 1988 archaeological survey of the area notes that 'there are settlements of one or more periods on all the ... hills in the area',[3] so perhaps there were farmers in Queen's Park, protected by a long-vanished hill fort. *The London Encyclopaedia* identifies the Brondesbury Ridge just above Queen's Park as the possible location of such a fort.[4]

Queen's Park is part of the only London borough whose name dates back to pre-Roman times: Brent. The borough is named after the River Brent, a tributary of the Thames that rises in the Borough of Barnet and flows in a south-west direction before joining the Tideway stretch of the Thames at Brentford. The river's name means either 'high' or 'holy' in the Common Brittonic tongue – the ancestor of modern Welsh, Cornish and Breton – which was once spoken throughout Britain.

---

3 www.brent.gov.uk/media/16403320/summary-of-archaeological-excavations.pdf
4 *The London Encyclopaedia*, p.104.

2

FROM THE ROMANS
TO THE GEORGIANS

At the dawn of the historical era, when the Greeks and Romans first began to record the history of Britain, two well-established highways passed close by Queen's Park: the Edgware Road and the Harrow Road, as we know them today. Bronze Age remains have been found near the places where these roads crossed the River Brent: funeral urns dating back to between 1800 BC and 600 BC were discovered at the Welsh Harp reservoir, where the Edgware Road meets the Brent, and a hoard of axes was found near where the Harrow Road crosses the Brent at Stonebridge.[1]

Streams and rivers were of great symbolic importance in pre-Roman British culture, often being used to deposit items of great value as offerings, and this area is surrounded by running water. The Westbourne rises on the Brondesbury Ridge above Queen's Park before running down to Kilburn, where it meets other tributaries from Hampstead, crossing the High Road by West End Lane and then flowing down to the Serpentine via Kilburn Park Road. One branch started around Willesden Lane, running down through the grounds of today's Paddington Cemetery and feeding ponds in the Queen's Park area before joining the main river south of Kilburn Lane. Most winters, the ghosts of these ponds reappear on the eastern side of the park, despite multiple attempts to eliminate them.

To the north and west, the River Brent follows a line now copied by the North Circular before joining the Thames at Brentford. Counter's Creek rises in the magnificently Victorian Kensal Green Cemetery (within walking distance of Queen's Park) and heads due south to Fulham. All of these 'lost rivers' have now been forced under-

---

1 www.brent.gov.uk/media/16403320/summary-of-archaeological-excavations.pdf

ground into culverts and storm drains for most of their course, and the only votive offerings the River Brent receives is the odd shopping trolley, but they have not been vanquished – they will carry on pushing against our attempts to contain them, until one or the other concedes.

Roman Rule

By the time the Romans arrived, regional kingdoms had developed. Julius Caesar noted that what is now outer north-west London and Hertfordshire was ruled by the 'Cassi' when he invaded Britain in 55 and 54 BC. They were a rich and powerful tribe whose leader Cassivellaunus led resistance to the Romans. When the Romans returned in AD 43, the tribe again provided stiff opposition under their leader Caratacus.

Among the many remarkable things that Julius Caesar noted about the locals was their use of war chariots (a weapon that was considered archaic by that time in most of the ancient world) and their love of animals: hares, geese and other fowl were sacred to them. He also described how they liked to cover themselves in woad (a blue dye extracted from plants), giving them a terrible appearance in battle. The word 'Britain' probably comes from the word 'Pretani', meaning 'painted ones' or 'tattooed ones'. 'Picts' has the same origin.

The Romans made a lasting impression on this part of London by 'metalling' (meaning they paved it with small pieces of gravel overlaid with flints) the Edgware Road, which they called 'the Second Route'. Surviving stretches of the road are between 7.5 and 8.5m wide. When you consider that the average Roman chariot was around 1.5m wide, that's the equivalent of a four-lane highway with space for a central reservation.

According to the Roman writers Tacitus and Dio, Boudica and her army travelled up the Second Route on their way back from torching much of London in AD 60. Although their estimate of the size of her army (230,000!) is an obvious exaggeration for polemical purposes, they must have made an impressive sight for any proto-residents of Queen's Park as they marched past with their booty-laden carts and war chariots.

Despite the charming remains of what some locals believe to be a Roman fort opposite Kilburn's Royal Mail sorting office, there's little evidence of permanent Roman settlement in the area. The 'fort', it turns out, was the imaginative creation of a local stonemason in the 1970s.[2] The nearest place to Queen's Park where any Roman remains have been found is Neasden.

---

2   https://twitter.com/lifeinkilburn/status/1161339959934107649

The Middle Ages

Over time, recognisable villages developed in an arc around Queen's Park. Neasden ('Nose-Shaped Hill') and Harlesden (probably 'Herewulf's Farmstead') are both mentioned in a ship's register around AD 1000. Willesden ('Hill of the Spring') appears in the Domesday Book of 1086. Kilburn (either 'Cow Stream' or 'Royal Stream' depending on your preference) isn't recorded until 1134 and Kensal ('King's Wood') not until 1253.

In a charter dated from the year 939 (now widely regarded as an eleventh-century forgery), King Athelstan supposedly granted ten manors in this area to the monks of St Erconwald's Monastery, which later became St Paul's Cathedral (which is how the council maisonettes called Athelstan Gardens on Willesden Lane got their name 1,000 years later). However they came about it, the monks of St Paul's certainly owned extensive property in the area by the time of the Norman Conquest. Much of the land to the south, on the other hand, was controlled by the monks of Westminster Abbey.

In 1086, the Domesday Book records that the hamlet of Willesden was owned by the canons of St Paul's and had a population of twenty-five villagers and five smallholders. Surrounding woodlands contained 500 pigs and the land was worked by eight plough teams. Harlesden (also owned by St Paul's) had twenty-two villagers, 2.5 plough teams and 100 pigs in nearly woods.[1] Between them and the third population centre in Willesden – Twyford – they account for around 2,800 acres of land that the Domesday surveyors could put a value on, out of a total land area of 5,000 acres. The rest, according to local historian Len Snow, will have been 'wasteland, marsh and common-land not identified with any particular ownership'.[2] This included the Great Marsh and the Little Marsh, where the Mitchel Brook still flows off Brentfield Road today.

St Mary's Church in Willesden is the oldest church in north-west London, supposedly dating back to Athelstan's grant of land to the monks of St Erconwald's in 939. The first documentary reference to it is from 1181, and the oldest surviving fragments of the building (a font and part of a window) date from that period. It is built on the site of a holy well – almost certainly the spring on the hill that gives Willesden its name – and may well have been a sacred site from pre-Christian times.

An audit of the church in 1249 refers to two large sculpted images of the Virgin Mary, and by the 1500s we know that the Black Madonna of Willesden was attracting pilgrims. The wife of Henry VII, Elizabeth of York, paid a pilgrim to visit the church in 1502 and Sir Thomas More visited it.[3,4] At a distance of just 7 miles from

---

1   https://opendomesday.org/book/middlesex/03
2   Snow, *Willesden Past*.
3   www.thetablet.co.uk/blogs/1/1440/canterbury-walsingham-and-willesden-4
4   https://andrewpink.org/2017/04/17/willesden

central London, the round trip to the shrine could easily be done in a day, making it very attractive for time-strapped penitents and a handy alternative to Canterbury or Walsingham until the shrine was destroyed in the Reformation in 1538. It was, however, a dangerous journey: the local woods were known as a haunt of bandits.

Willesden Lane (also known as Mapes Lane) must have connected Watling Street with the village of Willesden since at least the 1100s, bringing developments right to the edge of Queen's Park. Kilburn Lane (also known as Flowerhills Lane for part of its course) is also very old. It started at the junction of the Harrow Road and today's Ladbroke Grove, and ended on Kilburn High Road near the start of West End Lane. Presumably it was part of a bigger communication system, possibly extending up to Hampstead.

Two other major changes occurred during the later medieval period: the beginnings of development in Kilburn, and the spread of the manorial system in Willesden.

At the time of Domesday (1086), there is no record of any occupation along the stretch of Watling Street now occupied by Kilburn High Road. Sometime before 1134, a hermit called Godwin set up his own religious establishment near the crossing point of the Kilburn stream (then called the Cuneburna) and the main road, near today's Belsize Road. Godwin transferred the hermitage and adjoining fields first to the abbot and monks of Westminster Abbey, and then to a trio of Augustinian nuns, reportedly named Christina, Gunilde and Emma. The resulting priory, dedicated to St John the Baptist, survived for 402 years, until it was dissolved by Henry VIII and its lands given to the Knights of St John. According to Edward Walford's *Old and New London*,[5] the priory lands covered 45 acres, or half as much space again as today's Queen's Park (the park, not the district).

Little is known about the history of Kilburn Priory other than that the establishment was so hard-up during the time of Edward III that the nuns were granted a dispensation from paying taxes. The importance of this lies in the reason why the king showed such generosity: the priory ministered to the needs of travellers, and above all to pilgrims on their way to St Albans (and no doubt to Willesden too). We know the priory had a *hostium* (guesthouse), probably on the site of the current Red Lion public house. The Old Bell public house on the other side of Belsize Road (and now on the other side of the railway lines too), is supposed to be the site of another part of the priory complex, which in total consisted of a church, hall, brewhouse, bakehouse, buttery, pantry, cellar, larder-house and various accommodations. The Old Cock, further up Kilburn High Road, also claims to have held a licence since 1486. By the end of the Middle Ages, Kilburn was clearly becoming an important rest stop on the way into and out of London, if not a go-to entertainment destination in its own right.

---

5   Walford, *Old and New London: Vol. 5*, p.243.

In the rural hinterland of Willesden, the division of the land into manors acceler-ated in the early 1100s under Bishop Maurice of London (1085–1107), when the parish was sub-divided into eight 'prebends' (a prebendary being a canon of St Paul's who was given a specific manor to manage). The key ones in this case were Brondesbury (or Brands, or Brownswood), named after a canon named Brand; Chamberlain Wood, or Chambers, named after canon Richard de Camera (Richard of the Chamber); and the manor of Willesden (also known as Bounds). This area was split between all three. Chambers included all of Queen's Park west of Peploe Road (approximately – the boundary snakes through the gardens between Peploe and Milman), Brands everything between Salusbury and Peploe (today's Salusbury Road was the manor boundary), and Bounds all the land east of Salusbury. The most notable prebend of Bounds manor was the Archbishop of Canterbury, Roger Walden, in 1397.

Some of these prebends were managed from substantial manor houses; Brondesbury's stood until the twentieth century. Willesden/Bounds' more modest manor house was demolished in 1825. Mapes also had a significant manor house, on Willesden Lane (which is why it was also called Mapes Lane). It also survived until the twentieth century. The Chambers estate was smaller and doesn't seem to have had a manor house as such.

The freeholds to this land were owned by St Paul's until 1840, when all the church land in Willesden was transferred to the Ecclesiastical Commissioners. The one excep-tion was a period between the end of the English Civil War and the Restoration, when the land was sold off by the victorious Roundheads. However, it wasn't managed by the church; tenants leased and worked the land.

In the early 1400s, a substantial amount of land in the Kensal area (west and south of today's district of Queen's Park) was sold to Thomas Chichele, Archbishop of Canterbury from 1414 to 1443. He used this to endow All Soul's College, Oxford, which he founded the year he died – hence Chichele Road, All Soul's Avenue, College Road and the continuing involvement of the college in the life of the community even to this day. When Brent Council closed Kensal Rise Library in 2012, the prop-erty reverted to the college, which leased it out on condition that space for a library is provided rent-free for 999 years.

Early Modern Times

When Elizabeth of York, Henry VII's queen and the mother of Henry VIII, sent an emissary to pray for her at the shrine of Our Lady of Willesden in 1502, he would have travelled on dirt tracks through a sparsely populated landscape dotted with the occasional small village or farmstead. By 1547 there were around 240 communicants in the parish of Willesden (ie people old enough to take communion in church, which at that time was between the ages of 14 and 16), so the total population can't have been much above 600.

Edward Harvist

Edward Harvist, after whom Harvist Road is named, was a London brewer and grocer, who was clearly a very successful businessman. In 1601 he bought a 20-acre package of land in Islington, described as 'two closes or parcels of meadows called London Fields', just above today's Emirates Stadium, and the following year he bought the manor of Thriplowe in Cambridgeshire from Queen Elizabeth for the sum of £1,162 and 10s.

On his death in 1610 he bequeathed his Islington property in trust to the Brewers' Company, on condition that they used the income to maintain Watling Street from Tyburn (Marble Arch) to Edgware, including the 1.1 miles of the Kilburn High Road. This legacy is still managed by a charity, The Edward Harvist Trust, which gives grants to organisations in Barnet, Brent, Camden, Harrow and the City of London for the benefit of children, young people and the elderly through the promotion of health and well-being, arts, culture, science and sport, and poverty relief.

The land that would eventually become Queen's Park would still have been at this time a mixture of pasture and woodland, the latter supporting a population of pigs and providing local people with whatever fungi, fruit or firewood they could harvest by hand (thought to be the origin of the phrase 'by hook or by crook').[1]

This was no wilderness, however. A series of beautiful maps were made for All Souls College in 1597 by Thomas Langdon on behalf of Robert Hovendon, the master of the college; they show the college's holdings in the Queen's Park area in incredible detail.

From these maps we can see that roads that still exist today were already there: Chambers Lane was there and named, as was Shoot-up Hill (where the Kilburn High Road starts to rise towards Cricklewood); what is now the Harrow Road was called 'London Waye'. Kilburn Lane is also visible; south of today's Queen's Park, where the Queen's Park Estate in Westminster (see Chapter 5) now stands, was a field called Flowerhills, and that that was the section of Kilburn Lane called Flowerhills Lane.

From these sixteenth-century maps we can see the name of every plot of land and the individual hedges that enclosed the fields. South of Kilburn Lane were Turnors (sic) Fields (both Great and Little), Bushefielde in Chelsey and the aforementioned Flowerhilles in Chelsey, and the wood of Bushefielde's Grove. West of Chambers

---

1   Snow, *Willesden Past*, p.12.

Lane were Highe Fielde, Ponde Fielde, Brooke Fielde and Long Reddinge.[1] There were small woods south of Kilburn Lane and up in Kensal Rise.

Thanks to the notebooks of the Victorian antiquarian FA Woods, who wrote up ancient charters in the archives of St Paul's Cathedral by hand, we can also identify the boundaries of the fields that covered Queen's Park in Tudor and Stuart times, and even name them. I have been able to identify the name of a long-forgotten track that ran through the middle of the area, linking Brondesbury Manor with Kilburn Lane: it was called Long Cross Lane (see map, p.14). The lower part of the park was a field called 'Butchers Leaze', the northern part was 'Great Kiln Field'.

These names were settled by the 1640s, and their names and boundaries changed very little between then and the time they were built over. The field where Woodville Road runs today was called 'Tanners Meade' in 1649 and 'Kilburn Meade' in 1840. 'Great Kiln Field' in 1840 was 'Great Keelefield' in the 1640s.

Long Cross Lane cut through the park on the eastern side. An ancient gnarled tree in the park, today surrounded by a protective metal fence, was part of the hedgerow than ran alongside the lane. When the park was first built, many more of these trees were still standing from both sides of the lane, and some of them survived until at least the 1950s. The bandstand sits in the middle of the route of the old lane – I am absolutely certain this was done as an intentional tribute to the ancient path.

We also know the names of all the tenants, from the 1100s to the point when the farmland was finally built over. The first recorded prebend of Chambers manor, from 1088, was called Robert de Lymeses. The first listed prebend of Bounds was a priest called Uctred. We don't know the date when he took charge of the property, but we do know that in 1115 it was handed over to Hugh, son of Generus. Brands manor first appears in the history books in 1104, when a priest called Ailwardus Ruffus was made prebendary.

By 1538, the area of Brondesbury (just north of Queen's Park) had a moated manor house, tenanted by a succession of absentee landlords and local gentlemen farmers. A family called Marsh worked the land from the early 1600s, and bought the freehold from the Cromwellian government in 1649. Although they had to hand the freehold back when the Stuarts were restored to power, they retained the leasehold until 1749.[2]

Bounds (or Willesden) manor was more modest in scope than Brondesbury and never had anything as fine as a moated manor house. Its nerve centre was a brick farmhouse known variously as Willesden Manor House, Kilburn Farm or Bounds Farm, down by where Kilburn Park tube station is today, between Cambridge Avenue and Oxford Road. It was leased to a wide range of tenants in the Tudor and Stuart periods, including City of London distiller John Heath (1694) and Southwark brewer Sir John Lade (1737).

1   http://library.asc.ox.ac.uk/hovenden/hovenden.php
2   www.british-history.ac.uk/vch/middx/vol7/pp208-216

During the Interregnum after the Civil War, the freehold to the land was sold off, like Brondesbury, this time to a Willesden yeoman called Ezechiel Tanner.

The manor of Chambers was the smallest of them all, and never had anything remotely approaching a manor house. It did, though, have a manorial farm: what became known as Chamberlain Wood Farm, on the north side of Kilburn Lane where the Noko building and Banister Road (named after its last tenant farmer) stand today. As the land would have needed working from the earliest days of the manor in the 1100s, and this is the only logical place for a manor farm (it would have needed to be by a road so the produce of the farm could be taken out and supplies brought in, and Kilburn Lane was the only road that crossed the manor until the twentieth century), it's reasonable to assume that today's district of Queen's Park has been continuously occupied for a millennium, and this is where our predecessors lived. A survey of the manor by the Church of England in the 1840s describes Chamberlain Wood Farm as 'ancient'.

During the Stuart era, Chambers manor was in the hands of the Roberts family, who bought the freehold as well during the Cromwellian fire sale.

Although the land was well managed, it continued to be sparsely populated throughout the Tudor, Stuart and Georgian eras. By 1831, there were still only 358 houses in the entire parish, and Willesden was attracting artists keen to paint rural idylls, including George Morland, Paul Sandby and Julius Caesar Ibbetson.[3]

In Kilburn, there were just ten houses and five cottages along the whole of Kilburn High Road and Shoot-up Hill by 1646. When a 'medicinal' well was discovered in 1714 down near the site of the old priory,[4] pleasure gardens were laid out, competing with fashionable spas such as Sadler's Wells (1693) and Hampstead Wells (1698). The water was described as 'a mild purgative, milky in appearance [with] a bitterish taste. It was said to be more strongly impregnated with carbon dioxide than any other spring in England'[5] and to be 'good against all scorbutic humours, blotches, redness and pimples in the face, for inflammation of the eyes and all impurities of the skin'.[6]

Joseph Wyld quotes the following 'panegyric' from an unnamed eighteenth-century magazine:

Where sweet sequestered scenes inspire delight,
And simple Nature joins with every art;
At Kilburn Wells their various charms unite,
And gladly all conspire to please the heart.[7]

3   www.british-history.ac.uk/vch/middx/vol7/pp182-204#anchorn14
4   www.british-history.ac.uk/vch/middx/vol9/pp47-51
5   *The London Encyclopaedia*, pp. 431–432.
6   Snow, *Willesden Past*, p.10.
7   Wyld, *The London and Birmingham Railway Guide*, p.9.

However, the spa did not stimulate the development of Kilburn the way that Hampstead's did; by 1762 there were still only ten houses on the high road, the number of cottages had increased from five to seven, and there was now a tollgate down by the Old Bell pub and a blacksmith's, plus several other public houses.[1] Very little had changed in 120 years – serious development in Kilburn only really began in the 1820s.

In the hinterland, the remaining woodland was gradually being cleared in order to grow wheat and then, from the 1700s onwards, hay.

In 1788, Brondesbury Manor was bought by Lady Sarah Salusbury, along with the manor of Bounds, uniting everything east of Peploe Road under one management. The Salusbury name is Welsh, and not a misspelling of Salisbury as is often thought. Sarah's late husband, Sir Thomas Salusbury, had been a judge in the Admiralty high court. She had the manor house remodelled in fashionable Gothic style, commissioning designs from William Wilkins, architect of the National Gallery, while the acres of walled parkland were laid out by the famous landscape designer Humphrey Repton, who produced one of his celebrated 'Red Books' for the project. The new estate was named 'Brondesbury Park'. The house stood where Manor House Drive sits today; the grand entrance was on Willesden Lane, with the aforementioned service road (Brands Causeway) linking it with Willesden Green for the use of servants and tradespeople. All that remains of the estate today is its orchard, which is in the grounds of today's Malorees School. The manor house became a girl's school before being demolished in the 1930s.

The land where the district of Queen's Park is now was all pasture for cows in this era, apart from a small section of arable land down in the south-east corner. The land on the Brondesbury estate was managed by Bounds Farm, down by Kilburn High Road, and Brondesbury Lower Farm, on the north side of Kilburn Lane (also known later as Higgins' Dairy Farm). The Lower Farm was next door to Chamberlain Wood Farm, which looked after the Chambers estate for its leaseholders, the Godfrey family from Paddington (1755–1823) and the Harpers (1823–60). The cows of the area produced much of the milk consumed by West London, according to petitioners opposed to the construction of Paddington Cemetery.

Meanwhile, the last of the common land in Willesden was being appropriated by wealthy families and parcelled up into fields and building plots, thanks to legislation that allowed landowners (often aiming to maximise rental from their estates) to lay legal claim to land that had previously been shared by a local community. The Enclosure Acts passed by Parliament (as the result of lobbying by landowners) between 1760 and 1870 transformed 7 million acres (about one sixth the area of England) of common land to enclosed, privately owned land. Millions of people had

---

1 www.british-history.ac.uk/vch/middx/vol9/pp47-51

their customary access to lands – where their livestock could graze or they could col-lect firewood, or cut turf, for example – stripped from them, depriving them of their livelihoods and driving many to the developing cities to find work. Landscapes that had lain unchanged for centuries were altered almost beyond recognition.

Around 800 acres in total were privatised in this way across the manors of Brondesbury, Mapesbury, Chamberlayne and Willesden, which surround modern-day Queen's Park.

In the 1800s, the population of Willesden finally began to grow, doubling between 1801 and 1821 from 750 to over 1,400. This was just the start of things to come.

SECTION 2

DEFINING
QUEEN'S PARK

The boundaries of today's Queen's Park were established in a forty-year period between the 1830s and the 1870s. To the north and south, the area is defined by railway lines; in the east and west, roads do the work. But the boundary roads of Queen's Park only join up convenient crossing points on the railways. The railways came first; they are the reason there is a park in Queen's Park, and they still define the area today, for good and for ill: they are a magnet for new residents looking for a home with great transport links, but also the source of the traffic bottlenecks that blight the area.

3

THE COMING
OF THE RAILWAYS

At the start of the 1830s, the final decade of the Georgian era, the fields of today's
Queen's Park were surrounded by country lanes, the land used for pasture for animals.
Although the sprawl of London was beginning to spread and engulf surrounding vil-
lages, this part of Middlesex was still deeply rural.

But change was coming.

The London and Birmingham Railway Company was established in 1830 –
following the success of George Stephenson's Liverpool and Manchester line – to
build a railway linking the capital and England's second city. Stephenson senior passed
on the opportunity to build the line, but recommended his son Robert to do the job.

Disgruntled landowners who owned property along the route initially opposed the
development and were successful in getting the first Bill for the new railway voted down
in Parliament in 1832. Surveyors mapping out the course of the new line often had a
tough time from the locals. Thomas Roscoe reports that even if 'he be not an opponent,
but happen to have had a bad digestion, or his bilious organs disturbed from any cause
whatever, he warns them off his land, and they are left to make their survey how they
can, while the measure in question, no matter how advantageous to the public, is put in
jeopardy through the want of one or two of Abernethy's blue pills'.[1]

One clergyman was such an irritant; the surveyors had to hide in the bushes until
he departed for church to deliver his Sunday sermon before descending on his property in force to get their measurements done.

---

1 Roscoe, *The London and Birmingham Railway, with the Home and Country Scenes on Each Side of the Line*,
   p.13.

In the end, the company increased the amount of compensation on the table and tweaked the route, and the new Bill was passed in 1833. Construction started the same year, with an average of 10,000 men working on the construction of the line at any given time by 1836 and 12,000 by 1837. The line officially opened to passengers between Euston and Hemel Hempstead on 20 July 1837, one month to the day after the death of the last Georgian king, William IV, and the start of the Victorian era.

Parliamentary approval did not end the company's problems, however; landowners were remarkably ingenious in their compensation claims. One demanded compensation for the damage that the railway would do to his land. When the company returned to buy an additional plot from him a few months later, he demanded even more money on the grounds that the railway had improved his land so much that it was now worth a lot more than before!

A Mr Charles Brett went to court seeking compensation for the damage the railway would do to his land in Willesden, which would be cut in two by the line. He had been planning to construct his own permanent residence on the land, he claimed, as well as sub-dividing some of the rest of it to sell for use as country villas. In addition, he was certain that the trains would kill all of his cattle, frighten off the game that he enjoyed hunting and blight his land with trains passing through day and night. 'A more compact, beautiful estate, of the size, was not to be found in the County of Middlesex,' he reported. He was looking for compensation of between £4,600 and £6,000; the court awarded him £3,208.[1]

The route began at Euston Station, fronted by the celebrated 'Doric Arch' which stood until the 1960s (its destruction gave a huge impetus to campaigns to preserve London's heritage). The original intention was that the line would start from Camden Town. Because the Act of Parliament enabling the railway did not envisage locomotives operating south of Camden, trains were hauled by a system of steam-powered ropes and pulleys for the first mile of the journey, until new legislation was passed extending the route to its final terminus at Euston.

The rope-and-pulley system took the trains as far as the iron bridge crossing the Regent's Canal north of London Zoo, where the carriages were released and allowed to roll to meet their engine at the Camden Town Depot, where goods were loaded (Euston was for passengers only). This vast depot took in most of today's famous Stables Market in Camden, the performance arts venue The Roundhouse (or The Great Circular Engine House, as it was known when it was built in 1846 as a turntable engine shed for the London & Birmingham Railway) and ended at the canal.

---

1   *Morning Chronicle*, 1 August 1834.

The line then proceeded via the Primrose Hill tunnel to Kilburn, 'celebrated for its retired gentility, the splendid residences in its neighbourhood, and pleasant air',[2] where a cutting was excavated through the remains of the former priory, unearthing various artefacts in the process. The railway travels under the Kilburn High Road through 'a remarkably elegant bridge of the Grecian Doric order'.[3]

Between Kilburn and Kensal, the railway continued in a cutting along the north side of the old Kilburn Lane, disappearing into a tunnel under the Harrow Road beneath the Masons Arms and then on to Harrow, the first stop on the line after Camden. Only second-class trains stopped at Harrow; first-class trains kept going until Watford.

The entire 112-mile journey to Birmingham took around three and a half hours, at an average speed of 20 miles an hour – considerably faster and more comfortable than travelling by horse-drawn stagecoach, which took an entire day. Tame though that 20 miles an hour might sound to us today, in 1837 it was thrillingly fast. Thomas Roscoe describes the experience of emerging from the Primrose Hill tunnel and seeing Hampstead in the distance:

Such … is the rapidity of movement that little time is allowed for any feeling but that of a pleasant kind – for the eye quickly glances over innumerable objects, instinctively seeking and resting where, as the poet aptly expresses it, 'Distance lends enchantment to the view'.[4]

Charles Brett told the compensation court that many people found the new locomotives terrifying, speeding as they did across the landscape belching steam and flames from their boilers – although he was quick to add that he had personally travelled on the Liverpool and Manchester line and had not been frightened at all.

The railway separated the fields of what would become Queen's Park from the two farms that worked the land, Chamberlain Wood Farm and Brondesbury Lower Farm. A footbridge was provided next to Chamberlain Wood Farm to allow the cows from the Kilburn Lane farms to access grazing land on the other side of the line. Maps suggest that there was also a track crossing the line from Lower Farm to the fields on the other side. This must have involved quite a scrabble down the embankment and up the other side.

The southern limits of Queen's Park had now been set, and so had the only ways of crossing the boundary.

---

2   Roscoe, *The London and Birmingham Railway, with the Home and Country Scenes on Each Side of the Line*, p.45.
3   Ibid., p.46.
4   Ibid., p.45.

There were no stations anywhere nearby to begin with. The first to appear was called Willesden Station, which opened in 1841 on Acton Lane roughly where Harlesden Station is today. Local legend has it that it was opened for the convenience of an official of the line, Mark Huish, who lived in a building called Harlesden House on Acton Lane. Although there is no evidence to support this being the reason the station was built, it would not have been out of character. Huish – a former captain in the East India Company – had a reputation for being 'an able but rather untrustworthy man, who exerted undue pressure to obtain agreements favourable to himself and his company, and broke them whenever he saw advantage in doing so'.[1] At the time of the opening of Willesden station Huish was Secretary to the Grand Junction Railway company, which operated the line. Five years later, after the company had merged with other rail companies to form the London and North Western Railway, he was appointed as General Manager on the exceptionally high annual salary of £2,000 – equivalent to £198,000 today.

The station was served by two or three trains a day and was managed by a man known as Old Spinks, who acted as guard, ticket collector and porter. It survived until 1866, when Willesden Junction Station opened at the meeting point of an increasing number of railway lines.

Kilburn High Road Station (originally called Kilburn and Maida Vale Station) was the next to open on the Euston line, in 1852, followed by Queen's Park in 1879 and Kensal Rise in 1916.

The Hampstead Junction Railway

The northern boundary of Queen's Park was set in 1860, when the North London Railway was extended from Chalk Farm to Willesden Junction via the new Hampstead Junction Railway bypass. The NLR began life as the East & West India Docks & Birmingham Junction Railway in 1846, its creators charged by parliament with the job of constructing a railway line from Poplar to Camden Town to carry goods from the Port of London.

Like the L&BR, the developers of the Hampstead Junction Railway had to wade through multiple compensation claims from leaseholders who rented the land before the line was completed, as well as negotiating with the Church of England's Ecclesiastical Commissioners, who now controlled the freeholds. A Captain White of Kilburn demanded £4,500 in recompense for land between Willesden Lane

---

1   Ashworth, Review of Mark Huish and the London and North Western Railway, by TR Gouvish, *Journal of Transport History* vol. 2 iss. 2, 1973, p.127.

and Kilburn High Road, which he said his family had rented from the Church of England since the restoration of Charles II (he was awarded £1,250).[2]

Although part of the line was underground, the section north of Queen's Park ran through a cutting. The Ordnance Survey map of 1865 shows bridges over the cutting at the junction with Chambers Lane (the future Chamberlayne Road), Tiverton Road and Salusbury Road. It's interesting that the Ecclesiastical Commissioners insisted on a bridge at this point, rather than at Long Cross Lane further west; whereas Long Cross Lane was an old, maybe ancient, track across the fields, with an obvious purpose (ie connecting Brondesbury Manor and Brondesbury Lower Farm on Kilburn Lane), the Salusbury Road bridge led nowhere: it simply stopped in the middle of a field. It's clear evidence that the Ecclesiastical Commissioners had already mapped out the future of the area; they knew where Salusbury Road was going to go, and farms were not part of their future plans.

The new stretch of railway included a station on the Kilburn High Road, now called Brondesbury Station, but originally called Edgeware Road (Kilburn) Station. A year later, in 1863, a new station was opened near the junction of Wrottesley Road and the Harrow Road. Kensal Green and Harlesden Station, as the name suggests, served visitors to Kensal Green Cemetery residents of Harlesden. It operated for twelve years, before being replaced by the current Kensal Rise Station (originally called Kensal Green) on Chamberlayne Road.

The most recent station to open on the North London Line was Brondesbury Park in 1908.

A year after the North London Line opened, in 1861, there was a terrible accident when a passenger train collided with a goods train between Gospel Oak and Kentish Town. The engine of the passenger train rolled down the steep railway embankment and four of the carriages fell off a bridge; sixteen people died and over 300 were injured. Charles Dickens remarked that 'there has been a terrible slaughtering of passengers ... that would in each case clearly have been averted by a proper caution in the management'.[3] He wasn't exaggerating – early rail travel could be a hazardous business. In 1860 there were sixty-eight accidents on the railways in which 515 people were injured and thirty-seven were killed.[4]

The person on duty at the time the accident happened was a 19-year-old called Raynor, who had only been working on the railway for eight months. The regular, more experienced signalman, a man named Fessey, had left work a little earlier than he should have, before the accident happened. He claimed when testifying to the

2 *St James' Chronicle*, 28 September 1858.
3 Dickens, 'Rather Interested in Railways', *All The Year Round*, 28 September 1861.
4 *The Lancet*, 4 January 1862.

subsequent inquiry that he warned Raynor, 'when the ballast train wants to come out, see that all the four danger signals are up'.

The inquiry concluded that 'more experienced signalmen than Raynor should be employed. The safety of the public should not be entrusted to a lad of 19 years of age, paid at the rate of 14s. or 15s. a week'.

The Footbridge

Once Queen's Park opened in 1877, the vast majority of users came from the districts south of the railway lines – many of them facing a long round trip to the nearest railway bridge to get to the park. It must have been particularly galling for people living on Allington Road, a vigorous stone's throw from the park as the crow flies, to have to walk the best part of a mile with small children.

A campaign therefore began to get a footbridge erected before houses could be built on the south side of Harvist Road, blocking the way. In 1892 the *Kilburn Times* reported that the Chelsea Vestry had appealed for funds for a footbridge to the Ecclesiastical Commissioners, the London and North Western Railway Company, Middlesex County Council and the Willesden Local Board. All of them had found reasons not to contribute. The Vestry said they supported the idea, but sadly couldn't find any funding as the bridge would start and finish on Willesden land. The directors of the Artizans Dwelling Company, which built the Queen's Park Estate, offered £500 towards the cost of construction on condition that the Vestry could find the rest.[1]

Six years later, the Chelsea Vestry were still plugging away, petitioning Middlesex County Council for funding. The council not only decided not to provide any funding, but passed the following motion: 'That an intimation be given to the Vestry of Chelsea that the County Council is not prepared to contribute towards improved means of communication between Queen's Park, Willesden, and the district south of the London and North-Western Railway, and that, under these circumstances, it does not appear necessary to trouble the Vestry to send deputation to the County Council on the subject.'[2] In other words, 'don't bother coming to see us, we won't change our minds'. In 1902 the new Paddington Council tried again, with the same result.[3]

The dream lingers on. In 1967, the *Marylebone Mercury* tried to imagine what the 1970s might bring to the area.[4] One of these scenarios was a footbridge across the

---

1   *Kilburn Times*, 20 May 1982.
2   *Kilburn Times*, 29 July 1898.
3   *Kilburn Times*, 28 February 1902.
4   *Marylebone Mercury*, 4 August 1967.

Euston Line, linking the two sides of the railway line. This wasn't entirely fanciful: in the late 1960s Westminster Council had considered a footbridge or subway crossing the railway as part of its strategic plan for the future development of North Westminster. Perhaps one day it will become a reality.

4

PADDINGTON
CEMETERY

After the railways, the greatest legacy the Victorians left in London was the creation of the necropoli: the cities of the dead.

By the middle of the nineteenth century, one of the biggest challenges facing London was what to do with its dead. London's churchyards were already overflowing by the 1700s; burial grounds on the then-edge of town were licensed to take the overflow, but by the early 1800s even they had run out of space.

In 1849 it was estimated that 52,000 Londoners were dying each year, yet the total capacity of the city's burial grounds was just 100,000 spaces. Bodies were dumped in communal graves, often inches from the surface, and body snatching was a common hazard.

There were reports of grave diggers dying from the noxious gases released by putrefying corpses. The Sunday periodical *Bell's Life in London and Sporting Chronicle* warned its readers that: 'The state of the churchyards of the metropolis is at once disgusting and dangerous, and calls loudly for legislative interference. To know that the population of London is exposed to the pestilent miasma of our burial grounds, situated as they are in the very midst of the most densely crowded neighbourhoods, is calculated to excite the most painful apprehensions for the public safety.'[1] According to the report, a pauper's grave had recently been opened at Aldgate churchyard, killing not only the gravedigger who opened it but also a member of the public who tried to help him. A witness told the newspaper that 'such graves as those were kept open until there were 17 or 18 bodies interred in them'.

---

1   'Churchyards in London: Horrible Deaths', *Bell's Life in London and Sporting Chronicle*, 9 September 1838.

Reformers like George Alfred Walker (known as 'Graveyard Walker') urged a maximum of 136 burials per acre. Few of London's burial places could keep to that target, and many buried closer to 1,000 people per acre.

The problem was given greater significance by the commonly held belief (that existed in many cultures dating back to ancient times) that diseases such as malaria and cholera were spread by 'miasma' from graves. Miasma was believed to be a poisonous vapour filled with particles from decomposed matter that caused illnesses. In 1842, a Dr Chambers gave evidence to a House of Commons select committee inquiry on the subject, reporting that he was in 'no doubt that typhus fever owed its origin to putrid miasma; that crowded grave-yards supplied such miasma in abundance, and that it was injurious not only to the persons living in the immediate neighbourhood of such grave-yards, but to those living in otherwise healthful neighbourhoods.'[2]

The wealthiest in society had a solution to hand in 'The Magnificent Seven' cemeteries, which were built in a ring around London. The first of the seven, Kensal Green, was designed as Britain's answer to Père Lachaise in Paris; it was opened in 1833 by the Bishop of London, and is therefore technically Georgian. Although it looks overwhelmingly Gothic today thanks to decades of Victorian burials, the main buildings are actually classical in style. The remainder of the Magnificent Seven London cemeteries opened between 1837 and 1841.

However, these were options for wealthier Londoners; the problem of what to do for the rest of the population was a major topic of parliamentary and public debate from the 1820s to the 1850s. Although a parliamentary inquiry of 1842 had recommended against the practice of 'burying the dead in towns', it took the best part of another decade for action to follow.

The Metropolitan Internment Act of 1850 was finally passed after a two-year outbreak of cholera in 1848–49 that killed over 14,000 Londoners. It was the straw that broke the camel's back; London's churchyards and burial grounds were unable to cope, and even recent burials were exhumed to make room for the newly deceased. The Act ordered the closure of London's urban graveyards. It was followed by the Burials Act of 1852, which enabled parishes to borrow money to create out-of-town burial grounds, and led to the proliferation of planned cemeteries on a more modest, and affordable, scale than the Magnificent Seven.

Paddington Old Cemetery – to give it its proper name – was one of the first of the new-style cemeteries to open. But it opened on the edge of Kilburn and not, as you might have imagined, in Paddington at all.

Paddington parish's burial board posted an advertisement in the *Morning Advertiser* of 9 January 1854, saying:

---

2 *London Evening Standard*, 9 April 1845.

Burial-ground wanted.

The burial board of the parish of Paddington, in the county of Middlesex, are prepared to consider PROPOSALS for the SALE to them, in fee, of Ten Acres and upwards of LAND, situate either to the North, North-west, or West of the Metropolis, for the purpose of a Burial-ground.

They successfully secured 10 acres of land just off the Edgware Road at Kilburn in the summer of 1854 and received permission from Lord Palmerston, the Home Secretary, to proceed. However, they did meet resistance. In February 1855, *The Examiner*[1] reported that a delegation of aggrieved locals had appealed on the grounds that:

They weren't told about the plans and therefore had not been able to object

It would blight the area

The site was closer to London than the legislation permitted

The heavy clay was unsuitable for burials and the ground was flooded for much of the year

Water from the site drained into a ditch which fed ponds that provided drinking water for the cows whose milk supplied much of West London

Said water then went on through Paddington to Hyde Park and the Serpentine, no doubt carrying malaria and all sorts of miasma-related diseases with it.

They were still appealing, unsuccessfully, to the new Home Secretary, Sir George Grey, in April 1855.[2]

The cemetery opened on Friday, 31 August 1855, to a design by the architect Thomas Little, who fifteen years earlier had designed the Anglican chapel in Nunhead Cemetery, one of the Magnificent Seven. His design for Paddington Cemetery included a horse-shoe, tree-lined path layout, two chapels made of Kentish Ragstone (one for Church of England burials and one for nonconformists) and a pair of Gothic gatehouses at the main entrance on Willesden Lane, with the whole site surrounded by a high brick wall. All these features endure to the present day.

At the time the cemetery was built, Kilburn was developing quickly, as the protesting locals indicated. WH Smith, the founder of the stationery empire, lived in a lovely old building called Kilburn House from 1839 to 1856 (where today's Priory Park and Glengall Roads are), and a chapel (soon replaced by a church) dedicated to St Paul stood where Kilburn Square is today. The area attracted wealthy people looking to

---

1 'Proposed Cemetery at Kilburn', *The Examiner*, 10 February 1855, p.87.
2 *Morning Post*, 28 April 1855.

build villas on the Edgware Road and Willesden Lane, combining the benefits of a rural setting and easy access to London, particularly after the opening of the Euston line railway station in Kilburn in 1852.

By 1865, Brondesbury Road and Brondesbury Villas were starting to spread west from Kilburn High Road, there was substantial development around Kilburn Park to the south and there was a shooting range – the Victoria Rifle Ground – at the back of Kilburn Square. This was used by the Victoria Rifle Corps, a City-based volunteer unit, for shooting practice, and was also used by the Guards regiments.

However, the area south and west of Willesden Lane was still agricultural at this time. Seen from Long Cross Lane, the cemetery must have looked like a strange interloper – a giant walled garden in the middle of fields.

In 1894, Paddington's burial board unanimously voted to build London's first crematorium in the cemetery, serving not just Paddington but the whole of the capital. It provoked a furious response from local residents, 1,129 of whom signed a petition opposing the plans, arguing that 'Their neighbourhood was one they prided themselves on, and they had taken a pride in making it what it was – the best conducted, the most sanitary, and the most economical in London or the suburbs.'[3] If it was such an inoffensive thing, they argued, why were the burial board not suggesting building it on Paddington Green? In the end, the burial board and the Cremation Society of England, which had offered to run the facility, were unable to raise the £5,000 needed for construction and so the idea was dropped.[4] London's first crematorium finally opened at Golders Green in 1902.

Commonwealth War Graves

The cemetery has a small memorial garden, with a cross, containing the graves of 130 Commonwealth soldiers, sailors and airmen who served in the First World War. Another twenty-seven are buried in individual graves throughout the cemetery, and fifty are interred at Paddington but have no grave markers.[5] The memorial was erected in 1920, and an additional plaque commemorating men from Paddington who died in the war and are buried elsewhere was erected in 1927.

The cemetery also contains the graves of four Commonwealth soldiers from the Second World War and forty-three graves of people who died in military service outside of wartime.

---

3   *Kilburn Times*, 30 November 1894, p.6.
4   *Kilburn Times*, 13 December 1895, p.4.
5   For more on the history of Paddington Cemetery see www.fopoc.com/new-page-4

Many of the 338 civilian casualties of the Second World War are also recorded (but not necessarily buried) at the cemetery, but these were residents of the old borough of Paddington, not of Queen's Park; the 448 Willesden civilians who died in the war are commemorated at Willesden New Cemetery on Franklyn Road.

Paddington Borough was folded up into the new Westminster City Council in 1964, the same year that Willesden and Wembley merged to form Brent, and the management of Paddington Cemetery went with it. Westminster sold the cemetery to Brent in 1986.

Today the cemetery is still used for burials, but is also a popular spot for dog walkers and people who enjoy the leafy melancholia of Victorian cemeteries, representing as it does one of the rare green spaces in the midst of heavy urban development (alongside Queen's Park of course).

It boasts around 500 mature trees, featuring many specimen trees from the original planting including oak, lime, horse chestnut, yew, field maple, London plane and Scots pine. At least one oak tree dating from before the cemetery was laid out still stands. Visitors can enjoy small wildflower meadows as well as formal bedding schemes and lawns.

The cemetery is recognised in Historic England's *Register of Parks and Gardens of Special Historic Interest in England* and received a special commendation in the Cemetery of the Year Awards in 1999.

Notable burials at Paddington Cemetery include:

THE TICHBORNE CLAIMANT

In 1854 Roger Tichborne, the 25-year-old heir to a substantial fortune, went missing when the ship he was travelling on, the *Bella*, was lost at sea off Brazil. Eleven years later, a man identifying himself as the missing Roger appeared in Australia. Despite being heavily overweight (when last seen Roger was very thin), the Tichborne Claimant as he was known was recognised as the missing heir by Roger's mother and a surprising number of his former friends and colleagues. He claimed to have been saved from the shipwreck by a boat bound for Australia, where he wandered for a while before working (unsuccessfully) as a butcher, marrying and putting on a considerable amount of weight.

Roger's mother might have been convinced, but the rest of the family were not. It was argued that the Claimant was actually a Wapping butcher's son called Arthur Orton, who had emigrated to Australia via South America and disappeared around the time that the Claimant emerged. Two court cases followed, both of which the Claimant lost, resulting in gaol time but much popular support.

When the Claimant died in 1898, he was buried in an unmarked grave in the cemetery. It is estimated that 5,000 mourners attended his funeral. The casket he was buried in bore a brass plate with the inscription 'Roger Charles Doughty Tichborne, born January 25th 1829, died April 1st 1898',[1] and the name 'Tichborne' was written in the cemetery's register.

THE PRINCESS OF OUDE

Princess Omdutel Aurau Begum, the baby granddaughter of the last queen of Oude (or Oudh, also known as Awadh), died on 14 April 1858 at the age of eighteen months. Her grandmother's country was a princely state with a population of around 5 million people, in the Awadh region of north India, that had been annexed by the East India Company on behalf of Britain two years before. Her grandmother sailed for England with a party including the princess's parents, intent on petitioning Queen Victoria for the restitution of her crown. In the meantime, Oude had become one of the epicentres of the Indian Rebellion of 1857, and what little chance the family had of recovering their possessions vanished. Princess Omdutel died while the party were in England. Her father, grandmother and a cousin died on the return journey and are buried in Père Lachaise, Paris.

EMMA PATERSON

Emma was a feminist, trade union pioneer (one of the first two women delegates to the Trade Union Congress in 1875) and indefatigable campaigner who established women's credit unions, newspapers, a printing society and swimming clubs. She died at the age of 38 of complications from diabetes.

CUTHBERT OTTAWAY

The first ever captain of the England football team and the England captain for the first international match in football history (versus Scotland), Ottaway also captained an FA Cup-winning team (Oxford University) and played first-class cricket for Oxford, Kent and Middlesex. He died of a respiratory infection in 1878 aged just 27. Contemporary news reports of his death talk about his prowess at cricket and racquets, but make no mention of his football exploits.

MICHAEL BOND

The creator of Paddington Bear was fittingly laid to rest in Paddington Cemetery when he passed away aged 91 in 2017. His headstone says 'Please look after this bear. Thank you.'

---

1 *Freeman's Journal,* 7 April 1898.

5

THE FIRST QUEEN'S PARK (A 'TOWN FOR WORKMEN')

In the 1860s, most of the land to the south of today's Queen's Park (on the other side of Kilburn Lane) was still agricultural. It belonged to the parish of St Luke's Chelsea, despite being entirely detached from it, and was sometimes referred to as 'Chelsea in the Wilderness'.

These kinds of detached pieces of parishes were quite common in the past, the result of ancient grants of land, before Victorian reformers tidied them up. The nearest buildings were on the bottom end of Kilburn Lane where it meets the Harrow Road, including the Paradise public house (which dates back to 1750) and St John's Church (1844).[1]

This area was developed by the Artizans, Labourers and General Dwellings Company (subsequently referred to as The Artizans) between 1874 and 1886. The company was part of a general movement driven by concerns about the appalling living conditions that many working-class people endured in the nineteenth century.

A delegation sent by the parish in 1859 to inspect living conditions in Kensal Town reported that 'the merest dogholes [are] let for rent'.[2] Charles Dickens described the Potteries district of Notting Dale, down by Grenfell Tower, as 'a plague spot scarcely equalled for its insalubrity by any other in London'.[3] The Potteries – no more than 7 or 8 acres in total – featured open sewers, stagnant ditches and a 1-acre-wide septic lake, left over from the excavation of clay for making bricks – a perfect environment for breeding diseases. The residents were the 'domestic servants, cleaners, wet-nurses,

---

1 Willesden Local History Society, https://willesden-local-history.co.uk/kensal-green
2 *West Middlesex Advertiser and Family Journal*, 26 March 1859.
3 Dickens, *Household Words*.

prostitutes, laundry-women, needlewomen, gardeners, night-soil men, chimney sweeps, odd-job men and builders' that kept Victorian London's economy going,[4] but in 1845 the average life expectancy there was just eleven years. These were the kinds of slums creeping closer to Queen's Park by the mid-century.

The first thing approaching a modern housing association was the Metropolitan Association for Improving the Dwellings of the Industrious Classes, founded in 1841 with the purpose of 'providing the labouring man with an increase of the comforts and conveniences of life, with full return to the capitalist'. It created affordable, decent quality housing in Clerkenwell, King's Cross, Stepney and as far west as Pimlico.

Further impetus was provided the following year, 1842, when Edwin Chadwick published his hugely influential report on public health, 'Sanitary Conditions of the Labouring Classes'. Following a commission from the government to look into the links between sanitation and health, Chadwick self-published his report, which found a clear link between poor living standards and the spread of disease, and made a number of recommendations including access to clean water, better drainage and municipal refuse collections.

In 1844 another housing association, The Society for the Improvement of the Conditions of the Labouring Classes, was formed by Lord Shaftesbury and Robert Benton Seeley, with the aim of providing sanitary accommodation for the respectable labouring poor. It built model housing and tried to improve some of the existing slum dwellings. The Peabody Donation Trust followed in 1862 and the Improved Industrial Dwellings Company in 1863.

However, housing and public health reforms did not go unopposed. A *Times* editorial of 1854 thundered: 'We prefer to take our chance with cholera than be bullied into health. There is nothing a man hates so much as being cleansed against his will or having his floor swept, his hall whitewashed, his dung heaps cleared away and his thatch forced to give way to slate.'[5]

It was against this backdrop that William Austin and a group of men who all shared modest backgrounds founded The Artizans in 1867. Austin, born in 1804, was a former navvy who was illiterate all his life; his first job, as a child, was as a scarecrow. Having given up alcohol at the age of 47 and become a home owner and building contractor (he specialised in laying drains) in his own right, he became fiercely committed to improving housing standards for working people.

The company's advertisements stated: 'The Company is especially formed to erect improved workmen's dwellings on the co-operative principle. No beer-shop or tavern to be erected on the Company's property.'

---

4   Dyos and Wolff, *The Victorian City: Images and Realities*, p.372.
5   *The Times,* July 1854.

In 1871, The Artizans published a pamphlet entitled 'The Terror of Europe and the Disgrace of Britain', which set out their credo: 'There is no question that can possibly engage the attention or claim the sympathy of thoughtful men more than "how are we to repress or at least mitigate the disease, intemperance, crime and pauperism existing to an appalling extent in our large cities and towns?"' These evils were an ever-increasing plague, which brought shame on England's civilization, not to mention its government, the pamphlet said, and despite the expenditure of tens of thousands of pounds of public money on Royal Commissions, Acts of Parliament and other measures intended to deal with these problems, 'the result has been almost nil'.

If a tenth of the money, energy and intelligence expended on Poor Law Boards, asylums and prisons had been directed at the causes of these problems, the pamphlet argued, England would not be subject to the reproach it was. The startling fact staring everyone in the face, according to The Artizans, was that overcrowded and neglected dwellings were largely responsible for 'the horrors of intemperance, typhus, diphtheria, scarlatina, small-pox and cholera'. These diseases could be almost eradicated if the will was there, the pamphlet continued:

> There is no law of nature more stern in its operation, more exacting in its demands, and dealing swifter and more uncompromising retribution than if people are permitted to drivel out a wretched existence in dwellings alike deficient of light, drainage, ventilation, water, and proper conveniences for natural wants – temperance, health, morality and religion are rendered impossible. If families have not the chance of observing the decencies of life, how are they to be expected to cultivate purity of life and morals? To preach, to lecture, to distribute tracts and send among them missionaries is simply to mock their misery.[1]

The Artizans began with very little working capital (Austin had to remortgage his own house to put funds into the business) and started small, building a few new houses in Battersea. The Queen's Park Estate was their second big venture, following the Shaftesbury Park Estate in Clapham. Sadly, Austin was no longer part of the company by then; he was ousted in 1870, later commenting that, 'I am no scholar, so they outvoted me.'[2] His successor was the unfortunately (or perhaps accurately) named William Swindlehurst, an engineer who became the company's manager and secretary as well as a director.

The first 67 acres of land for the Queen's Park Estate in the borough of Westminster was bought on 3 June 1874 for £685 an acre from All Souls College, which owned

---

1   Bee-Hive, 7 January 1871.
2   www.locallocalhistory.co.uk/mp/p050/page081.htm

property on both sides of the Euston Line, with the remainder of the 80-acre site following in August.

On 26 September 1874 the *Kilburn Times* reported that the Artizans company would be developing 'a town for workmen' south of what was commonly known as 'Kilburn Lane or Canterbury Lane', on land that 'maintains its primitive state of green pasture'. The importance of providing decent quality housing for working people in order to 'spread moral influence over their class, tending to foster habits of industry, sobriety, and frugality' was one of the most pressing questions of the age, the paper said. 'Week by week our newspapers disclose sad facts of the outburst of disease in our crowded alleys and courts, which appear to set our sanitary measures at deffance [sic].'

As well as planting trees on the roads, the Artizans Company intended to offer inducements to residents to keep both their front and back gardens as beautiful as time permitted, the paper reported – although they doubted that this would be necessary, as the occupants of the Company's first venture, the Shaftesbury Park Estate, were already vying with each other to see who could create the most attractive displays.

The new estate would be equipped with a lecture hall and institute, co-operative stores, a coal depot, a dairy farm, baths, wash-houses and other buildings, and Queen Victoria herself would be asked to lay the foundation stone of the estate, which would be named in her honour.[3] The name 'Queen's Park' was clearly adopted at an early stage, the first part in honour of the monarch and the second because it was the latest in a series of 'park estates' planned by The Artizans.

The designs for the new estate were initially the work of Robert Austin, the company's self-taught architect and surveyor, who started out as a company carpenter, and later of Roland Plumbe. According to *Artizans and Avenues*, Erica McDonald and David Smith's history of the Queen's Park Estate, many of the materials needed for construction were brought in on the Grand Union Canal; a temporary tramway was constructed linking a wharf on the canal with the building site to carry supplies brought by narrow boat. Bricks were brought in from the company's brickworks in Alperton, as well as being manufactured on site from local clay. A saw mill was set up where Ilbert Street is today.

On the whole, however, 1877 was a difficult year for The Artizans. Swindlehurst was accused of taking bribes and inflating the value of shares; he was arrested, tried at the Old Bailey along with the company chairman and another defendant, found guilty and gaoled. Swindlehurst was sentenced to eighteen months with hard labour for his crimes, one of which was allowing an associate to buy the land for the Queen's Park Estate at its market value, and then immediately selling it on to The Artizans at a 20 per cent mark-up, which was shared between the three conspirators. The company

---

3   *Kilburn Times*, 26 September 1874.

sacked Robert Austin and a number of more junior employees, including the Queen's Park Estate's assistant collector, but work continued, despite the scandal.

Further problems emerged in subsequent years, including dry rot, a couple of collapsing ceilings, issues with sub-standard plasterwork, roofing and defective bricks from Alperton, and excessive charging for repairs. Toilets were finally provided for the construction teams in July 1881, seven years after work started.[1]

Nevertheless by 1882, over 1,500 houses had been built, with a further 450 under way. The roads were unusually wide and tree-lined for working-class dwellings of the time, and many regard them as the inspiration for the garden suburbs of the next century. At the time, most companies building affordable housing for working people were constructing blocks of flats; the tree-lined estates of terraced housing were The Artizans' signature innovation. The houses were small cottages in the distinctive Gothic revival style with polychrome brickwork, pinnacles and turrets. They originally came with cast-iron railings on their front walls; these were removed during the Second World War to supply the war effort. Similar railings can still be seen on houses on the Shaftesbury Park Estate.

One of the most striking features of the Queen's Park Estate is its division into numbered avenues (First to Sixth) running north to south and alphabetically ordered streets running east to west. At first these were simply called A Street, B Street and so on down to P Street, but in 1883 the company proposed naming them after people associated with The Artizans. A few of these made the final cut after negotiations with the authorities, including Ashurst, Droop and Evelyn.

The houses were originally planned for sale, not for rent; The Artizans needed to recoup the cost of building quickly so they could move on to new projects. A typical house might cost 1s 2d per room per week, spread over fourteen years.[2] However, following the financial scandal of 1877, the company switched to letting out the properties, which were organised into five price bands.

The first occupants included railway workers, employees of the Gas Light and Coke Company works (where Ladbroke Grove Sainsbury's is today), laundry workers (a major occupation in the area at the time) and skilled tradespeople. The company sought to attract tenants with reliable incomes and 'respectable' lifestyles.

In 1888, the company acquired some of the land north of Kilburn Lane, constructing more artisan-friendly maisonettes on Allington Road and Kilburn Lane itself.

The Artizans made good on their promise to endow the estate with a 'lecture hall and institute', although the company didn't get around to selecting the site, on the corner of the Harrow Road and First Avenue, until 1882. The Gothic Queen's Park Hall was

1 *Artizans and Avenues: A History of the Queen's Park Estate*, p.9.
2 www.locallocalhistory.co.uk/mp/p050/page082.htm

a great success, hosting all manner of alcohol-free entertainments including theatrical performances, dance classes, children's parties and temperance meetings. The downstairs is now shops and the first-floor hall has been a boxing gym since the 1970s.

The promised library – managed by Chelsea vestry – opened in 1890 and the estate was well served by schools and churches. However, the baths pledged in the original prospectus were much delayed, finally appearing (on the other side of the canal) in the 1890s.

By 1926, the Artizans Company was managing 9,200 properties around the country. Before the Second World War started, it had begun to modernise some of its properties on the Queen's Park Estate, installing electricity and baths, but all work stopped with the outbreak of the war, which saw considerable damage to the area. Peach Street was completely destroyed by a parachute mine, with considerable loss of life, and damage was also done to other parts of the estate. Modernisation began again after the war ended, although it started slowly due to shortages of materials.

In 1951 the Artizans set up a subsidiary company, the Artizans Housing Association, to build new properties on the estate to replace those destroyed in the war; this is when Queen's Park Court was erected, with funding from Paddington Council, where Peach Street used to stand. Five years later the company began selling off vacant properties to the council; the 1950s were a tough time for landlords due to rent controls and high tax levels.[3]

By 1964, Paddington Council owned 195 properties on the estate, and in September of that year an agreement was reached for the council to buy the whole of the estate, including 1,800 houses, eighty shops and two halls. The price was £2.5 million. The company's maisonettes on the north side of Kilburn Lane were sold to Brent for £175,000.[4] A 1965 study by Westminster Council into housing conditions in the north of the borough concluded that most of it should be torn down and redeveloped, although it accepted that the Queen's Park Estate might be an exception, requiring only partial destruction.

In 1967, the Greater London Council bought 3 acres of the estate through a compulsory purchase order. This included Mozart Street and sections of Herries and Lancefield Streets – a total of sixty houses, nine shops and a number of businesses. The properties were demolished and, over the next decade, replaced by the Mozart Estate.[5] Initially award-winning for its design, the estate soon experienced problems with crime, as well as with damp and 'black mould'. In 1985 Alice Coleman, in her seminal work on public housing *Utopia on Trial*, put the Mozart Estate in the worst

---

3 https://discovery.nationalarchives.gov.uk/details/r/a3a1dae2-836a-4e4d-8db1-fd67396620b6
4 *Artizans and Avenues*, p.29.
5 www.locallocalhistory.co.uk/mp/p150/page175.htm

4 per cent of estates in the country. As a result of her recommendations, the problematic walkways on the estate were removed and other improvements, including landscaping, were introduced.

The 1970s and '80s were not a great time for the Queen's Park Estate, with problems including petty crime, vandalism and squatting. However, it was not all bad news: in 1977 Farrant Street was demolished and the open space originally promised by The Artizans nearly a hundred years earlier was finally delivered in the shape of Queen's Park Gardens, and the Jubilee Sports Centre opened the same year (hence the name).

Since the 1980s, and the introduction of right-to-buy policies, the estate has been rejuvenated, with houses in demand and asking prices heading towards a million pounds.

Queens Park Rangers

Queens Park Rangers football club (QPR) was founded in 1886 following the merger of two boys' clubs – Christ Church Rangers and St Jude's. Christ Church was an Anglican mission, an offshoot of St John's Church on the Harrow Road, set up in 1882 to minister to the growing population of College Park, the triangle of roads south of the Harrow Road, where the Mayhew veterinary clinic is today. St Jude's was also an Anglican mission, set up in 1884 on Ilbert Street to serve the new Queen's Park Estate.

Not everyone was happy about the merger; some of the Christ Church Rangers players felt that the new team was a takeover by St Jude's rather than a merger of equals (the new team relocated to the St Jude's headquarters and took their name), so they left to form Paddington FC. Divisions were healed when the new team was renamed Queens Park Rangers, in honour of the estate where most of the players lived and the 'Rangers' part of Christ Church's name.

QPR have a reputation for being one of the most nomadic football teams in history – they have changed grounds more often than any other team in league history. Their first matches, in 1888–89, were played on a patch of open ground called Welford's Fields, behind the Paradise pub on Kilburn Lane. They carried the uprights for the goals (the crossbar was made of tape each time) from their headquarters on Ilbert Street and changed at a now-vanished pub, The Case is Altered, on the Harrow Road. They played other local teams including Brondesbury and Kensal Rise.[1]

From 1889 onwards they played games at the London Scottish rugby ground in Brondesbury, Home Farm in Kensal Green, Kilburn Cricket Club and the Kensal Rise Athletics Ground – an impressive stadium built in 1890 where Leigh and Whitmore Gardens stand today.[2] The club finally moved out of the area in 1901.

1   www.kilburntimes.co.uk/news/qpr-history-in-125-years-3678606
2   http://kilburnwesthampstead.blogspot.com/2021/06/sports-in-kensal-rise.html

6

THE ROYAL AGRICULTURAL SHOW OF 1879

At the start of the 1870s, the land in between the railway lines that would become the eponymous park of Queen's Park was still used as pasture for cows. It comprised 100 acres of greenfield space that on the face of it seemed perfect for the needs of one of the most popular annual events in the country: the Royal Agricultural Show. The reality, however, was to prove very far from perfect; the show of 1879 would certainly prove memorable, but for all the wrong reasons.

The annual Royal Agricultural Show was the ultimate showcase for the farming industry, a mix of competitions, displays of the latest technology and entertainments for curious lay people. It was hosted in turn by the RAS's regions, each finding a new venue every time for the ever-growing event.

The 1879 show was the fortieth run by the Royal Agricultural Society and the first to be held in London since the Battersea show of 1862. On 31 July 1878 the society's governing council, chaired by Lord Skelmersdale, authorised its secretary to sign a deal with the Ecclesiastical Commissioners to rent the land between Salusbury and Chamberlayne roads for the following year's show.

All the indications were that it would be a great success. It had royal patronage – the Society's President was Prince Albert Edward, Prince of Wales, and the scheduled visit of Queen Victoria on the second day of the show was sure to attract big crowds – it was within easy reach of everyone in London, then the largest city in the world, and (by train) most major provincial centres, and it had more livestock, machines and agricultural instruments on display than any Royal Show in history. Additional attractions included a steam-driven tram, using the very latest transport technology, to ferry visitors from one end of the 100-acre site to the other; a competition between two refrigerated railway waggons to see which could keep food fresh for longest; a museum of ancient and modern agricultural tool; and the cutting of a gigantic cheese from Canada. Omnibuses transported visitors from Charing Cross to the showground around the clock, and the site had superb rail and road access. The organisers had every detail covered – except the London Clay beneath their feet, and its astonishing ability to hold water when it rains.

In theory, the showground site was an inspired choice. It was a huge site – around a mile wide – and had excellent transport links. The London and North West Railway, linking Euston station with Birmingham, Liverpool and Manchester, agreed to open a station especially for the show (the present-day Queen's Park station, then called Queen's Park (West Kilburn) named after the housing estate to the south). One of the three entrances to the showground came directly off the station platforms. The North London Railway connected stations in west and east London, with more routes accessible from nearby Willesden Junction; the local stop was Kensal Green station (now Kensal Rise), on the north-west corner of the showground, which had been open since 1873. The third entrance to the showground was just by this station. (Brondesbury Park station would not open until 1908.)

The Times noted approvingly:

> Thus, from all parts of London, a return ticket and a direct journey to the show will be as handy as to the Alexandra or the Crystal Palace; the show is within the cab-fare radius from Charing-cross; it is a couple of miles from the Marble Arch, straight up the Edgware-road; any number of omnibuses convey passengers from any part of the metropolis more or less directly to Kilburn; and tramcars approach it by numerous lines converging from the east and north.[1]

The showground was the largest the Society had ever rented, and the scale of the show was immense: it had 24,000 sq. ft of shed space, 3,000 animals on display and nearly 12,000 implements exhibited, including an electric cheese cutter. The Royal Box was part of a grandstand complex seating 3,000 people.

Entering the ground from the main turnstiles on Salusbury Road – roughly where the junction with Windermere Avenue is today – visitors would have seen a grand processional avenue in front of them leading to the main parade ring. A steam-driven tram took visitors down this avenue to the parade ring and on to the other side of the showground; this was erected by the Leeds-based agricultural engineering firm John Fowler & Co., which also supplied the steam engine that drove the tram. The tracks were supplied by the French engineering firm Decauville, still only 4 years old.

---

1   *The Times*, 25 June 1879.

Thirty-five years later Decauville's portable rail systems were the standard kit used by the Allied armies to move equipment on the Western Front.

To the right and left, visitors would have seen refreshment tents (temperance and non-temperance respectively), and beyond them a vast sea of canvass-roofed stalls displaying the latest agricultural implements – seventy-eight of them in total, divided by fourteen rows running north to south and four avenues running east to west. End to end, these stalls would have measured 16,000 sq. ft – a third larger than the previous year's show in Liverpool.

Behind them, hugging the boundary wall on Salusbury Road, visitors would have seen 2,200ft of stalls displaying 'seeds, foods, manures, models and other objects of interest'[2] – twice that of any previous show – and in the far corners of the show-ground, more tents displaying 'machinery in motion'.

Beyond the lines of stalls displaying instruments were the 'loan collections'. The *London Evening Standard* noted that:

> Not by any means the least interesting department, however, will be the collection formed for the purpose of illustrating the progress made in mechanical science as applied to agriculture, wherein the most primitive appliances will be seen beside the latest triumphs of modern ingenuity.[3]

The report went on:

> Thus an old bill reaper, the patriarch of the tribe, will be brought into comparison with a Hornsby self-raker, Messrs Hornsby having been chosen to represent modern pro-gress from the fact of their holding all the latest first prizes for that class of machinery. Their Parragon mower also, which equally distinguished itself, will be found placed in juxtaposition with the most primitive grass cutters that could possibly be obtained.

Other curiosities included a Saxon plough, a Java plough and a plough from Cyprus (brought home recently by the first Lord of the Admiralty).

On the far side of this huge, regimented tent city, roughly in line with the Queen's Park bandstand today, there was a strip of open ground, housing more refreshment tents, the 'members' club', the President's tent, a clocktower and various administrative offices.

After this the serried ranks of tents began again, this time housing the vast numbers of sheep, cattle and horses that competed for prizes at the show. In between them stood the parade ring, with its grandstand and royal box.

---

2   Ibid.
3   *London Evening Standard*, 26 June 1879.

The far north-western corner of the showground was home to an international exhibition, displaying overseas livestock and dairy produce; the *London Evening Standard* seemed particularly taken with 'the buxom dairymaid whose deft hands are continuously employed in the making of cheese according to various German methods'.[1] One of the highlights of the show was the cutting of a gigantic Canadian cheese, weighing three-quarters of a ton, with a battery-powered cheese-cutter. 'The cutting wire having been connected with a battery, a stupendous cheese ... was completely severed in a few minutes, in the presence of a number of scientific gentlemen, and to the great surprise of a large number of spectators.'[2]

The land to the west and south-west of the site, where the Ark Academy is today, was unoccupied.

The show was due to open formally on Monday, 30 June 1879 and to run for one week, closing on Monday, 7 July. Her Majesty Queen Victoria was scheduled to visit on Tuesday, 1 July. Tickets were set at half a guinea (equivalent to around £52 in today's money) for a season ticket allowing unlimited admission every day, 5s (£25) for a day ticket for Monday, 30 June and Tuesday, 1 July, 2s 6d (£12.50) for Wednesday, 2, and Thursday, 3 July, and 1s (£5) for the remaining Friday, Saturday and Monday (the showground was closed on Sunday, 6 July).

The crucial importance of the weather was clear from the start. *The Times* noted:

> That fine weather during the show week is anxiously looked for may be understood, when it is remembered that the show will lay the Royal Agricultural Society under a liability of probably £40,000 ... And though the society has expended above £2,000 in draining the level site ... there is little doubt that much mud and water on the constantly trodden surface would sorely inconvenience visitors in case a heavy downfall of rain should be again blown over the Atlantic.[3]

That was an understatement, to say the least. By the time this report appeared in *The Times*, five days before the show was due to open, the showground was already a quagmire of mud and standing water thanks to days of heavy rain.

On Thursday, 26 June, the *London Evening Standard* struck a resolutely optimistic tone: 'From something that bore a very close resemblance to an absolute and impassable quagmire, the show yard at Kilburn is rapidly developing into a township of broad thoroughfares that will be perfectly practicable even for the most lightly shod of feminine visitors, and a few more days of well-directed labour will probably prove

1   *London Evening Standard*, 3 July 1879.
2   *London Evening Standard*, 8 July 1879.
3   *The Times*, 25 June 1879.

sufficient to place it in such a condition as to be little affected even by the persistently adverse weather that now prevails.'[4]

Although the society's governing council had spent a considerable sum on installing land drains, the paper continued:

> They had reckoned … without a due knowledge of London clay, and when the downpour of Tuesday came they were dismayed to find that the lower-lying surface of the ground became submerged to the depth of many inches, and there faced them the terrible prospect of seeing visitors to the show wading more than ankle deep through a Slough of Despond.

In response, thousands of old railway sleepers were brought to the showground, over which roadways were laid to enable the transport of the heaviest machinery across the site; without them, the *Standard* acknowledged, they'd have simply stuck fast in the mud. Fanning out from these wooden trackways, down the paths between the tents, pathways of planks were laid as improvised duckboards, and gravel was spread on the worst-affected areas. With four days to go to the grand opening, a spell of good weather might actually salvage the situation and result in a successful show.

Friday's *Times* was far less sanguine: 'anything more unpromising than the present condition of the ground cannot well be imagined,' the paper reported. 'Water and clay together form a combination which no executive ability and no power in the world can reduce into comfort and pleasantness.'[5] Progress on foot over any part of the showground where vehicles had travelled was 'a veritable plunge', the report went on, 'for the mud and water of the principal avenues, and indeed, of almost every square yard of the area where machinery is being fixed, vary from a few inches to a foot in depth.'

At least a dozen wagons containing heavy machinery were stuck in liquid mud up to their axles, and less than half the machinery that was going on display was correctly positioned. Outside the showground, a mass of machinery and equipment was backing up; inside, some exhibitors were dumping rubble on the ground in an effort to create a more solid base for their displays. Workmen were walking around bare-legged, because they knew they would lose their boots in the mire. Still, the paper concluded, 'if only a hot sun will look upon the scene during today [Friday], Saturday and Sunday, the well-drained grass on which the animals will be stalled and penned may be passable for well-dressed company on Monday.'

On Sunday, the day before the formal opening of the show, the Prince of Wales visited the showground, with his wife Princess Alexandra and daughters Louise,

---

4   *London Evening Standard*, Thursday, 26 June.
5   *The Times*, 27 June 1879.

Maud and Victoria, for a special church service for the organisers and exhibitors. The Dean of Westminster, Arthur Stanley, gave a sermon based on Genesis 1:26–27. 'And God said Let us make man in our image, after our likeness: and let him have dominion over the fish of the sea, and over the fowl of the air, and over the cattle, and over all the earth, and over every creeping thing that creepeth upon the earth. So God created man in His own image, in the image of God created He him.'[1] He reflected on the noble qualities of many animals – their patience, courage and strength – and urged his congregation to treat the animals in their care with gentleness and mercy.

Around them, the showground was undergoing an astonishing transformation. Against the odds, by a Herculean effort all the machinery had been moved into position in time for the opening, including all the wagons backing up outside the showground. The following day's *Evening Standard* was triumphant: 'Those who have so confidently predicted nothing short of utter failure for the forthcoming Show of the Royal Agricultural Society, simply because the ground has been covered with deep slush for a few days, must by this time begin to regret their persistent croakings,' the paper thundered, perhaps having a dig at *The Times*:

> They either had not allowed for, or were ignorant of the fact that beneath the surface of mire, through which heavily laden waggons and cumbersome traction-engines laboured heavily, a complete system of subsoil drainage had robbed the stiff London clay of its worst characteristic. The water which gave the grumblers so much concern last week was thus held only in a shallow pan by a thin crust of clay, that would be sure to crack under continued sunshine, and thus moisture would have a double chance of escaping, either to the channels beneath or by a rapid process of evaporation above ground.[2]

In short, the paper was telling its readers that there was nothing to get excited about, all would be well. However, the *Standard* did acknowledge that 'such moisture-holding soil as the London clay which prevails in the immediate neighbourhood of Kilburn is quite unsuited for an agricultural show ground.'

Fortunately, the 'gloomy forebodings of misfortune' had not deterred the show's executive, which had risen to the challenge. However, the paper worried that the predictions of the doom-mongers might deter visitors and exhibitors:

> In strolling round the pens and stalls on Saturday we could not fail to notice a very large number of empty spaces or avoid the reflection that these were in a great

---

1   *London Evening Standard*, 30 June 1879.
2   Ibid.

measure the result of the exaggerated rumours to which such wide currency was given a few days ago. Very naturally owners of valuable hunters or livestock of any kind hesitated to send their animals where according to assumption they would have to stand hock deep in water and mud.

As far as the implement makers were concerned, the *Standard* said they were never worried: the worst that could happen to their machines was a spattering with mud, 'which would entail a little additional labour in furbishing up'.

In an uncharacteristically dark note, the paper did accept that 'a return of heavy rain now would seriously mar the success of the exhibition,' although it immediately brightened up and declared that:

> The surface of the exhibition yard, which could be justly described as a quagmire a week ago, has hardened enough for heavy rollers to be applied, and thus the whole area will be quite fit for visitors to walk on this morning, or at all events such portions as people who are dainty in the matter of boots will be likely to favour with their presence. Should heavy rain come, they will only have to restrict their rambles to the points that are reached by the wooden thoroughfares or planked pathways, and even then they will be able to see all the chief objects of interest without much discomfort.

On Monday, 30 June, the Prince of Wales returned to the showground to formally open the show. He was again accompanied by 'Alix', the Princess of Wales, and by their daughters Louise, Victoria and Maud (the future Queen of Norway). The royal party travelled by carriage from Hyde Park up the Edgware Road and Maida Vale and then down Cavendish Road to the main entrance on Salusbury Road, arriving at a quarter past twelve.

Along the route, enthusiastic residents hung bunting from their windows and waited on balconies to cheer the royal party. An enterprising local florist erected a display of flowers on one side of the entrance and a grandstand on the other, which had become a 'garden of girls' by the time the Prince and his family arrived.[3] In fact, the *Standard* noted with surprise that there seemed to be more women than men at the show on the first day, and that there was nothing like the throngs that had been expected, which they put down to the fact that most Londoners were not engaged in agriculture, and many would have been put off by all the talk of mud. Around 4,300 people paid for admission that day.

It was a perfect day for the opening of the show: the sun shone and it was a warm day with enough of a breeze for people to be comfortable. The Prince's party was

---

3 *London Evening Standard*, 1 July 1879.

taken on a tour of the showground, including a demonstration of butter making, before having lunch with foreign dignitaries including the Russian and Austrian ambassadors. They then boarded Decauville's steam-tram and were carried to the grandstand at the main parade ring, before returning home at four o'clock.

The fine weather continued until the first day of the show closed – and then the heavens opened. Heavy rain started in the evening of Monday, the 30th, and although hopes were raised when it let off for a couple of hours after midnight, torrential rain returned in the early hours of Tuesday the 1st – the day of the Queen's planned visit – and continued to fall in Biblical proportions well into the afternoon. High winds added to the misery, causing havoc with the tents.

Jacob Wilson, the director of the Royal Agricultural Society, was onsite at the showground from 4 a.m., but all efforts to minimise the damage were hopeless; his workforce eventually laid down tools, and no one could blame them, according to the *London Daily News*. 'Such a contrast as that between the showyard of the Royal Agricultural Society as it was on Monday and as it was when the gates opened yesterday morning has never been seen, and one must most fervently hope never will be seen again by any person now alive,' said the *Daily News*, with only slight exaggeration.[1]

The Times reported that:

> The wretchedness of the showground under the heavy driving rain of yesterday morning passes description; the whole area was reduced to a shelterless mudhole, for even the implement sheds, in spite of the devices of sundry exhibitors for insuring some degree of firmness in the surface trodden on, were largely bottomed with water, and covered with roofs which dripped distressingly from the eaves.[2]

The parading of prize animals was 'almost a cruelty'. In fact, *The Times* argued, 'the ground has all along been totally unfit for the proper standing of animals while passing through the ordeal of inspection by the judges.' Only 3,300 visitors turned up.

Queen Victoria, unsurprisingly, cancelled her visit to the show that day.

Wednesday, 2 July started promisingly, with blue skies and sunshine, and the better weather, combined with the cheaper entry fee that day, saw visitor numbers soar to 21,000. Large parts of the showground were still a quagmire resembling Glastonbury festival at its worst, and the prize animals were kept indoors all morning, to the disappointment of the relatively few visitors who turned up and hung around the parade ring in hope. After lunch a few passing thunderstorms became progressively heavier and more frequent, with one ten-minute deluge in particular dropping a huge amount

---

1   *London Daily News*, 2 July 1879.
2   Ibid.

of water on the showground, and in the Council tent the society's executive had started discussing the possibility of extending the show beyond its original one-week residency.

In the afternoon, one of the highlights of the show was the announcement of the winner of the competition between the refrigerated railway waggons of the Swansea Waggon Company and the American Civil War veteran and inventor William D'Alton Mann. Both were filled with carcasses of beef, mutton, pork and game, freshly slaughtered on 18–19 June, and sent to Holyhead and back. On Saturday, 28 June, the waggons were opened. The contents of the Swansea waggon were found to be 'perfectly sweet and in thoroughly marketable condition,' while Mr Mann's beef and pork showed traces of mould and the kidneys of the sheep were 'somewhat affected'.[3] The £50 first prize therefore went to the Swansea Waggon Company. Both waggons used ice to keep the temperatures down. The Swansea waggon recorded an average temperature of 3° Celsius; the American one nearly 9°.[4]

On Thursday, 'the rain continued from morning to eve with depressing monot-ony', the *Standard* reported.[5] Heavy wagons moving around the showground had cut up the ground to the point where the mud was knee-deep in places. Visitor numbers were sharply down again – to 9,400 – and the *Standard* noted that the large number of women visitors who had come to see the butter-making displays could only get around 'under difficulties that must have taxed their good humour to the utmost'. As expected, the organisers announced that the show would run for an extra three days to compensate the exhibitors for the disappointing visitor numbers, although the animals would start leaving the site on the coming Monday.

Friday saw better weather, with sunshine and longer intervals between the thun-derstorms. As this was the first 1s day, visitor numbers rose considerably, to 36,000, although this was 22,000 fewer than visited the Birmingham show of 1876 on the equivalent day.

During the afternoon, large amounts of gravel were poured into the ruts left by wagon wheels, and thousands of wattled sheep hurdles laid on the ground to stop people sinking into the mud, in anticipation of even bigger crowds turning out for the Queen's rearranged visit the next day. But even the normally upbeat *Standard* was forced to admit that anyone 'tempted by a few faint gleams during the morning into a belief that peregrination of the yard would be a pleasant pastime … must have been awfully disappointed'.[6]

Saturday, 5 July saw the long-awaited visit of Queen Victoria, who travelled by royal train from Windsor to the new Queen's Park station via Acton and Willesden

---

3   *Morning Post*, 3 July 1879.
4   *Wilts and Gloucestershire Standard*, 5 July 1879.
5   *London Evening Standard*, 4 July 1879.
6   *London Evening Standard*, 5 July 1879.

Junction. She was accompanied by her children, Princess Beatrice and Prince Leopold. At Queen's Park Station they were met by a royal carriage for the short trip up Salusbury Road to the main entrance to the showground, where they were met by the Prince of Wales, who escorted them on horseback to the parade ground. Victoria was known for her good luck with the weather when she had official duties to perform – so much so that the phrase 'Queen's weather' was coined. On this occasion, that luck was tested; although the day was generally fine, a heavy shower of rain fell just as she made it from her carriage to the royal box. The *London Daily News* reported that the Queen, dressed as ever in a black mourning outfit, looked especially well and 'received with radiant smiles and unshaken courage, the oft-repeated tokens of her people's loyalty'.[1] Over 52,000 people visited the show that day – the largest number on any day of the show.

The showground was closed on Sunday, 6 July. The next day saw rain in the morning but brightened up in the afternoon. The highlight for the 45,000 paying visitors (the second highest of the show) was the cutting of the great Canadian cheese with the famous battery-powered cheese cutter. The *Standard* reported that, 'The improved state of the ground enabled the visitors to get about into more remote portions of the show-yard than has hitherto been possible,' so for the first time they could get to see the display of carriages, 'which is described as the finest collection of vehicles of every description that has ever been brought together'.[2] On Monday afternoon, the first of the livestock was moved off the site; although it was to stay open for another three days, the Royal Agricultural Show of 1879 was beginning to wind down.

Visitor numbers on the remaining days (all 1*s* days) were 10,000, 5,700, and, on the final day, 4,500. In total, under 200,000 visitors had paid to enter the show, well below expectations. The Prince of Wales, in his retirement letter from the presidency of the Royal Agricultural Society, wrote to the officers to congratulate them and commented that their labours had been 'crowned with success', although he went on to note that the Society's funds had probably been 'materially crippled' by the commercial failure of the show. The show lost £14,000 – equivalent to around £850,000 today.

Although the show was a wash-out, it left one very important legacy: it paved the way for the creation of Queen's Park.

---

1   The *London Daily News*, 7 July 1879.
2   *London Evening Standard*, Tuesday, 8 July 1879.

CREATING QUEEN'S PARK

The mud-drenched 1879 Royal Agricultural Show played a key role in the history of Queen's Park because of the passionate campaign that followed to preserve the showground site as a public open space. In a little over twenty years, Queen's Park went from green fields to the district much as we see it today, with the eponymous park at its heart.

7

THE PARK

Before the dust – or more accurately, the mud – had settled on the Royal Agricultural Show, it was clear that the land would not be returning to its former use as pasture for cows for long. Development was threatening to encroach from all directions. To the east, Brondesbury Road, Brondesbury Villas and Victoria Road had been completed as far as Algernon Road (then called Victoria Villas), while on the other side of the railway lines Albert and Denmark Roads were fully built as far as Salusbury Road.

In the west, the Church Commissioners and All Soul's College were planning extensive development. The tenants of Chamberlain Wood Farm finally surrendered their lease in 1888, while Chamberlayne Road was turned from a country lane to a navigable road between 1893 and 1895.[1]

It seemed highly likely that before too long, the 100 acres between Salusbury and Chamberlayne would be completely filled with housing.

However, the same forces that had driven reform in the care of the dead and in housing were now building support for the preservation of open spaces. The first milestone in this movement was the government's select committee report of 1833 on Public Walks, called due to rising concerns about the unplanned spread of towns and cities.

Moving the proposal for the inquiry in parliament, the Whig MP Robert Aglionby Slaney (who went on to chair the inquiry) told the House that:

At this time [London] contained a greater number of inhabitants than any city in the world had ever possessed. Within a circle of eight miles from St. Paul's, there were no less than 1,750,000 persons, and the population of the town itself amounted to one million and a half. In that population were mixed the richest and the poorest

---

1 https://willesden-local-history.co.uk/kensal-green

men – men whose wealth had never been surpassed by that of any other men, in any times whatever, and the most wretched outcasts, whose miserable condition was not equalled by that of the poor of any other city in Europe.

This population was served by three parks, only one of which was open to everyone, he pointed out, and this situation was mirrored in the other great cities of the country.

'It was said by Mr. Wyndham [Wadham Penruddock Wyndham, the MP for Salisbury], that the parks were the lungs of London; and if they were then so necessary to the ventilation of the city, how requisite was it now, that its present vast population should have increased means of recreation,' Slaney added.

This idea that parks and open spaces were the lungs of cities resonated with people. The select committee report did indeed find that there was insufficient open space being provided for the fast-growing urban working classes, and that access to green spaces had positive effects on family relationships and health, while reducing drunkenness. Among other things, it recommended opening Regent's Park to more visitors and preventing plans to enclose and build over Primrose Hill.

The drive for accessible open spaces was also driven by concerns over moral rectitude and social cohesion. The committee's report observed that 'a man walking out with his family among his neighbours of different ranks will naturally be desirous to be properly clothed and that his Wife and Children should be also … it is by inducement alone that active, persevering and willing industry is promoted; and what inducement can be more powerful to anyone, than the desire of improving the condition and comfort of his family.'[1]

As with the government's previous inquiries into burials and housing, legislative action was slow to follow and proposals for municipal action met resistance from opponents who felt sure that it must be someone else's responsibility to address the problem. A further government inquiry in 1840 – this time looking at the Health of Towns – highlighted the need for action 'not less for welfare of the poor than the safety of property and the security of the rich'.[2]

Fear of the working class was never far below the surface in Victorian times, as we will see later in this chapter, and not entirely without reason: in July 1866 demonstrators, denied access to Hyde Park for a protest in support of electoral reform, created their own entrances to the park by tearing down the railings all along Park Lane. The *Evening Mail* was in no doubt as to the sort of people who were responsible:

Between 9 and 10 o'clock a number of the lowest rabble of the metropolis assembled

---

1   Select Committee on Public Walks, p.9.
2   Report from the Select Committee on the Health of Towns, pp.xiv–xv.

in the park near the Marble Arch, and as time wore on their ranks were swelled by fresh arrivals until they presented very formidable appearance. They evinced their zeal for Reform by doing as much injury to the park as they possibly could, and insulting everybody who appeared to be more respectable than themselves. They wreaked their vengeance on the flowers and shrubs by wantonly plucking them up by the roots.[3]

The American Civil War had just ended, leaving over 600,000 dead; European capitals were regularly being engulfed by revolution, and in London the 'respectable' classes were shocked by an incident of flower-picking!

In 1848 the Public Health Act was passed, giving local authorities responsibility for promoting public health – including the provision of green spaces. Article 74 of the Act gave councils the power to 'provide, maintain, lay out, plant, and improve Premises for the Purpose of being used as public Walks or Pleasure Grounds'. In other words, to borrow money to pay for parks.[4]

Although some government money was used to promote healthy open spaces – buying Primrose Hill from Eton College, for example – the development of parks was largely left to local authorities and philanthropically minded wealthy people. The local experience suggests that the emerging municipal authorities of the 1880s were far from enthusiastic about shouldering the costs of building and maintaining new parks, while the Metropolitan Board of Works – an appointed (rather than elected) body responsible for London-wide government from 1855 to 1899 – constructed parks in every part of London apart from the north-west.

Paddington Park

Queen's Park was not the first park to be proposed in this part of London: that title goes to 'Paddington Park', which was under discussion at least as early as the summer of 1879, if not before.

The idea was to preserve an 80-acre plot of open land south of Carlton Vale – the last remains of the Bishop of London's Paddington Estate – as a public park. The area was under serious threat from developers: Reginald Brabazon, the Conservative peer and philanthropist, who supported the scheme, reported to the *Kilburn Times* that 'each month sees this open space become more and more contracted', with 15 acres disappearing of the original 95 since the park had first been suggested.[5]

---

3 *Evening Mail*, 25 July 1866, p.8.
4 Public Health Act 1848, p.755.
5 *Kilburn Times*, 19 August 1881.

A committee with some heavyweight backers was set up, and Paddington Vestry was petitioned to support the proposal. The vestry agreed to forward the proposal to the highest tier of local government in London, the Metropolitan Board of Works. One member of the vestry commented that he had no objection to parks, but the poor quality of housing for working people was an even greater cause for concern. *The Kilburn Times* dismissed this as 'facetious', since – according to them – housing conditions were a matter between landlords and their tenants, and therefore outside the scope of parish authorities.[1]

In November 1879, the Metropolitan Board met to consider the proposed Paddington Park. *The Kilburn Times* reported:

> They had no hesitation in at once admitting that a proposition, having for its object the increase of open spaces and recreation grounds in the Metropolis, most especially command itself to the sympathy of this Board, which had for years devoted a not inconsiderable share of its attention to the securing of open spaces, parks, and commons for the public benefit.[2]

There were, however, other factors to be taken into consideration, not the least of which was the cost. The price of the land would be four times what it cost the Board to acquire Southwark Park and eight times the cost of Finsbury Park. And anyway, Kensington Gardens, Regent's Park and Wormwood Scrubs were all pretty close to Kilburn, so maybe the poor could go there instead, argued the Board.

Their decision triggered a furious response from a local barrister's clerk and part-time organist called George Higgs, who wrote:

> The refusal of the Metropolitan Board is in every way a very serious matter. It is absurd to talk about Kensington Gardens and Regent's Park being within easy distance from the locality. They are both about half-an-hour's walk, which, I submit, is much too far for working men and hard-worked clerks after their day's labour is done. As for the immense number of children here it is quite impossible for them to walk far: and unless we secure the proposed site, or a fair part of it, I suppose they must, poor little things, be content to play on the streets or in the areas of their houses; thus being liable to be run over, or (what is perhaps worse) to an attack of fever through the foul air from the sinks. This is not exaggeration. There is not a single place for them to play in, not even a small recreation ground.[3]

---

1   *Kilburn Times*, 13 June 1879.
2   *Kilburn Times*, 21 November 1879.
3   Ibid.

He ended his blast by urging the park's supporters to 'begin again with renewed energy to secure, if not all the proposed site, still a good portion of it, that our homes may not only be happy but healthy', promising, 'I am quite ready to work hard and with all my heart for this real necessity.' He was true to his word, as we'll see later.

Francis Heath, the renowned expert on ferns, expressed hope that the Board would think again if enough matched funding could be raised from 'some of the wealthy and public-spirited residents in the richest city of the world', and this was the strategy the Paddington Park committee decided to follow. It was soon estimated that they could raise £100,000 of the £436,000 required, and according to Brabazon, the Metropolitan Board indicated that this would be enough for them to put up the rest, to be funded by the ratepayers, with a commitment to pay up to £1,000 per acre. Brabazon urged better-off Londoners to donate, arguing, 'I trust that some who are enjoying their holidays in fine air and amidst country scenes will remember the thousands who are unable to leave the town.'

Freehold ownership of all the land owned by institutions like St Paul's Cathedral, Westminster Abbey and the Diocese of London (including the manors of Chambers, Brands and Bounds) had passed from St Paul's Cathedral to the Church of England's Ecclesiastical Commissioners in Acts of Parliament in the 1840s. The commissioners were appointed to run the church's finances in a more professional way, and to raise the funds for a major programme of church building to minister to the needs of the growing population of Britain. Farmland like the fields around Maida Vale and Queen's Park was prime real estate, and they began parcelling it up into streets and individual lots for sale to builders (the leasehold, that is – they held on to the freehold until the 1950s). All Soul's College Oxford was doing the same with its property in the area at the same time, although down on the Queen's Park Estate (see Chapter 5) it was the Artizans Company that planned the street layout, not the college.

As a result, it was the Ecclesiastical Commissioners and a trust who managed the land in Paddington on their behalf who would ultimately decide whether the land in Paddington would be built over, or become a public park. Both the commissioners and the trust indicated a willingness to sell the land for use as a park, and even though their initial asking price was 'considerably more than the value of it', the committee was confident that they would eventually sell for a fair amount. However, the terms of the trust meant that an Act of Parliament was required to approve any sale,[4] so a parliamentary bill was duly prepared.

In February 1882, a 'stormy' public meeting was held by the committee backing the Paddington Park Bill in Paddington. The first resolution, in favour of the purchase of the remaining 80 acres to build a park, was passed by a large majority. The terms

4   *Kilburn Times*, 19 August 1881.

of the parliamentary bill were then explained to the meeting and a second resolution put, expressing approval of the bill and authorising the committee chair to sign a petition in its favour. The committee's barrister – the celebrated social reformer John Westlake – explained that by agreeing to this motion people would also be agreeing to an additional tax of sixpence for wealthier districts and tuppence for less well-off areas to pay for the park. This motion was also passed, although not without a lot of debate and opposition.[1]

The following month, the Willesden Board met to consider whether to support the bill. The meeting was told that a crowded meeting of South Kilburn ratepayers had been held to discuss the proposals ('indeed many were turned away from the doors, unable to gain admission'). It was the 'clear and unanimous' mood of that meeting that residents would rather have no park at all than have to pay an additional rate. With the Kilburn representatives strongly opposed to the proposal for additional rates, the Willesden Board resolved to write to parliament to object to the proposed bill.[2]

The Paddington Park Bill was subsequently rejected by a parliamentary select committee, as Westlake had warned, and efforts to preserve the 80 acres fell. The idea of a park in South Kilburn was revived in 1888, when the remaining 27 acres (centring on Paddington Cricket Club) that hadn't been built over were laid out as Paddington Recreation Ground.

Queen's Park

In August 1882, an extraordinary letter was printed in the *Morning Post*. Written by a J Huntington (a local Conservative activist) and entitled 'Queen's Park v Paddington Park', the author urged readers to consider the merits of an alternative to Paddington Park; he called this alternative Queen's Park. He had, he said, been corresponding with the Metropolitan Board of Works since 1879 about this idea. His proposal was to take the 100 acres of the Royal Agricultural Showground and combine it with another 200 acres to the west and north, including the whole of the Brondesbury Park estate, making a new park covering 300 acres. (For comparison, Hyde Park is around 350 acres and Regent's Park 410.)

The new park would have 'planting …, recreation grounds, a cricket-field, and garden, and, most important of all, ornamental ponds for birds and for bathing', the latter covering 10 acres, to be screened by the ornamental gardens of Brondesbury Manor on one side and by the mounds of earth excavated to make the new ponds on

---

1   *Kilburn Times*, 17 February 1882.
2   *Kilburn Times*, 10 March 1882.

the other. 'The last-named advantage is one loudly called for by the working population, which desires to enjoy the same facility for the healthy pleasure of swimming and bathing afforded in other metropolitan parks,' he explained.

Huntington had produced detailed drawings, which had been provided to the Metropolitan Board, and had been assured by the Board's chairman, James Garel-Hogg, that it would be duly considered. Despite this, the Board had pressed ahead with their assurance of a £1,000-an-acre subsidy to the Paddington Park scheme, with no offer of support to Huntington's counter-proposal. Worse, he had been told that because the Board was now backing the Paddington plan, it couldn't consider his.

He had landed on the name, he said, 'partly out of loyalty to her Majesty, partly from the contiguity of the estate of 80 acres so called, containing the dwellings of artisans and workers of all descriptions [the Queen's Park Estate] and partly from the North-Western Railway Station of that name'. (This was five years before Queen's Park formally got its name, having laboured under the working title of 'Kilburn Recreation Ground' until the Queen gave her royal assent to the name.)

He had no doubt that the excellent transport links of the area would bring visitors from all over London, including from the other side of the Thames, while, 'The character for good conduct and for hearty appreciation which the toilers of London have earned at ... other parks will effectually silence the expression of fear of a contrary conduct in the new space for enjoyment.'

His proposals were fully costed. The purchase price of the land (303 acres in total) would be £390,000; 'planting, path and road making, excavations and embankments, lodges and other buildings, fencing, draining, stocking, superintendence, and compensations would together amount to £40,000; the total being £430,000.' Annual maintenance would be about £4,000, including gatekeepers, police, gardeners, repair bills, maintenance of the bathing and ornamental ponds and other costs. He estimated that the whole amount could be repaid within twenty-eight years with a modest addition to the rates.

In comparison, he argued, the Paddington Park plan was expensive, was driven by wealthy people who didn't want poor people on their doorsteps, and was in a 'hole' that would not afford wonderful views over London of the kind that you would get from a park occupying the Brondesbury Ridge.

Huntington and his associates were still arguing the case for his inspirational vision of a 300-acre park in front of the Metropolitan Board in November 1883,[3] months after a new actor had come on stage.

3 *Pall Mall Gazette*, 3 November 1883.

The North-West London Park League

As we've seen, one of the local campaigners fired up by the dismissive attitude of the Metropolitan Board of Works to the Paddington Park concept was George Higgs. Higgs was a local man who lived in Barnsdale Road, a turning off Ferndale Road in what was then known as St Peter's Park, initially a wealthier part of the area than Kensal Town or the Queen's Park Estate. Higgs was 34 when he wrote to the *Kilburn Times* to argue passionately for public parks. He and his wife Jane, who was born in the Channel Islands, had at least eight children between 1871 and 1890, so he knew what he was talking about when he said that local children struggled to find places to play.

George Higgs: 'Health is impossible without adequate breathing room'

Born in Marylebone in 1845, George Higgs grew up in Nutford Place, just off the Edgware Road between Marble Arch and Paddington. He was brought up by his mother, Mary, a dressmaker. He had left school and was working as a clerk by the age of 16. He married Jane Elizabeth (Eliza) de Gruchy in St Saviours, Jersey when he was 24 and she was 22.

Their first home was in Walthamstow, but by 1881 they were living in St Peter's Park with their numerous children and George's mother. They were still there in 1891. They then moved to Harlesden, before settling at 98 Harvist Road, a short walk from the park. Once the children had left home, they retired to Cricklewood.

In May 1885, George was elected to the Metropolitan Public Garden and Boulevard Association, in recognition of his campaigning work, and in 1889 he was appointed honorary secretary of the equally successful campaign to establish a polytechnic in north-west London, which resulted in the creation of Kilburn Polytechnic in 1881.

George kept campaigning for an extension of Queen's Park for years after the park formally opened in 1887. Surviving letters show he was still urging expansion westwards as late as 1897, arguing that the increasing popularity of the park would soon make it too small to accommodate all the people who wanted to visit it.

In the summer of 1887, a committee was formed to organise a testimonial for George, in recognition of his work on the park campaign. It was organised by Sir Algernon Borthwick and his fellow MPs John Aird (Paddington North), Lord George Hamilton (Ealing) and Frederick Seager Hunt (Marylebone West). The treasurer was the Middlesex Coroner, Danford Thomas.

George died in Willesden in 1930, aged 86. Eliza survived him by three years, dying in Tendring, Essex, in 1933 at the age of 87.

Higgs was elected as the inaugural honorary secretary of the North-west London Park League, established to secure the 100-acre site of the Royal Agricultural Show for a new park for the people of Kilburn, St Peter's Park, Kensal and the other surrounding neighbourhoods. Public meetings were held at various locations on the Harrow Road, Westbourne Park and at the Cobden Working Men's Club and Institute on Kensal Road in the summer of 1883 to gain public support for the proposal.[1] The latter meeting was chaired by Daniel Grant, the Liberal MP for Marylebone, who spoke in favour of having a number of smaller parks across London rather than the kind of super-park proposed by Huntington, and also attended by his fellow Liberal MP JB Firth. However, the League seems to have tried to avoid becoming party political; the Cobden Club motion 'affirming that a park for the use of the inhabitants of North-West London was absolutely necessary, and that the site occupied by the Agricultural Society's Show in 1879 was admirably adapted for that purpose', was seconded by Algernon Borthwick, a Conservative politician, and the Unionist coroner for Middlesex, Danford Thomas, also lent his support. It was at this meeting that the idea first surfaced of asking the City Corporation to get involved, using a levy on corn to provide the necessary funding. Borthwick told the meeting:

> It was painful to think that the hundreds of children who had for one day been amusing themselves in the country should have to go back to the close quarters of narrow crowded streets without any prospect of enjoying themselves on the greensward or amongst the flowers and trees until perhaps another year had passed.

He added that, 'He was glad to give his hearty support to this movement, which was one in which men of all shades of opinion and political views could take part. Too much time was devoted to acrimonious discussion, to the disadvantage of plans which were calculated to advance the health and morals and happiness of their fellow countrymen.'

The meeting duly resolved to write to both the Metropolitan Board and to the City Corporation to ask for their support, and the League were soon notified by the Chelsea Vestry that they were supportive of the new campaign.[2]

In September, hopes were raised when Parliament passed the City Parochial Charities Act (1883), which centralised the administration of over a thousand charitable funds in the City of London, creating a pot estimated to be worth £70,000 a year for funding good causes. It was expected that both the League and the Paddington Park committee would appeal to it for support.[3]

---

1 *Morning Post*, 27 July 1883.
2 *Morning Post*, 28 July 1883.
3 *Kilburn Times*, 14 September 1883.

In February 1884, George Higgs led a deputation to the House of Commons to meet James Bryce (the author of the Charities Act), JB Firth and a 'Mr Holland' (probably Samuel Holland, the Liberal MP for Merioneth) and ask for their support. The Ecclesiastical Commissioners were happy to sell the land at market value, he reported, and the City Corporation were happy to buy it and take responsibility for the new park as long as they were guaranteed the income from corn duties to fund it; the City had written to the Treasury accordingly. Unfortunately, the MPs did not have good news for Higgs and his colleagues. Bryce told them that this was a question for the 'new municipality' (presumably meaning the London County Council, which was being debated at the time), and Firth said the proposal would require a Private Members' Bill, which couldn't be done in the current session of parliament. He even doubted if the City Corporation could find the necessary funds to buy the whole of the showground site even if the grain duty were extended.[1]

The League despatched another delegation in August 1884, this time to meet the Ecclesiastical Commissioners and their chairman, Earl Stanhope. (Chevening Road in Queen's Park is named after Stanhope's ancestral estate in Kent, which is now government property and occupied by a member of the Cabinet nominated by the PM.) Stanhope 'expressed his sympathy with the object of the deputation and spoke approvingly of the scheme suggested',[2] and agreed to delay negotiations with prospective builders for a further six months while the League continued their efforts to find the funding needed to buy the whole site.

In December, however, Higgs learned that builders were preparing to start work on the west side of Salusbury Road. He complained to the Ecclesiastical Commissioners, who said the strip in question had been sold back in 1880.[3]

In January 1885, the commissioners' estate agents, Cluttons, recommended that the site be sold for development, but the central section of 30 acres should be reserved for a park, as this would enable higher rents to be charged. On 22 January 1886, the commission's Estates Committee approved this plan, and Stanhope wrote to the City Corporation to offer them the 30 acres plus Gravel Pit Wood in Highgate.

With his characteristic generosity – and optimism – Higgs wrote to the commissioners saying: 'My joy on receiving your letter last night ... was so great that I passed a sleepless night, but my mind has now been relieved by this most Christian-like offer, for nothing can, I should think, prevent its being accepted.' He added that he still hoped the City Corporation might buy the whole of the showground site, and that he was particularly keen to save the Salusbury Road frontage.[4]

1   *Morning Post*, 22 February 1884.
2   *Kilburn Times*, 15 August 1884.
3   Cummins, *How Queen's Park Came into Being*, p.16.
4   Ibid., p.17.

In a letter to *The Times*, Higgs spoke in favour of the planned sale of the 30 acres, but added:

> Still more anxious am I that those to whose generosity you appeal may not forget the wants of the teeming population of Kilburn, St. Peter's Park, Kensal New Town, and Brondesbury, etc., to which the 30 acres so kindly offered by the Ecclesiastical Commissioners will, indeed, be a valuable boon, but to which the acquisition of the whole of the 94 acres for which we have agitated so long is still of incalculable importance.[5]

The elected members of Willesden, meeting at White's Hotel on Shoot-up Hill on 27 February, could scarcely conceal their excitement at the prospect of getting a park at no cost to them. A letter was read out from John Marrian, one of the leaders of the North-west London Park League, signalling George Higgs's role in getting the concessions they had won, and urging once again that someone – anyone! – should try to secure the whole 100 acres for a park. The vestry endorsed Marrian's sentiments but agreed to write to Stanhope and the commissioners to express their 'warm approval and appreciation of their wise munificence', generally agreeing that there was no point picking a fight with either the commissioners or the corporation.[6]

Some members did speak up in favour of a more ambitious project: a Mr Pryor and Mr Stewart, both members of the League's committee, said they hoped that the City Corporation might yet decide to bid for more land, and both spoke movingly about how George Higgs had kept plugging away when everyone else was losing heart. Without him, they suggested, there might not have been a park at all.

The Paddington Vestry also expressed their delight at the proposals.

It was not over yet. In May 1886, the City's Coal, Corn and Finance Committee, who were being asked to fund the purchase out of corn duty revenues, reported that they had visited both Gravel Pit Wood and the Royal Agricultural Show site. While they would happily approve buying the former, which required little work, they were unhappy at the likely expense of turning the latter into a full-blown park with decent drainage and modern conveniences. They recommended rejection.[7]

The Ecclesiastical Commissioners, however, were not budging: the offer was both or neither. They gave the City until New Year's Eve to find the funds.

On 4 June, the League held a mass gathering on the site to demonstrate public support for the park; 800 to 900 people attended, despite bad weather, including large

---

5   *Kilburn Times*, 20 February 1885.
6   *Willesden Chronicle*, 27 February 1885.
7   Cummins, *How Queen's Park Came into Being*, p.17.

numbers of children. The rally was eminently respectable, and was presided over by the Middlesex Coroner, Danforth Thomas.

In October, the City finally came up with a solution: divert a bequest left to the Corporation by one William Ward in 1881, part of which was intended for 'some fund for the benefit of the Poorer Classes'. The Common Council and Court of Chancery both gave their approval (this was, after all, taking place just thirty-odd years after the publication of Dickens's *Bleak House*) and the deal with the Ecclesiastical Commissioners was done. It was ratified in the Highgate and Kilburn Open Spaces Act of 1886.

Sixteen months later, the indefatigable George Higgs was still trying to get the park extended. The Ecclesiastical Commissioners even granted an extension until Lady Day (25 March) 1887 on the disposal of the remaining 30 acres to give the League the opportunity to double the size of the park to 60 acres. Appeals were made to the Paddington Vestry and the Willesden Board, and to people's patriotism: 'I cannot imagine a more worthy mode of commemorating Her Majesty's Jubilee than the extension of this Queen's Park, which is excellently situated, and will undoubtedly be a great boon to this densely populated district of London,' Higgs wrote.[1] If 'the opportunity for acquiring an additional breathing space for this extremely poor and overcrowded district [is] irretrievably lost' it would be a 'catastrophe', he added.[2]

No one took up this offer, and so the park proceeded at its present 30 acres. It was a remarkable achievement by Higgs, who had negotiated with some of the most formidable institutions in Britain – Parliament, the Church of England, the City of London – to get a park for the children of this area.

The Development of the Park

The Act of Parliament enabling the sale gave the responsibility for creating approach roads to the new park (Chevening Road and Mortimer Road, which was subsequently renamed Harvist between Salusbury and Chamberlayne) to the Ecclesiastical Commissioners, with a deadline of 1 January 1888.[3] The cost of the two new roads was £16,000.[4] Work commenced on the roads in 1886, shortly after the Act received parliamentary approval. In November of that year, George Higgs informed *The Times* that 'roads around this park agreed to be constructed by the Ecclesiastical Commissioners are being rapidly proceeded with'.[5]

---

1   *West London Observer*, 5 February 1887.
2   *Hampstead and Highgate Express*, 12 March 1887.
3   Highgate and Kilburn Open Spaces Act 1886, section 3.
4   History of Queen's Park, p.11.
5   *Hampstead and Highgate Express*, 6 November 1886.

The job of designing the new park was given to Alexander McKenzie, a leading designer of parks and gardens at the time. His previous work had included Alexandra Park, Southwark Park, Finsbury Park and the Albert Embankment. He was part of an influential group of designers who took Victorian landscape design away from the style of parterres and formal geometry towards a more natural sensibility.

McKenzie's original design featured the two circles that still exist today, one of them apparently intended for tennis and the other for cricket. The use of circles in park design, with planting to separate the different zones and activities, was first introduced at Sefton Park in Liverpool in the 1860s by the influential French designer Edouard Andre.[6] Around the outside of the park, where the circles brushed the boundaries of the park, were six densely planted triangles; today only the Quiet Garden gives an impression of what this must have been like.

Major works on the park took place between March and June 1887, ready for its official opening in November. These works cost £3,000, including laying out, drainage and planting. Plans for a head gardener's house were not submitted to the City Corporation for approval until after the park opened, although 'The Lodge' was up and running by 1889. An outdoor 'gymnasium' was sited where the children's playground is now.

In the final run-up to the opening there was much discussion of the by-laws for the new park. Contentious issues including whether perambulators would be allowed in the park (they were) and the closing time (shortly after sunset).[7]

Today's by-laws for the park still forbid people bringing in 'cattle, sheep, goats, pigs, or any beast of draught or burden'; and forbid that people 'brawl, fight, quarrel or create any disorder'; 'use profane, indecent, obscene or offensive language'; 'gamble, bet or play with cards or dice'; or bring greyhounds or whippets into the park that aren't muzzled (the latter of which I admit to breaking on a daily basis). There's also a by-law against landing helicopters, which is a more recent addition.[8]

In August, the *Kilburn Times* reported that the City Corporation had decided to name the space the Kilburn Recreation Ground, and noted that, 'Already the newly-laid road, parallel with the London and North-Western Railway, is a favourite promenade between Salusbury-road and Station-road, Kensal Green, on Sunday evenings.'[9]

However, on 4 November 1887, just in time for the opening of the park, a response was received to the request to Her Majesty Queen Victoria to be allowed to name the park in her honour. The letter read:

6   History of Queen's Park, p.20.
7   *Kilburn Times*, 11 November 1887.
8   www.cityoflondon.gov.uk/things-to-do/green-spaces/queens-park/queens-park-rules-and-byelaws
9   *Kilburn Times*, 5 August 1887.

Home Office, 4th November, 1887. Sir,—l am directed by Mr. Secretary Matthews to inform you that he has had the honour to lay before the Queen the application of the Corporation of the City of London for permission to use the Royal title in connection with name of the Kilburn Recreation Ground, which is about to be opened, and I am to state that her Majesty was pleased to accede to the request, and to command that the said Recreation Ground shall be called the Queen's Park. — l am, Sir, your obedient servant, Godfrey Lushington.[1]

The Opening of the Park

The new park was formally opened on Saturday, 5 November, a 'fine and bright' day, by the Lord Mayor of London, Sir Reginald Hanson. The Lord Mayor and his retinue, including sheriffs and under-sheriffs, travelled in full state by ceremonial carriage from the City to the park, via Kilburn High Road, Willesden Lane and Winchester Avenue. Other City dignitaries, including members of the Coal, Corn and Finance Committee, travelled by special train from Broad Street to Kensal Green station (today's Kensal Rise), where they waited with a large number of other notables for the Lord Mayor's arrival at the north-eastern entrance to the park.

Guests included G Bolland Newton, general manager of the North London Railway; F Dunn, the superintendent of the line; FA Wood, the chairman of the Willesden Local Board; John Aird, the MP for North Paddington; and Danford Thomas, the Middlesex Coroner. A guard of honour was provided by the Victoria Rifles, commanded by Major Mann and Lieutenants Weekley and Sandeman. They were accompanied by their regimental band, and the Queen's Park Brass Band also attended.

A temporary platform and a marquee were erected for the occasion 'at the foot of the park's northern slope' (presumably where the café is today), and 'people were massed not only immediately in front of the platform, but covered the rising ground alongside, this part having the appearance of a portion of a huge amphitheatre, thickly packed'.[2]

EJ Stoneham, the chairman of the City Corporation's Coal, Corn and Finance Committee, welcomed the Lord Mayor and said 'he should hardly be doing justice on this occasion were he to conclude without referring to the exertions of a gentleman present who had so long been prominent in that neighbourhood in endeavouring to promote the good cause so happily brought to a successful issue that day, and who, in connection with the securing of that ground, and in his attempt to obtain a similar boon for his own district of Paddington, had deserved a hearty recognition at their

1   *Hampstead and Highgate Express*, 12 November 1887.
2   *Kilburn Times*, 11 November 1887.

hands'.[3] (He was of course referring to George Higgs.) This was met with loud cheers from the thousands of local people who had turned up for the opening.

The Lord Mayor – who had previously lived in the area – said that 'he trusted and believed that as time went on there would be a considerable improvement in that open space, now so vastly improved from what it was eight or nine years ago, when a good many of those present visited the exhibition there, and a great part of the ground was a swamp'.[4]

After the Lord Mayor read out the message from Queen Victoria sanctioning the name 'Queen's Park' and declared the park open, a vote of thanks was moved by FA Wood on behalf of the Willesden Local Board, and seconded by George Higgs.

Wood perhaps caught the true meaning of the event best when he thanked the City Corporation not just on behalf of the Willesden Board but also:

> the many thousands of poor people, especially the children, who could now enjoy the park when they wanted a place of recreation or amusement. Anyone who went into the houses round that place, would know better than he could tell them, of the close streets, the confined houses, and the stuffy rooms the people had to live in day by day; and for these people, the women and children especially, the opening of this park would be the best work that had been done for many a day.[5]

There was then a surprising outbreak of Bonfire Night-related banter when the Lord Mayor said he thought he had heard someone say on his arrival, 'Here's another guy.' 'I wouldn't object to being a "guy" many times for the performance of similar tasks to this, and I certainly shall long "remember the fifth of November",' quipped the Lord Mayor, to loud cheers.[6]

The Lord Mayor and EJ Stoneham then planted a tree each in commemoration of the occasion, following which the dignitaries returned to town to attend a banquet at the Guildhall. During the toasts that evening the Lord Mayor revealed an unsuspected interest in football, 'which he had noticed was extensively played in Kilburn'. He said he would be delighted to encourage the game, and would be happy to provide a prize for the best local team.[7]

The City had paid the Metropolitan Police £4 1s for the services of fifteen constables and a sergeant following rumours that 'the cream of London ruffianism' were planning to show up, but their services weren't needed. The 'vast' crowd was good-

---

3 Ibid.
4 Ibid.
5 Ibid.
6 Ibid.
7 *Evening Standard*, 7 November 1887.

natured and well behaved, the great majority 'composed evidently of the respectable class, working people and their children predominating'.[1] Once the dignitaries had departed, large numbers of people stayed on for the forty-five minutes or so until closing time, being entertained by the two brass bands.

The whole ceremony must have lasted about an hour; it started at 3 p.m. and sunset that day was at 4.30, with the park closing shortly afterwards. Despite the work done on laying out the park, tarmacking the paths and planting, it must have been still quite rough on that day, judging by the Lord Mayor's comment that in eight or nine years, he hoped it would be 'much more of a park than it was now'.[2]

As the revellers trooped home, they would have had an unobstructed view across the fields towards Kilburn. As late as 1893, Salusbury Road was still empty of buildings apart from the police station, fire station and library at the very bottom, the 'Igar Hotels' buildings halfway up and the Maria Grey women's teacher training college at the very top of the road. At every other point there was a clear line of sight across open ground from the wooden palisade fence around Queen's Park to the brick wall of Paddington Cemetery.

Improvements

In October 1888, the diligent MP for Paddington North, John Aird, presented 'a handsome drinking fountain' to the City Corporation for the enjoyment of visitors to the park.[3] This fountain was located in the middle of the park where the two circles met.

In 1890, a 'rustic-style chalet' opened near where the children's playground is today, serving refreshments.

The bandstand followed in 1891. The park had a long tradition of brass-band music. As we have seen, the Queen's Park Brass Band (from the Queen's Park Estate) played at the opening ceremony, and George Higgs noted that the band '(composed entirely of working men, and most efficient they are) has played in the park since its opening … to the intense delight of at least 30,000 artisans and their families every Sunday'.[4] They were careful not to play during the hours when church services were under way so as not to tempt church-goers.

The band was founded in 1883, and had a membership of around forty, of which thirty would generally play at any one time, conducted by a Mr Cope. In November

1   *Kilburn Times*, 11 November 1887.
2   Ibid.
3   *Hampstead and Highgate Express*, 13 October 1888.
4   *Morning Post*, 31 October 1891.

1890 the band had 'got into low water in the matter of funds', so a public meeting was called. The ever-reliable Danford Thomas chaired, supported by John Aird. In addition to raising money for the band, this meeting also agreed to lobby the Corporation for a bandstand and enclosure in the park.

As a result of this petition, the cast-iron bandstand, manufactured by MacFarlane and Co. of Glasgow, was commissioned, at a cost of £342.[5] It was placed on the old route of Long Cross Lane, the track that had carried local people for hundreds of years across the fields where the park now stood.

---

5 *Kilburn Times*, 7 November 1890.

8

BUILDING
QUEEN'S PARK

Apart from the farms on Kilburn Lane – at least one of which was probably occupied in the 1100s – the earliest buildings in Queen's Park went up in the 1850s and '60s on Willesden Lane. At that time, Willesden Lane was still a rural retreat for well-to-do Victorians who wanted to live in 'villas' within easy distance of a train station that could take them into London, without the disadvantages of living in that smoky, overcrowded and fast-growing metropolis.

The lodges by the entrance to the Paddington Cemetery (see Chapter 4) were constructed in 1854, shortly after the land was acquired by Paddington's Burial Board. The Prince of Wales Public House next door opened in 1864. A terrace of six imposing homes called Lincoln Villas (where the block of flats called Athelstan Gardens is today) was built in 1865, and in 1866 the Church of England opened Christchurch a short distance up Willesden Lane to serve the expanding community.

In 1868, twelve houses were built between the Prince of Wales and the Lincoln Villas terrace, and in 1872 a small street called Lincoln Mews was added. Around the corner, on Winchester Road (now Winchester Avenue), a small number of houses were built in the late 1860s.

We can tell a fair amount about these properties from the 1871 census. In that year, one of the cemetery lodges was home to Henry Bailey, the manager of the cemetery, his wife Mary and their four children, and the other to David Pittack, a missionary who preached in the City of London. Next door, the Prince of Wales public house (since renamed the Kilburn Arms) was home to the Midgeley family, who ran it.

Lincoln Terrace and Lincoln Mews were working-class homes: the breadwinners had occupations like laundress, coachman and stonemason. Lincoln Mews still exists today (although not the original houses).

The villas, on the other hand, were home to higher-class residents. The chief earners in 1871 were a farmer, a butcher, a brewer, a solicitor, a warehouseman, a tea taster (they performed quality checks – there were also professional ale tasters) and a schoolmistress.

Winchester Road had an eclectic mix of residents in 1871, including a cow keeper, a railway signalman, a plate layer, a plasterer and a Keeper of the Royal Exchange. Most of the current houses on the road were erected between 1898 and 1901 by a number of builders including W Walters (27–43), WH Buftow (14–36) and David Dakers (38–54).

Victorian Builders

Most of the buildings in Queen's Park were the work of entrepreneurs who often had little or no experience of construction when they started out. Solomon Barnett, the master builder responsible for most of the roads between the park and the eastern edge of the Queen's Park area, was a trader in glass and lead before he went into the construction industry. He invested his own money in both buying the land and building on it.

The houses on the west side of park, on the other hand, were erected by a number of local builders. In some cases they both owned and built the properties, but in Kempe and Keslake Roads in particular they were contractors for the owners of the land and the buildings that went up on it.

This was typical of the Victorian housebuilding market, which was dominated by small firms, and was highly speculative: at the time when most of Queen's Park was built, for example, there was an over-supply of homes designed for middle-class families, so many went straight into multi-occupancy and didn't become single-family dwellings until the 1980s.

As we've seen, landowners – in this case the Ecclesiastical Commissioners – parcelled off the land into streets and individual development plots for sale. They retained the freehold, and sold the leases to developers, who then had to get approval for both the street fronts they were planning and the individual buildings they wanted to construct from the surveyors of the relevant planning authority. Brent Council's archives, at Willesden Library, hold the handwritten, leather-bound registers of Willesden's planning department from Victorian times. Thanks to these we know that EA Warfield of the William IV pub on the Harrow Road secured planning permission for the outline frontage of Chamberlayne Wood Road in August 1895, and that the local school board (dominated by nonconformists) was twice refused permission to build a council school on the road by the planning committee (dominated by Church of England activists) before they finally got the go-ahead (as we'll see in Chapter 12, education was highly politicised in late Victorian England).

Most building firms were small-scale enterprises, hiring local labour and crafts-men as and when needed rather than permanently employing skilled workers. The labour force they needed lived locally: around a third of local men in jobs in 1900 worked in manual occupations, many of them in building trades. Their employers were also local people: almost all the firms responsible for building Queen's Park were headed by men who lived in Queen's Park itself or at the furthest, in West Hampstead or Paddington. The only significant exception was in the case of large, municipal or church projects, and even some of these went to contractors from Willesden Junction and Acton.

For example, we know that local builder Thomas Pessell was responsible for 124 houses in Queen's Park over five years; William Riley 116; EH Elyatt 26; and Joseph Huish 12. Some of these builders only executed one type of house design, even if they were building houses on behalf of the leaseholder, suggesting that they had a high degree of control over their work. Others worked as sub-contrac-tors, finishing off jobs for other builders to their specifications, and built multiple types of house.

All of them would have had an architect involved in the design, although the term was a bit more elastic than we would recognise today. Solomon Barnett must have had a designer in his team; F Costin of Harlesden designed one of the signature types of houses in the west of Queen's Park (including the ones on Milman facing the park) and GA Sexton designed houses on Chamberlayne Wood Road and Salusbury Road, as well as owning building sites in his own right. There were two architects living on Chevening alone in 1901, including William Dakers, son of Scottish-born builder David who we'll meet later in this chapter.

Before construction could start, the drains had to be laid. On Montrose Avenue, this was done around two months before the foundations were laid, and construc-tion of the actual houses started two months after that. The houses themselves took around six months to complete.

The workers who built the houses had to shift everything by hand, starting with the soil (or in this case clay) excavated to lay the foundations. Bricks were sometimes fired locally (we know this was the case when the Queen's Park Estate was built) or brought in by canal or by road from George Furness's steam-powered brick factory at the top of Chambers Lane. Skilled brick workers were expected to lay around 1,000 bricks a day, but walls were not supposed to rise by more than 4ft a day in order to give the mortar time to set.[1] Wooden scaffolding surrounded the emerging properties, lashed together with ropes until the roofs were in place.

Salusbury Road

The earliest buildings on Salusbury Road, the main shopping thoroughfare of Queen's Park, also date back to the 1860s, and like most of the buildings on Willesden Lane, they have now vanished. In the 1860s and '70s, houses were built between the Falcon public house and hotel and the railway lines on both sides of Salusbury Road. There was no 'Premier Corner' or station car park; it was all a continuous line of houses. It must have made an imposing entryway to Salusbury Road – certainly more interesting than the present visual mess. The inhabitants were working class: many of the men worked in building trades and many of the women in laundries like the Linen House on Kilburn Lane. The houses, built between 1869 and 1879, were the work of local speculative builders.

The railway station, which first opened in 1879 to serve the Royal Agricultural Show, was a single-storey, solid building with tall chimneys at either side and two doors, as there are today. The original police station across the road, on the corner of Harvist and Salusbury, was built in 1884. It was home to a sergeant and seventeen unmarried constables between the ages of 22 and 36 in 1901. Married men lived out: there was a sergeant and a constable living on Harvist and the same on Kempe (not together). The station didn't take up the whole block between Salusbury Road and Dudley Road, as it does today: there was space for a row of houses at the Dudley end.

At the top end of Salusbury Road, the block of houses now occupied by the Igar Hotels, but then known as Halse Terrace, was built in the 1880s (although they look like detached houses, they are in fact a terrace). In 1901, six out of the eight occupied buildings on this block were single-family dwellings. The heads of the households included an army officer, a retired civil servant and an evangelist. Arthur Horstead (a gas inspector) and his wife Fanny occupied No. 9 together with their ten children and a nephew. The block – which would have had an unimpeded view across open ground towards the chapels in the middle of the cemetery for several years after it was built – was clearly prime property in the early years of Queen's Park.

By the 1890s, building was taking place at a fast pace at both ends of Salusbury Road.

A teacher training academy (Maria Grey) and associated girls' school (Brondesbury and Kilburn High School), both designed by James Osborne Smith, opened in 1892 on the corner of Chevening Road. Winkworth Hall, on the opposite corner of

---

1   Wedd, *Victorian Housebuilding*, 2012.

Chevening Road, opened at the same time, as a hall of residence for the trainee teachers at the academy. It was named after Emma Winkworth, the first woman to climb the Jungfrau in Switzerland in 1863. At the time of the 1901 census, there were fourteen student teachers living in Winkworth, between the ages of 19 and 30, supported by seven domestic staff, all under the supervision of a warden. The school itself was home to a male housekeeper and his wife and two servants.

The new Kilburn Fire Station, with a mortuary and coroner's court at the back, opened on 3 August 1894 next to the police station. It was a project of the local authority, Willesden Urban District Council, designed by the firm of Edmeston and Gabriel. The whole complex cost £7,000 (equivalent to £969,439 in 2022) and was built by local builders Kellet and Co. of Willesden Junction. It housed two new horse-drawn fire engines and had accommodation for four married couples and three single men, as well as stables for the horses. On the Thursday prior to the official opening, a drill was performed in front of luminaries from the Willesden Local Board. The tenders raced to the scene of a mock 'fire' in Winchester Avenue, where 'the water from the hose was sent up a tremendous height, and the practice caused considerable interest to the general public'.[1]

The library next door, which opened the same year, was also commissioned by Willesden Council and designed by James Edmeston and Edward Gabriel. It was built by Godson and Sons of Granville Road, and was opened by the headmaster of Harrow School, the Rev. JFC Weldon, on 30 January 1894. It cost nearly £3,000 (equivalent to £415,473 in 2022).

The site next door, where St Andrew's Presbyterian Church was built, was vacant for at least a decade after the library opened. The church was designed by the non-conformist architect AO Breeds.

Kilburn Grammar School (now the Islamia Schools) opened in 1900, Salusbury Road School, as it was originally called, opened in 1902 (see Chapter 12) and the permanent St Anne's Church[2] in 1904 (there was a temporary corrugated iron church there from 1900 – see Chapter 11).

The rest of Salusbury Road is largely the work of Solomon Barnett, and later of Barnett and Brotchie, the joint enterprise he set up with his son-in-law. Barnett built the shops on the lower part of Salusbury Road built between 1895 and 1900 (his estate office was first at No. 81 and then at 93). The buildings on either side are identical apart from the fact that the ones on the east side have a small roof terrace over the shop front, while the ones on the west side go straight up.

---

1   *Willesden Chronicle*, 3 August 1894.
2   This isn't the one we see today. The Edwardian church was demolished in 1996.

The next couple of blocks on the west side (either side of Montrose Avenue) were mixed-use buildings; the ground floors could be converted into shops or residential properties as necessary, and the upper floors were flats.

The middle section of Salusbury Road was non-residential, apart from the odd live-in caretaker; Barnett built workshops and warehouses on both sides of the road between 1899 and 1900. Many of them have now vanished, thanks to a major fire in the 1930s (see Chapter 22), but Queen's Studios on Salusbury Road offers an excellent idea of what they would have looked like. (That building was originally a furniture depository – you can still see the original signage painted on the side.)

The top section of Salusbury Road is a mix of houses, flats and shops and the work of multiple builders. College Parade was built in 1900–02 by David and William Dakers, who also built stables around the back. Next door to College Parade were the offices of Willesden Council's electricity department, where locals could pay their bills. The houses either side of 'Halse Terrace' were built in 1901–03 by Ernest Harvey of 1 Harvist Road, and designed by another local builder, GA Sexton. But most of this section of Salusbury Road was built by Barnett and Brotchie. The block of three-storey houses between Windermere and Brooksville, for example, has Barnett's signature sash windows, a 'Chinese-influenced "ladder" type [with a] floating frieze configuration'.[3] These were purpose-built as flats, with multiple apartments in each building, and appear to have attracted a well-heeled clientele. In 1911, 86a was home to Bertie White, the managing director of a firm of gun-makers, his wife Nellie, their two children and Nellie's sister Lydia. In flat B was a Scottish widow called Jessie Macfarlane and her three children, while C was home to the Randall sisters, Alice and Georgina, who lived off private means, with their servant Rose Scott.

Salusbury Road follows the line of the old manor boundary between 'Brands' and 'Bounds' manors, and the west side of the park (and therefore Milman Road) is close to the boundary between 'Chambers' and 'Brands'. I don't believe this is a coincidence: much of the road layout of the Willesden area closely follows the old manorial boundaries and field patterns. I think the Ecclesiastical Commissioners deliberately replicated the old manors in the way they designed the new districts. When they agreed to sell 30 out of the 100 acres between Salusbury and Chamberlayne Roads to the City Corporation, they could have placed the park anywhere in that space – it's not even vaguely centred on the space between the two roads. I think the fact that they aligned it with the old manorial boundary on the west was a deliberate nod to the history of this area.

---

3   Queen's Park Conservation Area Appraisal, Brent Council, 2006.

To Let Advertisements for Salusbury and the Roads East, 1901

Furnished bedroom for one or two young ladies engaged during the day, comfortable home, moderate terms, bath. 108 Victoria Road

----

One or two rooms to let furnished or unfurnished, 24 Donaldson Road

----

One room to let unfurnished, or two small rooms. 71 Hartland Road, Kilburn

----

Unfurnished three large rooms, redecorated, water and gas, use of bath. 85 Hartland Road, Kilburn (two minutes Queen's Park station)

Business young lady wanted to share bedroom with another, terms moderate. L, 17 Lynton Road, entrance in Victoria Road

----

Flat of three rooms, unfurnished, to let, one sorted as kitchen, two newly decorated, pleasant view from front and back, bathroom (h and c), WC etc, one child not objected to. 35 Lynton Road

----

Upper part of business (milliner's) premises to let, six rooms with every convenience, no children. 83 Salusbury Road, Queen's Park

East of Salusbury Road

In the 1880s, development in the south-east corner of Queen's Park crept closer as two local builders – George Henry Wickes and George German – extended Brondesbury Road as far as No. 74 (north side) and 77 (south side) between 1884 and 1885. They also extended Brondesbury Villas to 112. This took construction right up to the edge of today's Queen's Park – where Donaldson Road, the eastern border of Queen's Park as I've defined it for the purposes of this book, is now.

Solomon Barnett

Solomon Barnett was born in 1845 in the part of Poland that was then occupied by the Russian Empire. His family emigrated to Britain when Solomon was a child, settling in the East End.

As a young man, Solomon set up a lead and glass trading business. There's a record of him giving evidence at a fraud trial at the Old Bailey in 1871 after one of his customers failed to pay him.[1] In 1872, he became a naturalised British citizen, and in 1873, at the age of 28, he married 21-year-old Florence Joseph, the daughter of a silversmith called Joseph Joseph. Although the Josephs were living in Islington at the time when Solomon and Florence met, they were originally from the West Country: Florence was born in Plymouth and her father and mother both came from Redruth in Cornwall.

Sometime after marrying Florence, Solomon changed profession, becoming a house builder. Many of the roads he built were named after Florence's favourite places in the West Country (and possibly further afield too), including Torbay, Honiton and Lynton.

In 1881 the couple were living at 19 Brondesbury Road, near Kilburn High Road, with the first five of their eight children, and in 1891 in Greville Place, off Abbey Road.

In 1900, Solomon and Florence moved into Restmorel, the huge house Solomon built for the family on the corner of Brondesbury Park and Christchurch Avenue. Named after Restmorel Castle in Cornwall, the house had a tennis court and an orchard and was set in an acre of grounds. It was maintained by five servants. The year they moved in, Solomon hosted the meeting of prominent Jewish people that led to the opening of Brondesbury Synagogue in 1905 (see Chapter 11).

In 1902 the couple's eldest daughter, Fanny, married a Scotsman, George Brotchie, who was living in Kilburn and working as an architect and surveyor. After the marriage George went into partnership with Solomon, and George took over the business when Solomon and Florence retired to the south coast in the 1910s. Their estate office was on Salusbury Road, first at 81 (now the Worldly, Wicked and Wise gallery) and then at 93 (now Provenance butchers).

According to Solomon's great-grandson, Chris Brotchie, there is a family tradition that their usual practice was to retain two out of every ten of the houses they built to rent out, and sell eight of them to raise income to fund the next round of buildings.

Solomon left a huge legacy in building, and naming, most of the streets around the Salusbury Road end of Queen's Park.

According to Kit Wedd's *Victorian Housebuilding*, 'Most building firms in late-Victorian London produced fewer than six houses a year ... only the very largest built houses by the hundreds.'[2] In 1898 alone, Solomon Barnett built at least 111 houses and shops in Queen's Park, acknowledged to be of the finest quality. He was, by any standard, a significant builder.

1 www.oldbaileyonline.org/browse.jsp?div=t18710227-190
2 Wedd, *Victorian Housebuilding*, 2012.

There are four main types of houses in the streets east of Salusbury Road. The first are the work of a builder called Thomas Pessell, and they can be found on Hartland Road,[1] most of Donaldson Road[2] and the northern half of Lynton Road. These houses are identical to each other, with the odd variation in the parapet above the front door. They all have distinctive decorative lunettes between the first and second floors on the bays, which are two-storey in all cases.

The second group of houses was built by Solomon Barnett, and they are very similar to the houses he built shortly afterwards on the other side of Salusbury Road – the main difference is they have 'florid' capitals on the columns on the bays and around the doors. These houses can be found on Victoria, and those parts of Donaldson, Honiton and Lynton roads between Victoria and Brondesbury roads. Like the ones on the other side of Salusbury, they are faced with yellow stock bricks and are arranged in groups with a run of houses with single-storey bays in between houses with two-storey bays.

The third group of houses, on the south side of Brondesbury Road and both sides of Brondesbury Villas, is the work of an architect/builder called AC Hendry Watkin and a builder called Moses Davis. At 76–90 Brondesbury Road, Watkins created red brick, double-fronted, three-storey houses with grandiose porches and balconies on the first floor, and at 114 to 134 Brondesbury Villas he built single-fronted, three-storey houses with arched windows on the first floor.

On Brondesbury Road, Davis built double-fronted, square-bayed, two-storey houses at 92–98; he built more houses in the same style, but with sloping roofs over the porch instead of metal balconies, around the corner at 136–148 Brondesbury Villas. He adopted a very different style at 100 to 148 Brondesbury Road: double-fronted, two-storey houses, with stucco on the first floor and tiled decoration on the gables – altogether more Arts and Crafts (a design movement inspired by William Morris, among others) in style. Sadly none of the houses on the south side of Brondesbury Villas have survived so we have no idea what they looked like, but in all probability they mirrored the ones opposite. Both sides of Brondesbury Villas were occupied by wealthy people when they were first built: 92 per cent had live-in servants.

The final group of houses in this area are again the work of Solomon Barnett. They are distinctively different from his other houses in the area; they are faced with red bricks instead of yellow ones, and often have triangular pediments, Dutch gables and scallop-shaped decorations above windows and doors. They are more closely related to the houses he built on the imposing Kingswood Avenue (that runs along the park) than to his other houses in Queen's Park. These houses are on Honiton Road and

---

1   Hartland was finished by a builder called Samuel Callow.
2   Apart from the shops immediately north of Lonsdale – they are Barnett's work.

on the north side of Brondesbury Road. The block between Lynton and Donaldson roads in particular is a riot of different styles, unlike anything else Barnett produced.

The area must have been a gigantic building site when these houses were built, with residents moving in as soon as houses were completed, while construction continued a few doors away. The new roads had very different characters. Hartland seems to have been rented out as shared accommodation from the beginning: nearly 60 per cent of houses in the road were in multi-occupancy in 1901, and only two had live-in servants. Many people in the road had manual occupations such as a stablemate, plumber's mate and an ironer in a laundry, but there were also white-collar workers including a stockbroker's clerk, a police inspector and a minister of religion.

Around a quarter of the houses in Donaldson Road were home to more than one family, but very few in Victoria Road were, and none at all in Brondesbury Road. Honiton Road seems to have attracted wealthier families than Lynton Road, despite both roads appearing identical; 44 per cent of homes in Honiton had live-in servants, compared with 16 per cent in Lynton. However, Patricia Griffiths's house on the corner of Lynton and Hartland still had a maid's room and a system of servants' bells in the 1930s. Over 80 per cent of households on Brondesbury Road had servants; the Marks family at No. 91 found space for four.

Lonsdale Road was another one of Barnett's projects. Although Lonsdale is often described as a 'mews', suggesting it was all stables for horses, it had a mixed use from the start. Work started in 1894, when Barnett was given permission to erect a wooden shed as a site office; soon after he was granted leave to erect twelve workshops on the south side of the road, numbered 1 to 23 (starting from the Donaldson Road end). Nos 25 to 51 (next door to today's Wolfpack pub) followed soon after, and the whole road was completed by August 1899.

No. 1's first occupant was an oil merchant, 23 was occupied by 'art metal workers' and 53 by printers. There *were* horse-related businesses in the road: 19 and 21 were the premises of a 'jobmaster', who hired out coaches by the day or week, and 33 was a coach maker. (For more on businesses in Lonsdale Road, see Chapter 14).

The Brondesbury Estate

The roads between Salusbury Road and the park were built by Barnett (and later by Barnett and Brotchie) between 1897 and 1904; the whole enterprise was titled 'The Brondesbury Estate'. Summerfield and Dudley roads were the first ones to be built, between April 1897 and August 1898; Dunmore was the last (June 1903 to April 1904).

The houses on Kingswood Avenue (and those around the corner on the south side of Chevening Road) were erected in batches at the same time as the adjoining avenues;

1–5 Kingswood (between Harvist and Summerfield) went up at the same time as Summerfield, the next block at the same time as Montrose and so on. The last houses on Kingswood were finished in 1904.

There are two basic designs in this area: the houses on the avenues between Kingswood and Salusbury, which are faced with yellow stock brick and are all single-fronted, and the ones on Kingswood and Chevening, which are faced with red bricks and are a mix of single- and double-fronted houses, some with their entrances off Kingswood. They all came equipped with fireplaces in the main reception rooms made of Belgian Rouge marble.

All the houses in the avenues were built with two WCs: one upstairs and one on the ground floor at the rear, accessed through an external door. They had coal bunkers on the back wall, and coal merchants accessed the properties through a lane behind the houses; Victorian and Edwardian families would have been horrified by the prospect of coal deliveries coming through the front door if it could be avoided. The door-steps and front paths of the Barnett (and Brotchie) buildings on Salusbury Road and the avenues were paved in terrazzo – multicoloured pebbles set in cement and then ground flat with specialist equipment.

Early photos show that the avenues had trees planted on the dividing line between every other house (these were removed by the GPO later to make way for telephone junction boxes) and the houses had tall metal gates to the height of the gate pillars and metal fences on top of the garden walls. These were removed during the Second World War, along with the park's metal railings, to support the war effort (see Chapter 19).

Few of the houses in the avenues were in multi-occupancy. Between a quarter and 30 per cent had live-in servants, rising to 80 per cent of properties on Kingswood. The first occupants of the avenues were typically white-collar workers – clerks, cashiers, and schoolteachers – or skilled manual workers, such as French polishers. On Kingswood, they included a bank manager, a stockbroker and an antiques dealer.

To Let Ads, the Avenues, 1901

Bedroom with use of sitting room, to let. E.R., 20 Montrose Avenue.

Comfortable bedroom, suit gentleman, partial or total board with family, terms moderate. Apply 41 Montrose Avenue

West of the Park

The first buildings west of Kingswood Avenue were actually the park-keeper's lodge and the refreshment kiosk (1887), but most of the houses between the park and Chamberlayne Road went up between 1898 and the early 1900s.

Unlike the avenues to the east of the park, which were all built by Solomon Barnett under a single master plan, the roads to the west were constructed by a number of builders, and this is reflected in the different architectural styles used, although the overall effect has a pleasing harmony to it.

The leases in Kempe and Keslake roads were owned by a City of London firm of architects and surveyors, Walter Hall and Co., who contracted local builders to do the actual construction. Elsewhere in the area, it seems that the builders owned the leases as well as doing the actual building work. However, given the uniformity of roads like Milman and Creighton, it seems likely that one builder was responsible for the overall project, sub-contracting the execution to other firms when they ran short of capacity.

Apart from the south side of Harvist Road, all the houses west of the park are two-storey buildings (some on Chevening also have basements), built to a relatively small number of designs. The first is the 'Costin'. These houses have two-storey, angled bays, arched porches, and the upper sashes have rows of small windows at the top, ranging from four to sixteen. The ones on Milman Road are faced in red brick, the others in yellow. Some of them have tiled gables, some have half-timbered gables, and some have a mixture of the two. A small number on Milman are double fronted, and a few on the south side of Creighton have 'Chinese ladder'-style windows. Some have coloured glass in the rows of small windows in the upper sashes, others have clear glass. Like the houses on the other side of the park, fireplaces in reception rooms are made of Belgian Rouge marble and they originally had bathrooms on the ground floor, accessed through an eternal door. They account for nearly half of all the houses west of the park, including all of Milman and Creighton roads, the north side of Chevening Road and half of the south side, the north side of Harvist Road and half of Keslake Road. Half of them were constructed by the builder William Riley, who did not build in any other styles in Queen's Park – the 'Costin' was his signature design.

The next most common type of house west of the park is the 'Hall', designed by Walter Hall and Co.; there are nearly 180 of them on Kempe and Keslake. Like the 'Costins', they have angled bays and are faced in yellow stock bricks. Their gables are tiled at the top and half-timbered below, like some of the Costins, but they have florid capitals and tiled sloping roofs over their porches. Like the Costins, they were the work of a range of builders including W Glanville, J Charlesworth, James Ball, EJ Webb and Joseph Huish. Glanville did a variation on this theme at 120–130 Kempe; these houses have flat-fronted, square bays instead of angled ones.

The third group of houses in this area have metal balconies above the front door. They come in two types: with square bays with elaborate parapets on top on Peploe and Chevening, and with angled bays with pointed roofs on Peploe and Keslake. The designer was probably GA Sexton.

Finally, there are five houses at the western end of Chevening Road that are quite different from anything else in the area: they have elaborate gables with a cross-shaped decoration in the middle. They were constructed by W Glanville.

Half of the shops on the corners of Peploe and Keslake were built by James Chamberlain and designed by Costin. They originally had stables. The other two are the work of FH Ellyatt, built between 1899 and 1902.

Creighton Road was originally called Sinclair, after the Anglican Dean of London at the time, but the name was changed to Creighton in honour of the Bishop of London following his death in January 1901.

All the roads west of the park had a high degree of multi-occupancy when they were first constructed – between 65 per cent (Milman) and 93 per cent (Peploe). The residents were more mixed in this part of Queen's Park. Single family dwellings were occupied by similar professional people to the ones on the other side of the park: teachers, clerks, and salespeople, but the houses in multiple occupation attracted more unskilled manual workers and live-out domestic servants.

To Let Ads, West of the Park, 1901

Three large rooms unfurnished, every convenience, fitted with gas and blinds, rent 11s. 15 Milman Road, overlooking Queen's Park

----

Two unfurnished rooms, one as kitchen, every convenience, use bath, no other lodgers, terms moderate. 27 Kempe Road

----

Bedroom or bed sitting room, furnished, use of bath, terms moderate. 82 Kempe Road, Queen's Park

----

Three rooms, first floor bath, every convenience, no children, none taken, near Kensal Rise Station, rent 10s 6d, 15 Peploe Road

The Mystery of Idstone Terrace

When Chevening was first being built, some of the houses were numbered sequentially, rather than having odds and evens on opposite sides of the road, and were listed as 'Idstone Terrace, Chevening Road'. (The same thing happened with Halse Terrrace, on Salusbury Road.) Within a few years, the houses were renumbered using the present system, so the location of Idstone Terrace is a mystery. We know it was west of Kingswood, and the only true terrace on Chevening is between Nos 2 and 34, so that's the most likely solution. Nos 2–10, built by W Glanville, are radically different from anything else in the area but are closely related to the three blocks he built around the corner on the east side of Chamberlayne Road – well worth inspecting if you get a chance. They have turrets on the corners and the same cross-motif on the gables as 2–10 Chevening.

The rest of the houses on Chevening west of the park, on both sides of the road, were built by two firms – the 'Costin' houses, at 1–107 and 76–106, were built by William Riley, and the 'Sexton' houses, with their balconies, by Bennett and Gimbrett. The remainder of the south side of Chevening, at the Kingswood end, is the work of Solomon Barnett (west of Carlisle) and Frederick Marks (architect of the synagogue, which opened in 1905).

The eastern corner of Tiverton was the site of St Laurence's Church, first erected as another corrugated iron temporary structure by Humphreys Ltd of Knightsbridge in 1901, and later as a permanent church designed by the Cutts brothers and built by local church construction firm Godsons. The impressive vicarage next door opened in 1909.

Between the vicarage and 197 Chevening Road, there are a series of red brick, two-storey houses constructed by S Kendall and JH Reeder between 1900 and 1905; the ones facing the park are double-fronted. The final stretch of Chevening, from opposite Carlisle down to Salusbury Road, was built by the firm of Rogers and Bevan in 1900–01. They have angled bays to the full height of the house and are faced in red brick.

To Let Ads, Harvist Road, 1901

Flats to let, overlooking Queen's Park, four rooms, range, gas, water and WC, 13s, apply Office, 1 Harvist Road

----

Flat to let, four rooms first floor, just re-decorated, WC, use of bath.
44 Harvist Road, Queen's Park

Down on Harvist Road, the first houses went up when the road was still called 'Mortimer' – no.s 14 to 22, between Dudley Road and Kingswood Avenue. There was another mysterious terrace on Harvist when the houses were first built: Western Terrace. Fortunately, we can locate this with a high degree of confidence. Western Terrace was the run of twenty-eight houses between 211 and 265 backing on to the railway lines at the westernmost end of Harvist Road. It ended at one of the two entrances to the goods yard where Queen's Park coal was stored.

The houses on the south side of Harvist are all three-storey buildings apart from a run of fourteen houses opposite Peploe. The first houses at the Kingswood end (from 1 to 71) were constructed by a builder called Ernest Harvey, of Saltram Crescent, between 1896 and 1901. He moved into No. 1 and ran his business from there as soon as it was finished. Some of these houses have the 'Chinese ladder' sash windows usually found on Solomon Barnett's buildings. Other houses on the south side were built by J Boatfield of Fernhead Road, Rogers and Bevan and C Blount of Saltram Crescent.

On the north side of the road, Solomon Barnett built three houses between the police station and the corner of Dudley in 1898–99. These were destroyed when the police station was bombed in the Second World War. The section between Dudley and Kingswood is the work of Henry Guest of Ashmore Road and F Williams of Bravington Road (1893–96).

West of the park, the north side of Harvist is an unbroken line of two-storey 'Costin' houses, erected by builders including William Riley, James Chamberlain, GF Kendall, J Boatfield and Bennett and Gimbrett. There were originally another twelve houses at the west end of Harvist where the school playground is today.

Chamberlayne Road

Chamberlayne Wood Road, as it was still called in 1900, was also the work of a number of builders, many of them familiar from their work elsewhere in Queen's

Park. In 1894, the only buildings standing on the road – which was still a farm track a few yards north of Kensal Rise Station – were on the west side opposite where Ark Franklin Academy is today: the block between Mostyn Road and Bolton Road and the first three buildings between Mostyn Road and Mortimer Road. Further west, Kensal Rise was taking shape – houses had been built on the north sides of Ashburnham and Purves, including Princess Frederica (a church school), plus most of College Road and a handful of houses on Mortimer Road. There was still a lot of green space, though, and the other side of the railway lines was largely fields apart from the National Athletic Stadium (see Chapter 13) and a nursery for plants just north of the station.

Kensal Rise School, a Willesden Board School like Salusbury Road, was built in 1898. The Methodist Church on the corner of Wrentham Avenue was constructed in 1899–1900 by Trant, Brown and Humphries in 1899–1900. The rest of the road in the Queen's Park area was constructed between 1898 and 1905. The shops on Chamberlayne Road were built by EA Warfield (who got planning permission for the outline frontages in the first place), Ernest Harvey (who built the block between Clifford Gardens and Leigh Gardens, including stables) and W Glanville. Charles Pinkham and his partner Charles Langler also built shops with stables on Chamberlayne Road, as well as the block of nine houses opposite Kempe Road (1904–05) and the courtyard with workshops and stables on the corner of Wrentham Avenue opposite the church. Station Terrace (originally called Station Road) was built by William Herbert Stone between 1898 and 1900.

By 1914, more national (or at least regional) businesses were getting established in Chamberlayne Road: the Whippet Inn (63 Chamberlayne Road) was a branch of Home and Colonial Stores Ltd, which had over 100 food stores across Britain at that time (by 1903 it had 500). The Rise pub (on the corner of Chevening Road) was a branch of the London and South Western Bank, a company founded in 1862 and later taken over by Barclays in 1918.

Back Where We Started

One of the last streets to be built in Queen's Park was Kimberley Road, named in honour of the diamond mining town besieged during the Boer War and located off Willesden Lane behind some of the very earliest buildings in the area. Starting in July 1901, the West End firm of AA Webber built two workshops with stables, one workshop with offices and one workshop with a house attached. The last one, Albion Works, on the south side of Kimberley Road overlooking the cemetery, was built for a firm of cardboard manufacturers, Lawrence and Aitken. In 1904,

Lawrence and Aitken sub-let some more land they owned on the other side of Kimberley to the Simms Manufacturing Company, for the construction of another workshop (for more on Simms, see Chapter 14). Braid Pater and Co. of Cheapside did the building work later that year. Two other workshops on Kimberley were built in 1902–03 by Joseph Sabey.

9

THE FIRST RESIDENTS

So who were the first residents of Queen's Park, and where did they come from? This chapter is based on my analysis of 1901 census data, examining information on residents who were living at – or in a small number of cases visiting – properties in Queen's Park[1] on the night of 31 March 1901.

The district was still under construction at this time: Carlisle, Radnor and Dunmore roads were yet to be built, there were twenty-seven houses on Chevening Road (compared to over 160 today), Kingswood Avenue was complete as far as Windermere Avenue and only the south side of Creighton Road was occupied. There were few buildings, and no people, on Chamberlayne Road. However, around 80 per cent of Queen's Park as we know it today was finished, and occupied, so the census of 1901 gives us an accurate picture of the first residents.

Here are the headline figures:

In total, there were 6,877 residents on the night of the census, living in 1,028 properties – an average of nearly seven people per house.
Around a third were under 18 (today the figure for England is around a fifth).
There were 1,039 school-age children (aged 5 to 14).
There were more women than men by a ratio of 53:47.
The oldest resident (who lived on Montrose Avenue) was 91.
Most households were headed up by men, but one in eight had a woman as the head.

The vast majority – 62 per cent – were born in what is now Greater London. Many of them came from Kilburn, Paddington, Marylebone, Notting Hill and Hampstead,

---

1 Based on the QPARA boundaries set out in the introduction to this book.

but they also came from Deptford, Woolwich, Dulwich, Dalston, Islington and many other communities that had either been swallowed up by the London sprawl or were about to be. Another 9 per cent came from counties in the South-East.

There's a commonly held belief that people mostly stayed in the communities they were born in until the 1960s, and that geographical mobility is a comparatively recent phenomenon. That's a myth: the Victorian and Edwardian era saw extraordinary movements of people thanks to the push of loss of jobs on the land due to agricultural mechanisation, and the pull of fast-growing industries in towns and cities. The economy needed people to be mobile.

Although over 70 per cent of the new inhabitants of Queen's Park were born within the wider region, others moved impressive distances to be part of the new community: 8 per cent came from the South-West, 5 per cent each from the Midlands and East Anglia, and 3 per cent from the North of England.

Others again found themselves very far from where they were born, as the table below shows. As a percentage they may not have been very significant, but culturally they played a significant role in shaping Queen's Park.

Scotland	111	Wales	80	Ireland	68
Germany	37	Russia	17	France	11
Australia	18	New Zealand	4	Canada	2
South Africa	8	India	5	Straits Settlements	1
Sweden	4	Norway	2	Denmark	1
Switzerland	6	Austria	5	Hungary	1
Channel Islands	8	Netherlands	3	Belgium	3
USA	12	Japan	6	West Indies	1
Gibraltar	1	Malta	1	Turkey	1
				At sea	1

Most, if not all, of the 'Russians' in Queen's Park in 1901 were Jewish people born – like Solomon Barnett – in the part of Poland that was annexed by the Russian Empire in 1795. They came to Britain because of the increasing persecution of Jewish communities in Russia that led to between 120,000 and 150,000 Jewish immigrants arriving between 1870 and 1914.

Among the Austrian immigrants, Marcus Lewy of Brondesbury Road, the Fieber family from Windermere Avenue and Hermann Frischmann of Kingswood Avenue are most likely of Jewish origin too.

Five of the six residents born in Japan lived in one house on Brondesbury Road: Renjiro Negishi, the London manager of the Japanese NYK shipping company, lived at No. 90 with his wife Fern and three children (one born in London). Negishi returned to Japan in 1911 to take up a position as a director of the company. They also had a student boarder in the house, Shinkich Kondo.

Two young Americans – Lilian and Joshua Levy, both born in San Francisco – were living with their widowed mother Agnes (a Londoner) at 60 Salusbury Road. Lily went on to work in retail and David became a journalist. Two more teenage Americans – Edward and Arthur Knight – were living with their mother Emily over on Kempe. Again, Emily was a native Londoner who had lived in America, started a family and returned. Also in Queen's Park that night in 1871 was an American visitor, an author called Josephine Lespinase.

Swiss-born Pietro Bini was working as a chef de cuisine, Hungarian Alexander Auer was a bank clerk and the inauspiciously named Irishman Ernest Slaughter was practising as a doctor of medicine.

On the night of the census, there were over 300 live-in servants in Queen's Park. All of them were women and girls, the youngest aged just 13. Altogether a quarter of households in Queen's Park had at least one live-in servant, with the highest concentration in Brondesbury Villas (92 per cent). Creighton had none at all. Like their employers, most serving staff came from London and the neighbouring counties, but by no means all. On Kingswood Avenue there were twenty-five servants, and whilst eleven of them were from London and six from the south-east of England, there were also two who were born in Norfolk, two in the West Country, two in Liverpool, one came from Staffordshire and one (a cook) was born in Germany.

Some of the couples in Queen's Park that night come from so far afield you wonder what brought them together in the first place. How did Lynton Road's Louis Mendola, born in the Netherlands, meet his wife Hannah, from Wandsworth? Or Frank Felloes, born in the Straits Settlements in today's Malaysia, meet his wife Maude from Bury St Edmunds before they ended up in Kempe Road together?

We know that some people gravitated to Queen's Park purely for work reasons. There were an impressive eighty-one people involved in teaching in the area in 1901. Most of them were presumably working at one of the two local authority primary schools, Kilburn Grammar or Brondesbury and Kilburn High School (including the fourteen student teachers living at Winkworth Hall). There was a cluster of police officers in Kempe Road and an impressive number of postal workers in the same road, and a smattering of employees of the Gas Light and Coke Company (the forerunner to British Gas, whose works were down on the Harrow Road where Sainsbury's Ladbroke Grove is at the time of writing).

Some – particularly those in the building trades – were probably drawn to the area because there was so much construction going on locally, and once it was completed they no doubt moved on.

In today's terms, rents were cheap. A whole house could be rented for £1 6*d* a week, which included free redecoration inside and out every four years – equivalent to around £525 a week today.[1]

But there were huge disparities in wealth and living conditions. Dr Slaughter, at 76 Brondesbury Road, shared his house with his wife and their two children, his sister from Ireland and her son, and three servants. It's a double-fronted, three-storey house with plenty of space for nine people. Around the corner at 57 Donaldson Road there were nine people living in the two-storey, single-fronted house: two couples (the Martells and the Majors), one with two teenage daughters, and three lodgers.

In the decade between the 1901 and 1911 censuses, there was huge churn in the population. On Kingswood Avenue, only four families were still in the same house on the two dates: Elizabeth Kimbler (a wealthy widow) at No. 6, the Solomons at No. 8 (Samuel, the chief earner, was a City accountant, and daughter Rebecca was an artist), the three Biggs sisters at No. 17 and Reverend Grant and his family at No. 26. Interesting incomers included a young Japanese mercantile clerk, Shinjiro Kambe, who was boarding with the Grants and the large Haythornwaite family at No. 13, with their ten children. There was a slight reduction in the number of families who had live-in servants on Kingswood Avenue but 70 per cent still did, and there were no houses in multiple occupation.

Victoria Road was less wealthy than Kingswood Avenue in 1901 but still pretty well off: 37 per cent of households had live-in servants and only one house was in multiple occupation. In the decade that followed, its fortunes seem to have declined: by 1911 one in five houses on Victoria had been divided into flats (as opposed to bedsits) and only 9 per cent had servants. Only six families out of forty-six were still in the same homes. The proportion of newcomers on Victoria Road who were from other parts of London was unchanged, but there was a big increase in people from the West Country, a significant French community and a housepainter called Morris Halpern and his wife, whose name is recorded as 'Tony', who were both born in Romania. Many Jewish people emigrated from Romania in the early 1900s in the face of economic hardship, and Solomon Barnett was noted for offering employment to many who reached London.

---

1   Interview with Minnie Arens in the Queen's Park Centenary Brochure, 1987.

On Peploe Road, only four families were there in both 1901 and 1911, out of twenty-six households. Roughly half the road was single-family units, and half housed two families, presumably one per floor. The occupational mix was similar in both 1901 and 1911: clerks, dressmakers, signwriters, carpenters and shopkeepers. There was only one live-in servant in 1901 and none at all in 1911.

So where did the 1901 residents go, and why? If the following three stories are any guide, some moved because of personal loss, some because of a change in career and some because they needed more space – and could afford it. And some moved around the corner, some further afield and quite a few (including the Negishi family) to the other side of the world.

Johanna Van Adleberg of 151 Victoria Road, who was born in Mulheim, Germany, left Queen's Park when her (considerably older) husband Michael died in 1907. She and her daughter moved to Maida Vale, then Kensington, and we last see her in 1920, arriving at New York's Ellis Island on the SS *Philadelphia*, ready to start a new life in America.

Newcastle-born William McDonald, who was living at 14 Kingswood in 1901 with his wife Elizabeth and seven children and running a laundry business, had moved to a more modest house in Finsbury Park by 1911. He was now working as a cinematograph salesman and the couple had eleven children.

Harold and Caroline Jutsum, a newly married couple in their early 20s, were renting half of No. 15 Peploe in 1901. Harold, who was born in Stockport, was working as a coal merchant. Caroline was a local – she was born on the Queen's Park Estate. In 1911 they had three small children and were living at 40 Wrentham Avenue, sharing a big house with Harold's mother Elizabeth and father Humphrey, a Methodist minister.

10

SHOPPING

We have a window into the shops and essential services of Queen's Park in the early years thanks to the detailed *Kelly's Directories* – an early version of the *Yellow Pages* (which for the benefit of younger readers, were printed telephone directories of businesses very widely used in the UK from the 1880s until the arrival of the internet made them obsolete).

In late Victorian and Edwardian times, food shopping was a daily necessity due to the lack of refrigeration in the home – hence the huge number of greengrocers, butchers and fishmongers in Queen's Park at the time. In 1914 there were five butchers on Salusbury Road alone.

Shop opening hours were largely unregulated, so shops would open at 7 or 8 a.m. every morning and close at 9 p.m. or later on weekdays. Thursday was early closing day, and on Saturdays shops were meant to close at 2 p.m. (although this rarely happened in practice according to the Early Closing Association), and all shops were shut on Sundays. The one exception was the West End, where shops closed between 6.30 and 7 on winter evenings and between 7 and 8 in summer.

Shop assistants selected, weighed and packaged the goods for customers – there was no such thing as self-service. The 1886 Select Committee on Shop Hours was told that in north London the average shop assistant worked between eighty and eighty-six hours a week.[1]

A number of the local shopkeepers had Jewish or German names. In 1914 these were the two largest immigrant communities in Britain. Local hairdresser Gaspare

---

1 Hosgood, 'Mercantile Monasteries: Shops, Shop Assistants, and Shop Life in Late-Victorian and Edwardian Britain', *Journal of British Studies, 1999*, vol. 38 no. 3.

Ravioli was one of the Italian diaspora; he was born in Faenza in the Emilia-Romagna region of Italy.

Salusbury Road

In 1899, Salusbury Road had only been developed up as far as Hartland on the east side and the library on the west. However, it started beyond the railway bridge by Queen's Park station, where Marks and Spencer and the station car park are today. Most of these buildings were houses; the only non-residential properties were at the far end. No. 1, on the M&S side, was a grocers and wine shop, and No. 4 was the Kilburn District office of Willesden Parish, where births, death and marriages could be registered.

Remarkably, there were two more shops on the bridge opposite the railway station than there are today – in 1899 they were a laundress and a tobacconist. They must have perched on metal girders; no traces are visible today.

However, shops weren't confined to the high streets. There were a number of retailers on both sides of Donaldson Road, some of which have now been converted from shops to residential; 40 Donaldson Road (the corner property on the north side of Lonsdale) was Mary Jane Lillywhite's corn chandlers in 1899, for example.

By 1914, a number of businesses had opened in the houses south of the station: chimney sweeps Edward Best and Arthur Stapleton operated out of 20 and 23 Salusbury Road, and an upholsterer, James Chamberlain, was based at No. 27. On Harvist Road, No. 1 was the premises of a builder, Ernest Harvey, and Nos 2 and 12 were home to makers of artificial teeth.

Up on Chevening Road there were two doctors, Thomas Wilson at No. 108 and Thomas Meyler at No. 115, and a solicitor and commissioner for oaths, Charles William Lyons-Pike, at No. 111, and another down in Harvist. Over in Lynton Road, Rose Shapter was running a lace-cleaning business at No. 33, 44 Donaldson Road was David Lewis Jones's dairy, and Ada Hunt, artist, resided at 20 Harvist Road.

The tables below show all the businesses on Salusbury Road in 1899 and 1914. In addition, we know there was a coal merchants (Thomas Lea's). There were no pubs at that time, but there were a number of wine and spirit merchants so the area was not 'dry' as sometimes thought.

Salusbury Road Shops West Side: Kelly's Directory

No.	1899	1914
Station	Queen's Park station, Henry Arthur Hutton station-master	Queen's Park station, Harry Amos Easter station-master; Frank Bevis, fruiterer (stall outside station)
26	E Jones and Co., bicycle and tricycle makers	
30	Frances Holemans, tobacconist	Frances Holemans, tobacconist
32	William Jeffery, butcher	William Jeffery, butcher
34	Payne and Co., dairymen	Payne and Co., dairymen
36	Francis Horn, baker and confectioner	John Miller, baker and post office. (Telegrams only – nearest telegraph office at 81 Kilburn High Road)

Harvist Road

Police station	Metropolitan Police X Division; sub-divisional inspector William Bell in charge	Metropolitan Police X Division; sub-divisional inspector Thomas Travis in charge
Police station	Willesden Urban District Fire Brigade, Salusbury Road; superintendent Thomas Edwards. Plus coroner's court and mortuary	Willesden Urban District Fire Brigade, Salusbury Road; superintendent Thomas Edwards. Plus coroner's court and mortuary
Library	Kilburn Public Library, James A Seymour librarian	Kilburn Public Library, James A Seymour librarian
44	Not constructed yet	St Andrew's Presbyterian Church. Rev. T Finlayson Darroch
46		Frederick William Tiller, watch maker
48		Samuel Aaron, butcher
50		Henry H Horne, ironmonger
52		Charles Hills, furniture dealer
54		Ambrose Allen and Sons, butchers
56		William Batchelor, chemist

Summerfield Avenue

58		Wetjen and Co., wine and spirit merchants

60		Fournier and Co., thermometer manufacturers; Thermo and Pressure Instruments Ltd, thermometer makers
62		The Quirie Co. Ltd, metal polish manufacturers
64		Frederick William Greenacre, slipper manufacturer
66		James Samuel Richard Weir, physician and surgeon

Montrose Avenue

68		Balchin and Son, printers; Risiocol Ltd, manufacturing chemists
70		Leo and Co. Ltd, manufacturing chemists
72–74		The Crossley Co., wire mattress makers

Hopefield Avenue

76		RS Currie and Co., engineers and vulcanisers
78		R Boyle and Son, ventilating engineers
80		Aron Electricity Meter Ltd; Musicus Ltd, player piano manufacturers
82		Frederick H Hallam and Son, dental manufacturers

Windermere Avenue

84–92		Residential
94		Frank Birch, solicitor
96		Residential

Brooksville Avenue

98–132		Residential
		Brondesbury and Kilburn High School for Girls, M Rees headmistress

Salusbury Road Shops East Side: Kelly's Directory

No.	1899	1914
Railway lines		
39	Amelia Boden, laundress	
41	Caroline Walton, tobacconist	
43	Arthur Henry Parsons and Co., dyers	
45	William Davidson, provision dealer	Albion James Rodges, boot and shoe maker
47	Eliza Gardner, grocer	Algernon Rolt, laundry
49	Gilbert Hine & Co., printers	Henry James Kirby, newsagent
51	Henry Porter Chambers, coffee rooms	George Rose, hairdresser

Brondesbury Road

53	William Baxby, furniture dealer	Elizabeth Baxby, furniture dealer
55	Thomas Thornton Gwyer, laundry	John Style, laundry
57	Rose Cook, haberdasher	Rose Cook, haberdasher; Jessie Weissel, dressmaker
59	Richard Gommez, confectioner	Zupraner Abrahams, bootmaker
61	Edwin Sisley, oilman	Alfred Joseph Rider, undertaker
63	Edgar James Aynscombe, grocer	Thomas Banford, grocer
65	Hawkins and Fotheringham, butchers	Harry Frank Steggall, butcher
67	John Dawson, fruiterer and greengrocer	Arthur Ernest Doran, fishmonger
69	John Parr, confectioner	Mary Parr, confectioner
71	Chalkley Brothers, dairymen	Arthur Gibson, dairyman
73	Edward Robert Marsh, chemist	George Nelson, chemist

Victoria Road

75	Richard Gommez, linen draper etc	Oborne and Co., bakers
77	Tremlett and Martin, grocers	Henry Norris, grocer
79	Pitcher and Co., fancy stationers	Sydney Mynors, boot repairer
81	Solomon Barnett, builder	Maddison and Co., house decorators; William Smith, hairdresser
83	Albert Henry Barnett, wine and spirits merchant	H Greenfield, laundry
85	Solomon George, oil and colour man	Louis Simon, greengrocer
87	Solomon George, oil and colour man	Julia Harrison, draper
89	Alfred James Beak and Co., cheesemongers	George Graham, upholsterers

Hartland Road

91	Not constructed yet	A Thorley and Son, tailors
93		Solomon Barnett estate office
95		Elizabeth Broadridge, confectioner
97		Herbert Maurice Thomas, tobacconist
99		Thomas Sullens, oil man
101		George Childs, dining rooms

Lonsdale Road

		Queen's Park Electric Theatre Ltd, cinema
School		Salusbury Road Public Elementary School, for 860 mixed and 460 infants. Head teachers J Mellor and Miss A Butler
107		Delacour Brothers Ltd, pipe manufacturers

117–121		Green and Edwards Ltd, furniture depository
Church		St Anne's Church. Vicar, Rev. Odell Newton Tribe, Curate, Rev. Leonard Stanley Beale
School		Kilburn Grammar School, headmaster Wilfred Bonavia Hunt
131	Willesden Council Electricity Department (payments office)	Willesden Council Electricity Department (payments office)
11–12 College Parade		William Henry Cullen, grocers and post office
13 College Parade		S Davison and Co., dyers
14 College Parade		Higgins Brothers, dairy
15 College Parade		Frances Shurly, stationer
16 College Parade		Sidney Coote, butcher
17 College Parade		Arthur R Pratt, chemist
18 College Parade		William Henry Hall, confectioner
19 College Parade		Octavius Scarff, greengrocer
20 College Parade		William Alfred Jenney, boot maker
21 College Parade		Joseph Sabey, baker

Chamberlayne Road

In 1899 hardly any buildings had been constructed on Chamberlayne Road: just a few were standing opposite Kensal Rise School. By 1914 Chamberlayne Road was complete up as far as today's Lexi Cinema.

There seem to have been a remarkable number of false teeth manufacturers in Queen's Park; as well as the two down the Salusbury Road end of Harvist, there were four on Chamberlayne Road alone, and another at 14 Wrentham Avenue. Perhaps this was connected to the number of confectioners (eight) and tobacconists (five) in the area.

No.	1914
52	Mayfield Farm Dairies
54	Cooper, Crook and Co., watch makers
56	John Breton, baker and post office
58	Galton Brothers, butchers
60	Alexander Reavill, bootmaker
Mortimer Road	
62	Ernest Bumstead, dyer and cleaner; Williams and Williams, house agents
64	Home and Colonial Stores Ltd, grocers
66	Francis George Jones, corn dealer
68	Ada Hyde, confectioner
70	John Pike and Sons, butchers
72	Charles Henry Williams, greengrocer
78	William Beavis, florist and bootmaker; Jessie Cooper, confectioner; James Smith, laundry
Mostyn Gardens	
80	Lancashire Coal Company; Wesleyan and General Assurance Society, superintendent Arnold Robinson

82	John Henry Ridd, artificial teeth maker
86	PJ Evans and Co., artificial teeth manufacturers
88	Dixon and Clark, physicians and surgeons
90	Edward Rowley, optician
94	David Harold Mayes, builder; George William Robert Skene, physician and surgeon
96	Thomas Banister, furniture remover; Bertie Hopkinson, boot repairer

Bolton Gardens

Station Road (now Station Terrace)	
30	
29	WS Chapman and Co., grocers
28	Florence Moody, dressmaker; John Nodes, undertaker
27	Herbert A Cole, dining rooms
26	John Radley, cycle agent
25	Sawyers Stores Ltd, oil warehouse
24	Agnes Hyde, confectioner
22	Welch Brothers, butchers
21	West London Industrial Co-operative Society Ltd

Dagmar Gardens

20	Charles White, builder
19	Joseph Spiegelhalter, watch maker
18	Alfred Howell Atkin, physician and surgeon
17	Herbert A Cole, dining rooms

16	William Turtell, French polisher
1 Keslake Mansions	Henry A Tarrant, grocer
2 Keslake Mansions	Frederick William Stone, tobacconist
3 Keslake Mansions	Henry John Marston, physician and surgeon
4 Keslake Mansions	Greenfield and Co., shirt and collar dressers
5 Keslake Mansions	Edith Davis, florist; Alfred Nunn, tailor
7 Keslake Mansions	Albert Henry Maryon, ironmonger
11	Charles Kubald, hairdresser
10	Henry Richard Lowe, confectioner
9	George H Tanner, boot maker
8	Frank Gibson, sign writer
7	Henry E Datz, baker
6	Samuel Norman, oilman
5	Harry Sharp, grocer and post office
4	Hartley Ernest Phillips, dairy
3	Allnutt and Hillman, stationers
2	George W Reid, boot repairer
1	George F Edwards, grocer

Railway Lines

98	Lee and Son, bakers; Spiers (Wallace) and Co., coal merchants
100	Florence House Laundry, laundry; Hanbury, Tomsett and Co., printers; Albert Jefcoate, stationer
102	Rapkin and Son, butchers
104	Mayfield Farm Dairies

Clifford Gardens

108	Lionel Frank Henwood, draper
110	John Johns, oilman
112	Hilda Nott, music teacher
116	Augustus John Askew, laundry
118	Laura Kammerer, confectioner
120	Rapkin and Son, butchers
122	H and B Sheppard, boot makers
124	James Anderson, builder

Leigh Gardens

132	Benjamin E Bantin, artificial teeth maker

No.	1914
37	Getgood and Co., pianoforte dealers
39–41	Alec Lee and Co., drapers
43	Bishops Stores Ltd, provision dealers
45	

Harvist Road

School	

Kempe Road

47	National Wine Company, wine and spirit merchants
49	Alfred Pain, greengrocer
51	William Chapman, fishmonger

53	Thomas H Kenington, grocer
55	Willie Howard, butcher
57	Lee and Son, bakers
59	Johns and Leach, fancy drapers
61	Walter John Hunt, stationer
63	James Percy Clarkson, estate agent
65	King and Co., chemists

Keslake Road

67	Walton, Hasell and Port Ltd, grocers
69	John William Clayton, artificial teeth maker; Frederick Curry, tailor
71	John and James, grocers
73	W Prince and Sons, provision dealers
75	Charles H Barty, outfitter
77	Freeman, Hardy and Willis Ltd, boot and show dealers
79	Higgins Brothers, dairymen
81	JW Carpenter Ltd, ironmongers
83	London and South Western Bank, manager Leonard B Gaywood

Chevening Road

85	Moore Brothers, hosiers
87	Lipton Ltd, provision merchants
89	Hannah Margaret Dale, milliner
91	Singer Sewing Machine Company Ltd
93	John Henry Hillier, builders merchant

95	Alice Lucas, dressmaker; Richard Vickery, confectioner
97	Madame Vee, laundry
99	John Henry Nicholas, tobacconist; Fraser Nott, music teacher; Williams and Williams, house agents
101	Willesden Central Liberal Club, secretary JH Hillier
103	G Ravaioli, hairdresser; Brereton Watson Ltd, coal merchants
105	Edith Daman, nurse; Hanbury, Tomsett and Co., printers
109	Eastman and Son (Dyers and Cleaners), dyers; Stephen Stevens, watch maker
113	Samuel Watkins, greengrocer
115	Frederick William Stone, tobacconist
117	Johns and Leach, fancy drapers
119	Kensal Rise Constitutional Club, secretary ES Harper

Wrentham Avenue	
Church	

There seems to have been a thriving community of music teachers in the area, including Lillie Bridges (a professor of music) at 82 Harvist Road, Rosa Tidbury at 263 Harvist, and Herbert Williams at 81 Keslake.

Down on Harvist Road, the London & North Western Railway Goods Depot, on the north side of the tracks behind the houses where the builders merchants is today, was a repository for coal and other heavy, dirty essentials: two coal merchants, a stone merchants and a purveyor of tar operated out of there. One of the two entrances to this emporium on Harvist Road has been filled in by number 71a, opposite the park; the other one was where 209a is now.

There were shops on the corners of Keslake and Peploe, including Samuel Walters's dairy at 39, Alice Latcham's grocery at 40 and Edith Pearson's drapers at 41.

Like the other side of the park, the west end of Queen's Park also had a smattering of businesses operating out of private homes, including doctors at 47 Okehampton and 2 Chevening, an insurance agent at 41 Milman and a midwife at 98 Keslake Road.

King's Parade, on Okehampton Road, was a mini high street in its own right.

King's Parade, Okehampton Road	
1	Nicholas Rolfe, grocer and post office
2	George Hook, confectioner
3	Benjamin James, dairy
4	Robert S Campbell, chemist
6	George Player, fruiterer
7	Ernest Lorden, butcher
8	Henry James Tilling, music dealer
9	Wyatt Brothers, bakers

11

FAITH

Church of England

For centuries, the area we call Queen's Park today was part of the parish of St Mary's, Willesden. The few inhabitants, living down on the farms on the north side of Kilburn Lane, would have had to trek up Chambers Lane to Willesden for Sunday services, weddings, baptisms and funerals.

Change started slowly, then began accelerating as the wider area developed. St Paul's Kilburn (located where Kilburn Square is today) first opened as a chapel in the 1820s and then as a full church in the 1830s. The church of St John the Evangelist opened in 1843 on the corner of Harrow Road and Kilburn Lane. In 1867, during a particularly vigorous sprint in Anglican church building, Christ Church opened on Willesden Lane, and Holy Trinity, Kilburn, opened on Brondesbury Road (opposite the junction with Algernon Road).

By 1899, it was clear that the local population was growing so fast, a dedicated Anglican ministry would be needed. In March 1900, a corrugated iron church was erected on the site where the present St Anne's Church stands on Salusbury Road. The builders were Lightfoot and Ireland of Stoke Newington. (You can get an idea of what these temporary 'tin' churches looked like from the example still standing down on Cambridge Avenue.) Presided over by the Reverend Odell Tribe, the former curate from Christ Church, the 'mission' covered the area between Kingswood Avenue and Donaldson Road, carved out of parts of the parishes of St John's, Christ Church and Holy Trinity.

The following year, the congregation decided to erect a permanent church. The architects JEK and JP Cutts were appointed to design it. The Cutts brothers were prolific church builders: between them they were responsible for forty-six places of worship. They produced plans for a Gothic-style church seating 750 people at a cost of £8,000.

The congregation were able to secure £2,000 from the Bishop of London's fund and other sources. The remaining £6,000 seemed like an ambitious target for local fundraising alone, so they decided to start by building the central section of the church, which would cost £5,000 in total.

Vigorous fundraising followed, including a three-day bazaar at Salusbury Road School at which the guest of honour was Her Royal Highness, Princess Christian of Schleswig-Holstein, the fifth child of Queen Victoria. According to the *Kilburn Times*, crowds gathered along the royal's processional route (the now well-established royal way of Kilburn High Road, Willesden Lane and Winchester Avenue), and bunting decorated local shops, stretched across Salusbury Road and even covered the West Kilburn omnibuses.[1] The princess was welcomed by the Bishop of Islington and a guard of honour formed by the Christ Church company of the Church Lads' Brigade, and the Queen's Park Military Band played the national anthem when she entered the main school hall where the stalls were set out.

Setting out the case for the proposed new church, Reverend Tribe told the princess that 'a few years ago, the greater part of the mission district of St Anne's consisted of little else than green fields. Since then the remorseless tide of bricks and mortar had rapidly covered them over with streets and houses until there was now a population of nearly 4,000 persons, while the work of building still went on.' They were quite a poor district, and if they were left to themselves it would take the congregation many years to raise so much money, he added. The fundraisers, and other parish-related groups, met in rooms at Solomon Barnett's offices at 93 Salusbury Road (Provenance butchers as of 2022).

The necessary funds having been raised, the foundation stone of the new St Anne's Church was laid on 2 July 1904 by another of Queen Victoria's daughters, Princess Henry of Battenberg (the queen's youngest child). Bunting and cheering crowds were again plentiful; this time the 18th Middlesex Regiment were called on to provide the guard of honour and play the anthem.[2] The builders were the aptly named G Godson and Sons of Pembroke Works, Kilburn Lane. The church was finally completed, and consecrated, in the summer of 1905. It stood where St Anne's Court is today, next to Queens Studios. The old cast iron church building was used as St Anne's church hall, surviving until it was destroyed by a flying bomb in 1944 (see Chapter 19). The vicarage was built by the Godsons in 1906.

---

1   *Kilburn Times*, 23 May 1902.
2   St Anne's Brondesbury: A Guide to the Church.

In 1950, Holy Trinity Church was destroyed by a fire, and St Anne's parish boundaries expanded all the way to Kilburn High Road (the ruins of Holy Trinity were demolished in 1970). A lectern, in the shape of an eagle, survived the fire at Holy Trinity, despite crashing through the floor into the crypt when the timbers gave way. It was used at St Anne's until the church was demolished in 1995 due to irrecoverable subsidence. St Anne's original font was also older than the church: it dated back to 1711 and originally belonged to an ancient church in Hampshire.

Reverend Tribe – the first vicar of St Anne's and the driving force behind its early success – led the congregation until 1915. He was supported by curates including Leonard Beale, who lodged with a family in Lynton Road (the Tribes lived at the vicarage on Salusbury Road). Odell Tribe left St Anne's in May 2015 for a new parish in Haddenham, Ely. Sadly, he died just two months later, and was buried just over the wall (behind St Anne's Church) in Paddington Cemetery. A memorial was erected to him in St Anne's Church in the 1970s when parishioners realised his original grave marker had vanished; this is one of a number of memorials from St Anne's and St Andrew's churches that were relocated to the new church on Salusbury Road when it was built.

Brondesbury Synagogue

St Anne's only just made it as Queen's Park's first consecrated place of worship: Brondesbury Synagogue was a matter of weeks behind. The Willesden area of Northwest London already had strong links with the Jewish community before any houses were built in Queen's Park; the Willesden United Synagogue Cemetery, which opened in 1873, served Jewish families from the City and West End. And as increasing numbers of Jewish people emigrated to Britain from the Russian Empire towards the end of the nineteenth century, the numbers of Jewish people living in Willesden grew significantly. With the nearest synagogues – Hampstead and St John's Wood – already at capacity, there was clearly a need for a place of worship for the growing Jewish community in this area.

In late 1900, Solomon Barnett (see Chapter 19) hosted a meeting at his house on Brondesbury Park, Restmorel, to discuss how to establish a synagogue in Queen's Park. Barnett provided the land on which the synagogue was to be built, on Chevening Road, for £1,020 – well below its true market value – and the United Synagogue lent £4,500 on condition that the balance needed could be raised locally.[1] An acting

---

1   https://jewishmiscellanies.com/2020/04/27/brondesbury-synagogue-semi-jubilee-celebration-record-compiled-by-dayan-harris-lazarus-1930

committee was set up and over £4,500 raised through fundraising events including a dinner, presided over by the Lord Mayor of London, Sir Marcus Samuel (who was himself Jewish and who founded the oil and gas company Shell) and a bazaar at the Portman Rooms.[2]

The synagogue was designed by Frederick William Marks, an Australian architect, and built by the firm of Gough & Co. It was consecrated by the Chief Rabbi on Sunday, 9 April 1905 and declared open by Mr Lionel de Rothschild. The memorial stone was laid by Sir Marcus Samuel.

The synagogue even had its own 'tin' structure, like St Anne's, where Hebrew classes were held. By 1908 the synagogue had 130 pupils in its religious classes, a social and choral society, a Dorcas Society and a company of the Jewish Lads' Brigade.

Brondesbury Synagogue was gutted in an arson attack in 1965, causing £120,000 worth of damage (in 1960s money). The perpetrators were supporters of the National Socialist Movement – in other words, British Nazis. The judge released them on the grounds that they were 'penitent', and had promised to stop their anti-Semitic activities. He told them: 'You are young men whose minds seem to have been snared by a philosophy which permits and even encourages the burning down of holy and venerated places. Having been so snared, you were used by unscrupulous people to further their own evil design.'[3]

According to the biography of the Metropolitan police officer who investigated the case, Francoise Jordan – the wife of the leader of the National Socialist Movement Colin Jordan and the niece of fashion designer Christian Dior – not only ordered the arson attack on the synagogue but actually watched it, telling police 'It was like *Kristallnacht!*'[4]

During the 1960s, National Socialist Movement supporters organised thirty-four arson attacks against buildings associated with the Jewish community, including synagogues in Bayswater, Clapton and Ilford as well as the one on Brondesbury Synagogue.

The synagogue was rebuilt after the fire, and in 1974 the building was sold to the Imam Khloei Islamic Centre.

St Laurence, Brondesbury

St Laurence's was founded as a mission church of Christ Church, Brondesbury, in 1901; its parish boundaries included all the streets between Kingswood Avenue and

---

2 *The Jewish Year Book*, 9 September 1907–31 December 1908.
3 *Detroit Jewish News*, 15 April 1965.
4 Dick Kirby, *Scotland Yard's Gangbuster: Bert Wickstead's Most Celebrated Cases*.

Chamberlayne Road. The first church on the site on Chevening Road (where St Laurence's Close is today) was a temporary iron structure; building of the permanent church, designed by the Cutts brothers like St Anne's, was started in 1906. It had a seating capacity of 537. Both the church and the vicarage next door (which was completed in 1909 and is still standing) were the work of the Godsons of Kilburn Lane. The first vicar was the Reverend WM Snook.

The celebrated novelist Barbara Pym and her sister moved to Queen's Park because of their friendship with the church's organist, and became active members of the congregation of St Laurence's.[1] The church closed in 1971 and was subsequently demolished. It is remembered in the name of Laurence's Larder, the food and clothes bank that operates out of Christ Church.

Nonconformist Churches

There was a Presbyterian church, St Andrew's, next to the library on Salusbury Road, and a Congregational church on the corner of Wrentham Avenue and Tiverton Road. The nearest Baptist chapel was Ebenezer, on Carlton Vale, and the nearest Methodist Church was on Chamberlayne Road, on the corner of Wrentham Avenue.

The Roman Catholic Church

The main Roman Catholic parish church in Willesden in 1900 was Our Lady of Willesden Church in Harlesden, which opened in 1885. When the church's capacity could no longer accommodate the growing Catholic population of Willesden, a new church – St Jude's – was founded on the other side of the Harrow Road near the Mayhew Animal Home. This was on the extreme edge of the new parish of Kensal Rise, which included Queen's Park.

In 1910 Restmorel, Solomon Barnett's home, was bought by a Catholic priest, the Reverend Doctor Herbert Vaughan, who renamed it 'Mission House' and turned it into a training centre for volunteer priests who would go out on missionary work in Protestant communities.

The centre had a flagpole in the garden from which the papal flag was flown, and a chapel that hosted several masses a day. A history of the building reports, 'Mission House won notoriety among Protestants and there were demonstrations at the gates

---

1 https://barbara-pym.org/wp-content/uploads/2020/12/FBF20_Suburbs.pdf

against the "Italian Mission".[2] The Missionaries, as they were known, despatched a Chapel truck across England to preach.

In 1915 Mission House was turned into a military hospital (see Chapter 19); when the war was over the Catholic Missionary Society reoccupied the building.

A report in *The Times* from 1932 gives a flavour of the kind of preaching the occupants of Mission House were trained to deliver. Father Owen Francis Dudley, one of the Missionaries, warned an audience in Liverpool that 'the Red Menace was a reality … not a fiction as some complacently imagined'. 'Bolshevism was a contradiction of human nature, a blinding of humanity to itself,' he warned, and 'were Bolshevism to succeed in overthrowing Christian marriage and the Christian family and home, we should have a world emptied of its own unique happiness.'[3]

The Missionaries continued there until 1939, when the building was requisitioned by the government for the war effort. In October 1940 Mission House was destroyed by a bomb, and the Mission Society never returned.

2   https://parish.rcdow.org.uk/willesdengreen/parish-history/mission-house-1910-40
3   *The Times*, 17 October 1932.

12

EDUCATION

By the middle of the nineteenth century, the Industrial Revolution – arguably the most profound social and economic change that Britain has ever experienced – was complete. The British Empire was continuing to expand. Acceptance gradually grew that in order for Britain to rise to these challenges and demonstrate its (supposed) superiority to the world, young people would need to be educated. Gone were the days when it was widely assumed that educating children from poor families would give them ideas beyond their station and be a waste of time, as literacy and numeracy were not important skills for working the land.

By the middle of the nineteenth century, most working-class children went to school for some of their childhood, while the children of the wealthy had governesses and, in the case of boys, were sent away to public school.

In 1870, the government passed legislation mandating that every child was to be given a place at school. Head teachers were now required to be qualified and school buildings had to be of a reasonable quality. School inspections were introduced and school boards were set up to manage schools, with the power (if they chose to exercise it) to make school compulsory for children between 5 and 10 years old. Over the next ten years, vast numbers of schools were established to make sure that all children could reach one easily.

The Elementary Education Act of 1891 went further, declaring that elementary education would henceforth be free for all children between the ages of 3 and 15 and not just for those in severe poverty.

The formal school leaving age up to the First World War was 14, although children could still leave from the age of 12 if they had jobs to go to. The school system was therefore heavily focused on primary education, with churches and local authority school boards competing with each other.

In Queen's Park, the development of so many new dwellings housing over a thousand school-age children in such a short time made the foundation of new primary schools an urgent necessity. The closest school east of the park was Christ Church School, which opened in temporary accommodation in 1878 and in its current, permanent home in 1889. This building – designed by James Brooks and built by Solomon Barnett – had space for 123 infants; a junior school with room for sixty-two boys and sixty-two girls opened next door to it in 1893. Brooks was a former vice-president of the Royal Institute of British Architects and a winner of its gold medal for achievements in architecture.[1]

On the west side of the park, the nearest school was across the border in the London School Board area: Kilburn Lane School opened in 1884, with space for 1,583 infants and juniors, on the site of the current Moberley Sports Centre.

Maria Grey Teacher Training Academy and Brondesbury & Kilburn High School

However, the first school to open in the area was actually a secondary school. Brondesbury and Kilburn High School for Girls opened in 1892 at the top of Salusbury Road, along with the Maria Grey women teachers training college, which was embedded in it; the new high school was designed for the trainee teachers to practise their skills in a real-life classroom.

The new buildings cost £11,500 and were designed by the architect James Osborne Smith, who had very progressive ideas on the importance of light and good ventilation for promoting learning. In a speech to the Royal Sanitary Institute, Smith pointed out that, 'In America, as much is often spent upon warming and ventilating a building as would have been spent on the whole building a few years ago,' and he looked forward to a time when 'it is recognised here, as it is in America, that it is sound policy for the State to give to every child the best education it is fit to receive, under the most healthy conditions possible'.[2]

The teacher training college originally opened in 1878, occupying temporary accommodation in the City of London and Fitzrovia before building a permanent home in Salusbury Road. It was one of the first buildings erected in the area; according to the college's magazine, 'we walked through wide hayfields and larks sang to us' when the staff visited the site.[3]

---

1   www.brent.gov.uk/media/16415196/locally-listed-heritage-assets-in-brent-full-list.pdf
2   'Recent Educational Developments', *Journal of the Royal Sanitary Institute*, 1904, vol. 24, no. 5.
3   Judith Knight's notes on OS Map of Willesden Green and Brondesbury 1893, Godfrey Edition.

The school received funding from Willesden Council and Middlesex County Council from 1909, by which time it had 300 pupils, with ten 'free' places reserved for girls from poorer families. It also had a kindergarten for both girls and boys. The school was taken over by the county council in 1938, becoming a girls' grammar school. The teacher training college moved out in 1940.

Kilburn Grammar School

Kilburn Grammar, a boys' secondary school, opened in 1898 in temporary premises at No. 1, Willesden Lane. It was founded by the vicar of St Paul's Church, Kilburn Square, the Rev. Dr HG Bonavia Hunt. An advert was placed in local papers announcing a new school 'For the Sons of Business and Professional Men', with fees of three guineas for seniors and two guineas for juniors. The first intake consisted of thirty-three boys.[1]

The school's links with the Church of England were clear from the start. The Bishop of London, Mandell Creighton, was appointed 'Visitor', an honorary role dating back to the Middle Ages; church and church-related institutions, such as Oxford colleges, have 'visitors' who provide advice and arbitrate in disputes. The school's badge was the emblem of the diocese of London – crossed swords on a red background, surmounted by a bishop's mitre. The school's motto – *Pasce Agnos Meos* (Latin for 'feed my lambs') – also has obvious religious roots.

This connection with the church resulted in some friction with local nonconformists, who argued that the school should be renamed St Paul's Choir School.

In January 1899 the school – now with eighty-five pupils – moved to 28 Cavendish Road, and by July there were over 100 boys enrolled. It was clear that larger, purpose-built premises would be needed, so a trust was set up tasked with raising £4,500, and the architect George Baron Carvill, of Brondesbury Road, was employed to design the new buildings. The builder was George Neal, whose offices were at 87–91 Willesden Lane, on the corner of Tennyson Road. (Neal was also responsible for the building opposite the entrance to Paddington Cemetery with Greek-style theatrical masks on the façade.)

Kilburn Grammar moved to its new premises (which were still under construction) in April 1900, and in June – the month work finished on the site – the Bishop of London visited to formally open the school's Speech Hall. The hall was named after Bishop Creighton following his death later that year, and old boys of Kilburn Grammar are still known as Old Creightonians. Creighton Road was also named in his

---

1   Brock, *A History of the Kilburn Grammar School, 1897–1967*.

honour. School sports were held at various locations including Kensal Rise Athletics Ground and Gladstone Park, where the boys used to change in an old tramcar. In 1921, Willesden Council purchased the former playing fields of the London Scottish Cricket Club on The Avenue for the school's use.

Like Brondesbury and Kilburn High School across the road, Kilburn Grammar was adopted by Willesden Council and Middlesex County Council during the 'noughties' – in this case, 1907. The two councils paid £6,500 for the school, splitting the bill down the middle.

The following year, two inspections by the University of London and the inspectorate of the Board of Education were highly critical of the school. The buildings were inadequate, the pupils' work was poor and the headmaster, Evan Evans, was 'obstinate, arrogant, unaware of his own limitations and without self-restraint ... His discipline of the boys was severe, compelling them to stand for over 40 minutes at a time.'[2] Evans stood down as headmaster in 1909; he was replaced by Wilfrid Bonavia Hunt, son of the vicar who founded the school, and future inspection reports were far more positive.

The Willesden School Board

Willesden Council established a school board in 1882, charged with ensuring there were enough school places of the right quality for the growing population. The board opened Kensal Rise School (now Ark Franklin Academy) in 1898 and Salusbury Road School in 1899.

This building programme was surprisingly contentious. Leading lights in the Church of England first tried to block the creation of the school board (preferring to see church schools open instead) and then took it over, before being ousted by nonconformists.[3]

In 1896, George Fuller of Mizpah House, Kensal Green, who described himself as 'a large ratepayer' wrote to the school board to protest about the sums of money being spent on Kensal Rise and other board schools. Although he accepted the need for extra school places, he queried whether it was necessary to build schools of the same quality as Oxbridge colleges 'in order to teach a few hundred poor children ... in the midst of laundries and low rated houses' and close to a dirty ditch. 'So soon as the high-class ratepayers feel the pinch that is coming they will move out,' he predicted. 'I can seem

2   Brock, *A History of the Kilburn Grammar School, 1897–1967.*

3   www.british-history.ac.uk/vch/middx/vol7/pp247-254

to see the ghost of your Board stalking forth now, with education in one hand and pauperism in the other.' Fuller was one of the elected members of Willesden's Board of Guardians, which oversaw the area's Poor Law Union; the guardians were planning to erect a major new workhouse on the Twyford Abbey Estate off Acton Lane at this time, and presumably saw the board schools as competition for scarce resources.[1]

John Cash, the vice-chair of the school board, thundered back: 'If the Board had placed these schools near the high-rated houses, all the "high-class ratepayers" would have fled before they had paid for them, and we should not now be able to look forward to the exodus of these unfortunate creatures.' Perhaps Mr Fuller could 'lead a purifying crusade for the purpose of cleaning [the dirty ditch] out', Cash added.

In 1914 the upper school at Kensal Rise, which had space for 400 boys and 400 girls, was supervised by WJ Dowdell ('master') and Miss Gledhill ('mistress'), and Mrs Morrall was in charge of the infants, which had a roll of 440.

Salusbury Road School was also a mixed primary, which opened in 1899. It was initially based in a corrugated iron building on the site where St Anne's Church stands today, a short distance up Salusbury Road. According to the school's informative and engaging online history, a large pond (it was drinking water for horses) had to be drained before the permanent school could be built on the corner of Salusbury and Lonsdale.[2] The new school was designed by the architect GET Lawrence and built by the firm of Cowley and Drake at a cost of £22,495 (plus £1,000 for furniture).

'The first Head [of the upper school], Mr. Mellor, was a charismatic and enlightened teacher, who wrote his own Arithmetic and English textbooks for the school and used "stereoscopes" (presumably a close relation of Victorian "lantern-slides") for geography teaching,' the school's website tells us. The headmistress of the infants' school was Miss A Butler. There was supposedly space for 860 juniors and 400 infants, but the fourteen classrooms were completely insufficient for anything like these numbers: it would have meant average class sizes of ninety. An additional class was therefore held in the hall from 1903 to 1909 (despite protests from the head teacher). In May 1905 this class contained eighty-four pupils!

The school had a pupils' parliament, a monthly school magazine, an orchestra, a school motto and song, and an association for former pupils, the Old Sols Guild. Empire Day (24 May) was a half-day holiday. The school day ran from 9 until 5, with a two-hour break at lunchtime to give children time to get home and back again.

'Salusbury School was ... part of a nascent drive to professionalise education, offering its diverse community of pupils – from crossing-sweepers' to clerks' and drapers' children – a rich, formal and very thorough education with the mandatory

1   www.workhouses.org.uk/Willesden
2   www.salusbury.brent.sch.uk/About_Us/Our-History

"3 Rs" and religious instruction, supplemented by games, music, some science-teaching and crafts. The school was particularly serious about sports and, among others, boasted winning swimming teams, whose exploits are celebrated in successive newspaper reports in the early decades.'[3]

---

3   Ibid.

13

LEISURE

Leisure time was a precious commodity in late Victorian and Edwardian England. Although the length of the average working day had fallen over the course of the nineteenth century and there was some legislative protection for employees, shop-workers still worked punishingly long shifts even on half days, clerical workers complained about the long hours they worked, and there was no limit on the working hours of women, who had to manage homes and children with no refrigeration to keep food fresh and very few mechanical aids to help with domestic tasks like washing and drying or house cleaning.

When Queen's Park residents did find time off, they had a number of options.

Queen's Park

The park offered multiple ways for people to spend their leisure time. When it was first constructed it had an outdoor 'gymnasium' where the children's playground is today. Mackenzie's original plans for the park show he kept the two circular spaces largely free of trees because he expected tennis to be played in the southern one and cricket in the northern circle.

From the start, there were weekly brass band performances by the band from the Queen's Park Estate. Some people came simply for a stroll and to enjoy the trees and flowers. Although George Higgs's estimate that 30,000 people were descending on the park every Sunday seems on the high side (by comparison, in modern times the most successful Queen's Park Day in 2019 attracted 18,000 people), the park was clearly a big hit from the outset.

The West End

Locals who wanted to go to the West End had a number of options prior to 1915: take the train to Euston and travel on from there, take a horse-drawn omnibus from down by The Falcon pub, or go down to the Harrow Road to take a tram. On 11 February 1915 the Bakerloo Line extension from Paddington to Queen's Park opened officially, allowing residents to get to Piccadilly Circus without changing trains. As it was wartime, all three stations between Queen's Park and Paddington were completely staffed by women.

Cinema and Theatre

Those who preferred to stay closer to home had a choice of cinemas by the end of 1914. The Acme Picture Theatre, which opened in October 1913, was on Chamberlayne Road near the corner of Kilburn Lane. In January 1914 its name was changed to the Kings Picture Palace. It was designed by the architects George Duckworth and Albert Howell, and had space for 300 cinema-goers.

Chamberlayne Road was also home to The Electric Pavilion Cinema, which opened in November 1914 where the Noko block is today. It was also designed by George Duckworth and could seat 800 people. In 1924, now called the Pavilion Cinema, it was expanded to take over 1,500 people at a time.

Over on Salusbury Road, the Queens Park Electric Theatre (also known as the Grand Electric Theatre) opened in 1911 on the corner of Salusbury and Lonsdale, where the Salusbury Rooms (part of Salusbury School) are today. In 1916 its name changed to the Old Boys' Cinema. It could accommodate 450 people.[1]

There were also another six cinemas on Kilburn High Road and the northern part of Maida Vale by 1914. Popular films of 1915 included DW Griffiths's racist epic *The Birth of a Nation*, which is credited with the resurgence of the Ku Klux Klan in the US, and Cecil B De Mille's *The Cheat*, which has a Japanese actor playing a sexual predator.

When not in use as cinemas, these buildings often doubled up as theatres, concert halls and settings for children's entertainment, and schools and churches were also used as venues. In February 1915, for example, Harvist Road School was the venue for a concert in aid of the Belgian War Refugees Relief Fund, including humorous songs performed by Mr Alf Morris, Miss Isabel Peachey and Mr Stanley Molland. *The Kilburn Times* reported that a performance of 'Cuthbert, Clarence and Claude' 'was quite one of the funniest numbers on the programme'.

---

1   For more on all three cinemas, see http://cinematreasures.org/theaters/14528

In April, St Anne's Church put on a pantomime – *Sleeping Beauty*.[1] The church had run pantomimes for several years before the war, but it only decided to continue the tradition in 1915 after 'very serious consideration' – not least because the male cast members from previous productions were all either serving at the front or in training. However, a new cast was recruited and it was judged one of the best ever staged by the church, with 'scarcely a dull moment'. Twelve months later a morale-boosting concert was performed at St Anne's by the 13th Hampstead Boy Scouts, based in Lonsdale Road. The scouts performed songs, piano solos and 'humorous sketches', including one entitled 'The N★★★★r Storekeeper'. The performance was attended by Alderman Budd, deputy mayor of Hampstead, who 'takes a keen interest in the scout movement', according to *The Kilburn Times*.

The nearest proper theatre was the Theatre Royal, near the corner of Belsize Road and Kilburn High Road. From 1909 onwards the Theatre Royal began showing films as well as staging plays, and by 1916 it had changed its name to the Picture Palace.

Sport

Late Victorian and Edwardian England was a great place and time for sports enthusiasts. At least two professional tennis players lived locally in 1901 – Arthur H Smith at 13 Harvist Road and 'Jimmie' Fennell at 34 Kempe Road. The two worked together at the real tennis court at Lord's cricket ground from 1890 until 1902, when Smith moved to Petworth House Tennis Club as their first club professional.[2] There's a photograph of Jimmie at an exhibition match that Arthur ran at Petworth in 1912.

From 1890 until the First World War, locals had first-class sport on their doorstep in the shape of the National Athletic Ground, which had tracks for cycling and running and also hosted walking races, football (it was QPR's home ground from 1896 to 1901 and again from 1902–04) and boxing (the famous Welsh boxer Jimmy Wilde, known as The Mighty Atom because of his diminutive size, fought a match there in 1916). It was taken over by the army in 1917 and never returned to being used for sports. It was demolished and replaced by Leigh and Whitmore Gardens in the 1920s, which explains why there are two streets of more modern houses in the middle of a predominantly Victorian and Edwardian district.[3]

---

1   It seems surprisingly late – or maybe early – in the year for a pantomime.
2   http://petworthrealtennis.com/history/professional-history
3   There's an excellent account of the history of the stadium, including the roles played by Norman Wisdom's great-grandfather and 'Jumbo' Ecclestone, 'the heaviest man to fly', in Dick Weindling and Marianne Collom's blog at http://kilburnwesthampstead.blogspot.com/2021/06/sports-in-kensal-rise.html

Boys' football was incredibly popular in the area in the early years of Queen's Park. All the local primary schools had their own teams, as did Keslake Road. Queens Park Rangers was, of course, formed out of the merger of two boys' teams down on the Queen's Park Estate (see Chapter 5).

London Scottish rugby club was based in Brondesbury (just north of Queen's Park) for a time, and there were cricket clubs in both Brondesbury and Carlton Vale in the 1900s.

Eating and Drinking

Queen's Park had no pubs in the 1900s apart from the Prince of Wales on Willesden Lane. (The Falcon also counts as a Queen's Park pub in my view, even though it is outside of the QPARA area.) It wasn't because of any restrictive covenants by the Church Commissioners who sold the land – it just doesn't seem to have occurred to the builders that pubs would be a particularly lucrative investment, plus they were trying to attract 'respectable' people to the new homes they were building. However, there were plenty of off-licences in the area from the start.

Similarly, Queen's Park was not a particularly inspiring spot for dining out. In 1899 'Mr Fish' was a coffee shop, and in 1914 'Jacks' was George Childs' dining rooms. And that was it – very unlike the Queen's Park of today where residents are spoilt for choice.

14

WORK

In 1900, London was the economic powerhouse of the world – the largest and most prosperous city on the planet – and its economic growth fuelled the expansion of Queen's Park.

Male unemployment was very low. In Queen's Park, only 3 per cent of working age men and boys were jobless – but the vast majority of those were under 18s, most of whom were probably still at school. When someone was genuinely unemployed, they are recorded as 'unengaged', and there are only three in the whole area in the 1901 census.

Female employment patterns were very different. Two-thirds of women in Queen's Park were not in employment in 1901, but that doesn't mean they were jobless: unless they were rich enough to employ servants, they were expected to do unpaid labour in the home, in a world with only a fraction of the labour-saving devices we enjoy today.

Those who did work were heavily concentrated in certain occupations – working in retail, manufacturing, dressmaking, or domestic service, for example. They were paid far less than men who did equivalent work, and when they got married they were expected to stop working and manage the home, regardless of their social class.

In Queen's Park, around 40 per cent of all women and girls in paid employment were working in some form of domestic service in 1901. A scan of the census for Kingswood Avenue in 1901 shows that twenty of the twenty-six households occupied on census night had live-in servants – twenty-five in total, all of them women, with an average age of 25. The youngest was 14, the oldest 54. Four of them were cooks and one was a professional nurse; the rest were general domestic servants.

It wasn't just the big houses facing the park that had servants; over in Honiton Road there were twelve general servants, two nursemaids and one cook, although there were only two servants on Milman Road in 1901 and just one on Peploe Road.

THE PRINCE OF WALES AT THE OPENING OF THE ROYAL AGRICULTURAL SOCIETY'S INTERNATIONAL EXHIBITION.—SEE PAGE 14.

The Prince and Princess of Wales arrive at the Royal Agricultural Show, 1879. *Illustrated London News*

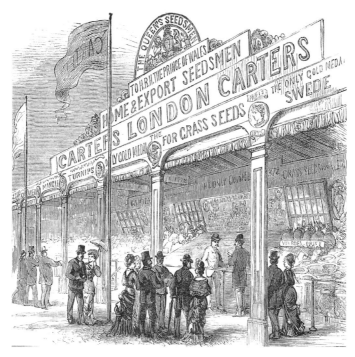

The Carter's Seeds stand at the Royal Agricultural Show in 1879. Carter's stand, along with others demonstrating 'seeds and models', was along the eastern perimeter of the showground facing towards today's park. This stand was on the site of today's police station.

Hayward, Tyler & Co. exhibited in the 'machinery in motion' section of the 1879 Royal Agricultural Show. Their stand was approximately where the north-east entrance to the park is today, facing north.

BAND STAND, QUEEN'S PARK W.

The bandstand, Queen's Park, 1904, surrounded by some of the trees that used to be part of the hedges alongside Long Cross Lane. www.images-of-london.co.uk

Vanguard Omnibus, Chamberlayne Wood Road, Kensal Rise.

Number 6 bus outside Kensal Rise Station, 1905. www.images-of-london.co.uk

Chamberlayne Road, 1906. www.images-of-london.co.uk

St Anne's Church, Salusbury Road, sometime between 1906 and 1914. Courtesy Brent Museum and Archives

H.R.M. Series, 69.

The Lodge, Queen's Park.

Park-keeper's lodge, Queen's Park, 1907. HRM series, Courtesy Brent Museum and Archives

The junction of Salusbury Road and Harvist/Brondesbury roads sometime between 1907 and 1910. The building on the left is the police station, destroyed by a bomb in 1940. Courtesy Brent Museum and Archives

The 'Quiet Garden' c.1910, with the vine-covered park-keeper's lodge on the right

Salusbury Road Council School, Kilburn.

Children in Salsubury Road School's hall, 1910. The class that met in this hall had eighty-four pupils in 1905! www.images-of-london.co.uk

Footpath, Willesden (leading to Kensal Rise.)

Footpath leading to Kensal Rise, 1910. www.images-of-london.co.uk

The drinking fountain, Queen's Park, c.1910. The fountain stood in the middle of the park near where the café is today. It was erected in 1898. There was another drinking fountain outside the 'gymnasium' (now the children's playground). www.images-of-london.co.uk

Salusbury Road, 1910. This photo was taken on the railway bridge outside Queen's Park Station, which can just be seen on the left of the picture. The first two buildings visible on the right have vanished. Bell's Photo Company, Courtesy Brent Museum and Archives

Corner of Chamberlayne Road and Kempe Road, around 1910. Courtesy Brent Museum and Archives

The Grand Electric Cinema on the corner of Salusbury Road and Lonsdale Road sometime between 1911 and 1916. Courtesy Brent Museum and Archives

Entrance to the park on the corner of Harvist and Milman Roads, c.1910. WJ Hunt, Courtesy Brent Museum and Archives

Father Dominic Dams and refugee children and teachers from the King Albert Belgian School on Wrentham Avenue. Photo taken in Queen's Park in 1916 or 1917. Arthur Dunn, Courtesy Brent Museum and Archives

Queen's Park, c.1919.

Willesden Council Electricity Department, top of Salusbury Road, 1926. WG Briggs & Company Ltd,
Courtesy Brent Museum and Archives

Commemorative postcard from the centenary celebrations of Queen's Park, 1987. Note the bandstand is
all white! Collection of the late Gwen Molloy

Across the whole of Queen's Park there were 312 live-in servants in 1901 and 64 who lived out; many of these were 'monthly nurses', who looked after newborn babies in the first few weeks.

The remaining 60 per cent of women who were in paid employment were split roughly equally between manual work (especially dressmaking, hat-making, and laundry work), retail, hospitality and leisure, and white-collar and professional occupations.

By the end of the Victorian era, increasing numbers of women were moving into office work. We see this reflected in the local population of Queen's Park. On Kingswood, the Grant sisters at No. 25, Dora and Lilian, were a shorthand clerk and a telegraphist. Around the corner in Montrose Avenue, Jessie Rose at No. 2 was a 'letter correspondent', and Nellie and Charlotte Riding at No. 20 were both telegraphists. The houses on the south side of Harvist Road alone were home to twenty-one women office workers, including two bookkeepers, an accountant, eight clerks, three stenographers, four typists, a telegraphist, a stock keeper and a travelling secretary.

When women did break into male-dominated workplaces, they were often subject to outrageous sexism. During the First World War, five women teachers were employed at Kilburn Grammar to replace male teachers who were fighting in the war (women teachers up to this point were normally only employed in infants' schools and girls' schools). In 1915 one of the senior (male) teachers recorded a formal vote of thanks to his female colleagues in the staff meeting minutes book for 'detention lists of magnificent proportions' and suggested that they spend less time on 'animated conversation' and more on 'the arduous feat of marking registers'.[1] Antipathy wasn't just limited to their male colleagues; some families took their boys out of the school in protest at the hiring of women teachers.

In January 1917, the *Kilburn Times* published an editorial complaining about the large number of bonuses paid to women teachers. In the following edition Ethel McKenzie, honorary secretary of the Willesden Women Teachers Association, hit back. She pointed out that 'girls, infants, and special schools have always been staffed by women, and in addition two-thirds, maybe more, of the present staffs of boys and of mixed schools are women teachers', who anyway were paid far less than male teachers. Under the circumstances it was hardly surprising that a large proportion of bonus payments should go to women teachers, she argued.

Since the majority of children left school at 14 (and often earlier if they had a job), most teaching jobs were in primary education and this was far more women-friendly: of the 130 locals employed in teaching and education-related professions in Queen's Park in 1901, eighty-seven of them were women, including twenty-three on Harvist Road alone.

---

1   Brock, *A History of the Kilburn Grammar School, 1897–1967*.

Despite the many barriers they faced, some local women did have successful careers; many of the businesses listed in Chapter 10 were run by women. Elizabeth Felton, who lived at 47 Donaldson, ran an omnibus company.

Young Workers

The number of very young workers in Queen's Park in 1901 was mercifully small – around thirty-five 13- and 14-year-olds. They included a 13-year-old office boy on Keslake, a 13-year-old messenger on Salusbury Road and a 14-year-old domestic servant on Montrose Avenue.

Older Workers

There was no formal state pension scheme until 1908, and no formal retirement age, so a fair few people kept on working well into their 70s. On Harvist Road there was a bricklayer still working at 74 and an estate agent aged 79. Walter Girling, at 37 Hartland Road, was still working in 1901 as a painter's labourer despite being born in 1819, four years after the Battle of Waterloo! However, some employers did have retirement schemes, particularly in public sector institutions like teaching, the post office and the civil service, and the vast majority of over 65s in Queen's Park in 1901 were no longer in employment.

Male Employment

Around 40 per cent of men in employment in Queen's Park in 1901 worked in professional and/or white-collar jobs. Late Victorian and Edwardian England had a huge need for clerks to copy and process documents, and Queen's Park was full of them: over 400 men and women had 'clerk' in their job title. More than a third worked in manual jobs, in the building industry, for gas and water companies, driving cabs or working on the railways. The rest worked in shops, restaurants, hotels and theatres.

Most seem to have worked locally. There were twenty-two men involved in stock-broking in the City of London, a couple employed by the royal family (a page and a messenger) and some secretaries to national companies, like the stationery suppliers Wiggins Teape. Some of the merchants and traders who lived locally traded in oriental goods, handled business in West Africa or managed Japanese shipping companies, but the majority worked in the local economy.

In addition to the shops, schools, fire brigade and police station and local coroner's court, there were a growing number of jobs available in businesses on Lonsdale Road in the early 1900s. The first businesses to open there included an oil shop at No. 1, run by a woman called Julia Elizabeth de Combe, Caslake and Co.'s 'art metal workers' at 23, a shoeing forge at 27 and a coach builder at No. 33. The workshops also housed a stonemasons and a decorating business. Two units were home to Charles Riggs, a 'jobmaster' whose business was renting out carriages by the day or week.

By 1914, Lonsdale Road was fully built and a great deal more mechanised. Nos 7–11 were occupied by Needham and Son, carriage and motor body builders; No. 27 was home to Motor Pistons; No. 6 was the NFH Motor Repair Co.; and Nos 10–12 were Wilkinson Motor Engineering Co., motor engineers. There was also a chimney sweeping business, a honey merchants, upholsterers and Carltona Ltd, a firm of baking powder manufacturers. No. 15 was the headquarters of the 13th Hampstead Boy Scouts Troop and No. 23 was used by the Harvist Orchestral Society for practice sessions.

Aron Electricity Meter Ltd bought all the land on Lonsdale between No. 18 and the corner of Salusbury Road (ie where the Salusbury Rooms, Lonsdale Medical Practice and The Minster Centre are today), intending to open a factory there. That didn't go ahead, but they did open premises on Salusbury Road, occupying a block and a half of the workshops between Montrose and Windermere avenues. The land on Lonsdale was used to build the Electric Theatre cinema and a garage for the London General Omnibus Company. In 1908, this bus company had established a near monopoly on bus services in London, having bought up most of its rivals, including presumably Mrs Felton's (see p.135) with whom 'the London General' had had a court battle over 'passing off' in 1896.

Kimberley Road also provided industrial jobs in the area. In 1904, Frederick Simms opened a car plant called the Welbeck Works on the site of the modern block of flats called Kimberley Court. The factory produced cars, commercial vehicles and engines, and was in business until 1920. In 1910, they were joined by the Grosvenor Carriage Company, which made car bodies and did coachwork for companies including Rolls-Royce. They were based in the building overlooking Paddington Cemetery.[1] There was also a business in Kimberley Road, Aero Motors Ltd, which made engines for aircraft.

Salusbury Road was also a manufacturing hub. As well as Aaron Electricity Meter Ltd, there was a firm of mattress makers, 'vulcanisers' (who worked with rubber), ventilating engineers and a piano firm on the west side, and on the east Delacour Brothers' pipe manufacturing business and Green and Edwards' furniture depository. A firm of printers set up in Salusbury Road later.

1   https://kilburnwesthampstead.blogspot.com/2020/06/frederick-simms-and-welbeck-works.html

Fine Arts

A number of residents worked full-time in the arts in the early years of Queen's Park. The 1901 census records nine full-time artists, two of whom (sisters Mabel and Maud Cockburn of 'Latton' (now No. 157) Chevening Road) exhibited in the Royal Academy's summer show in 1895. There were also professional musicians, journalists and authors, an actor and two professional entertainers including popular music hall star Tom Clare, who lived on Montrose Avenue' at the end of the sentence.

15

HEALTH

Healthcare in 1900 was on an upward trajectory. The death rate per thousand people had fallen from 22.5 in 1870 to 18.2 at the end of the nineteenth century, and doctors, surgeons and midwifes now had to be medically qualified thanks to the 1886 Medical Amendment Act. (But not dentists – alarmingly, you didn't have to be professionally qualified to work on someone's teeth until 1921.)

However, healthcare in 1900 was still a commercial enterprise (and would remain so until 1948), and the care you got depended on how much you could afford to pay, and where you lived. Wealthier patients expected to be treated in the home by GPs who worked hard on their 'bedside manner', listening to the patient's description of their symptoms and diagnosing accordingly. Poorer patients were more likely to be hospitalised.

Hospitals were often established as charitable enterprises, or paid for out of public subscriptions, like St Mary's in Paddington or the Willesden Cottage Hospital, which opened in 1893 thanks to a donation from the philanthropist John Passmore Edwards. Others were municipal foundations, like St Charles' Hospital off Ladbroke Grove, which started life in 1881 as the St Marylebone Union Infirmary for treating the poor of the parish.

Mary Wilson Carpenter, in her *History of Health in Victorian England*, writes:

Hospitals were feared, rightly, as places where patients with internal complaints would die of 'hospital fever' (contagious diseases), while surgical patients would die of 'hospital gangrene' (wound gangrene). Like the puerperal fever which killed so many women who gave birth in hospitals, these were hospital-acquired infections spread by the contaminated hands or clothing of doctors, or simply by bacteria present everywhere in the air and on patients' bodies.[1]

Wealthy women, like Solomon Barnett's wife Florence, therefore gave birth at home rather than in hospitals. Minnie Arens, one of the earliest residents of Queen's Park, remembered her mother helping the midwives when local women went into labour:

> Most confinements were in the house then, but she wouldn't let me go near the gate, because she didn't want me to hear the screaming ... She told me years afterwards that she used to stuff something in their mouths to stop them screaming.[2]

Some working-class people joined 'friendly societies' that covered the cost of medical treatment, but many were dependent on charities or the Poor Law Union for their treatment. Many simply put up with their ailments rather than facing the costs of healthcare.

Early Queen's Park was home to many medical professionals. There were physician/surgeons living on Winchester Avenue, father and son medical practitioners (a surgeon and a GP) on Brondesbury Road, and a medical nurse on Kempe.

In 1911 a doctor called James Samuel Richard Weir was both living and practising at 66 Salusbury Road (the corner of Montrose Avenue). There were two doctors on Chamberlayne Road, including George William Robert Skene at number 94. Weir was born in County Down, Ireland; Skene in Colombo, Sri Lanka. Also on Chamberlayne Road were an opticians and a false teeth company. There was a surprising number of false teeth manufacturers in the area at the time, probably reflecting the fashion for having all your teeth taken out to avoid the inconvenience and cost of tooth decay and remedial treatment later on.

---

1 *Carpenter, Health, Medicine and Society in Victorian England*, p.26.
2 Margaret Chambers, Queen's Park Centenary Brochure.

16

CRIME AND PUNISHMENT

A number of Queen's Park roads are said to have changed their name as a result of the reputational damage caused by horrific murders; Creighton/Sinclair is an example. In most cases, these are urban myths – but one of them is absolutely true, and most likely the dimly remembered inspiration for all the rest.

The Ladysmith Murder

Until 1904, Wrentham Avenue was called Ladysmith Road, in honour of the South African town where a British army was besieged for four months during the Boer War. The previous year, a 29-year-old man called George Crossman was living at a house called 'Sunnyside'. Crossman was working as a commission agent (ie a salesman who received no salary, only commission on successful sales). He had struggled to find his vocation, previously working as baker, a barber and a barman. He was also a serial bigamist, 'marrying' seven times.[3] Although the first three were legitimate (his first wife died, the second divorced him), the last four were not. Crossman had actually been found out and convicted for bigamy, and was reporting monthly to the police station in Salusbury Road when he committed his most heinous crime.

In January 1903, Crossman 'married' two women within a week. He first married Edith Thompson, who he met when he responded to an advertisement she had placed looking for work as a 'mother's help'; he told her he was a reporter with

---

3 *St James' Gazette*, 29 March 1904.

the *Morning Post* on a salary of £150 a year. They were married at Holy Trinity on Brondesbury Road and moved into the house on Ladysmith together. A few days later, he told her he had to go to Manchester on business, and she went to stay with friends in Peckham. In fact, he travelled down to Blackwater in Hampshire, where he went through another marriage ceremony, this time with Ellen Sampson, a widowed nurse who worked at a cottage hospital nearby. He called himself 'Charles Seymour'. The two returned to Ladysmith Road, where it appears Crossman murdered Ellen the following morning.

Crossman put Ellen's body in a tin trunk, poured concrete into the trunk and stashed it in the cupboard under the stairs. Meanwhile, Edith returned home and – suspecting nothing – resumed her married life. During the following year, Crossman married twice more, first to a woman from Richmond called Venables, and then, in January 1904, to Annie Welch, who he met when she answered a 'matrimonial advertisement'. Annie seems to have been a great deal more inquisitive than Crossman's other victims. While they were on honeymoon in Herne Bay, she found a letter in his pocket from Venables addressed to a 'Mr Weston' and starting 'My dear husband'. Although she dragged Crossman down to Richmond to confront Venables, his sixth wife denied being married to him. They then returned together to Ladysmith Road, where he told Edith Thompson that Annie was someone interested in adopting his eldest child, and asked Edith to pretend not to be his wife in case that complicated the adoption process.

Things spiralled out of control very quickly for Crossman. After he'd kept Ellen's body secret for a year, a new lodger called William Dell became suspicious of the tin trunk the same day that Annie arrived at the house. Looking for something in the cupboard under the stairs, Dell was appalled by the stench coming from the trunk (Crossman had poured cement around and on top of the body, but not underneath so the smell was able to escape.) Dell was not convinced by Crossman's claims that the smell was caused by old chemicals, and urged him to go to the police.

On Thursday, 24 March, Dell came home from work in the City and was appalled to see Crossman dragging the massively heavy tin trunk down the hallway toward a waiting van parked outside. He ran to Kilburn Police Station on Salusbury Road, where he persuaded the station sergeant, Smith, and a police constable, Reeves, to accompany him back to Ladysmith Road. They found Crossman smoking a cigar on the street outside, next to the trunk and the waiting van. Crossman ran, but was cornered in Hanover Road, where he drew a cut-throat razor from his pocket and slit his own throat, dying instantly.

The council responded with a speed that would be unthinkable today. Just three weeks after the murder *The Globe* reported: 'The Willesden Council have altered the name of Ladysmith-road, Kensal Rise, where the recent murder was committed, to Wrentham-avenue, in response to the wishes of the inhabitants in consequence of the murder.'[1]

The Tin Trunk Murders

A tin trunk was involved again the following year. Arthur Devereux, a 34-year-old chemist's assistant, murdered his wife Beatrice (35) and 2-year-old twins Evelyn and Lawrence. Devereux was said to be devoted to the couple's oldest child, a 5-year-old called Stanley, but disappointed with the twin boys, who were disabled.[2] He placed the bodies in a tin trunk, which he sealed hermetically using wood and copious amounts of glue to prevent them decomposing. He then had the trunk taken to a storage facility in Buller Road, Kensal Green, and decamped to start a new life in Coventry. His crimes were only discovered thanks to the persistence of Beatrice's mother, Ellen, who suspected foul play and had the trunk opened. Devereux was tried, found guilty of his wife's murder (by poisoning) and hanged at Pentonville Prison. His executioner was Henry Pierrepoint, father of the celebrated hangman Albert Pierrepoint.

Following this run of killings, one London evening paper launched a campaign to drop the name 'Kensal Rise' altogether because of its association with dark deeds. *The Kilburn Times* objected on the grounds that 'the accidental occurrence of one serious crime in their midst' hardly justified changing the name of a whole area.[3] The proposal was debated by the Kensal Green Ratepayers' Association, where – amid much laughter – a Mr Evans declared that 'this was the silliest of all silly season discussions that had ever been raised, and how any level-headed men could mix themselves up in a discussion of this description passed his comprehension'.[4]

Death in Dundonald

A year later, there was a tragedy around the corner from Wrentham Avenue at a house inDundonald Road. Early in the morning of 7 September 1906, 38-year-old Alfred Robert Rogers killed two of his children, 9-year-old Florence and 14-year-old May, and attempted to kill his wife Jessie and 3-year-old daughter Ethel. He was prevented from doing so by his brother, Albert, who also lived in the house. A furious fight ensued between the brothers, in the course of which Albert was slashed in

---

1   *The Globe*, 14 April 1904.
2   *Daily Telegraph and Courier (London)*, 15 April 1905.
3   *Kilburn Times*, 1 September 1905.
4   *Kilburn Times*, 22 September 1905.

the throat, chest and back with a cut-throat razor. The fight started in the bedroom and continued down the stairs and into the kitchen, where a rolling pin and couple of balusters were used as weapons. At one point Albert disarmed his brother and threw the razor out of a window, but Alfred got hold of a kitchen knife and the fight continued.[1]

When a couple of neighbours – Albert Elliott, who lived next door, and Andrew Ralph, from No. 15 – broke down the front door, Rogers tried to kill himself by cutting his own throat, but failed and was restrained until the police arrived. He told the police:

> I do not know what made me do it, but I have had a lot of worry over money matters lately [his upholstery business in Kilburn had failed in June]; I was in fear that my wife and children would be in want, and rather than see that, it caused me to do what I have done, but I wish now I could undo what I have done. I wish now I had killed myself and let my family alone. When you take me away go down Milman Road to the police station.[2]

A detective who investigated the crime scene said there was 'blood everywhere; the whole place was like a slaughterhouse'.

Alfred Rogers's wife, youngest daughter Jessie and brother Albert were taken to St Mary's, where they all recovered, despite terrible injuries. The couple's other surviving child – an 11-year-old boy called Willie – was unharmed. Rogers was found guilty of murder in a trial at the Old Bailey, but found to have been insane at the time of the attacks. He was committed to Broadmoor, where he died in 1920.

The Quarry Murder

Three decades passed before Kensal Rise was in the news again for all the wrong reasons. In June 1935 Philip Quarry, a 22-year-old joiner, stabbed his wife Angela (also 22) to death after a violent quarrel at their basement flat in Chevening Road. Quarry ran off, but handed himself in at the police station on Salusbury Road later the same day. Quarry attempted a defence of insanity, but was found guilty of murder. His death sentence was later commuted to life imprisonment.

---

1 *Kilburn Times*, 14 September 1906.
2 www.oldbaileyonline.org/browse.jsp?div=t19061022-28

Shooting in Esmond Road

On the other side of the park, the 'usually quiet' Esmond Road was shaken in November 1894 by an attempted murder and a suicide. A married man and father of five, William Carter, turned up on the street to press his attentions on a Mrs Alice Sims, a married woman with three children. They had known each other when the Sims and the Carters were tenants in the same house in Maida Vale, during which time Carter became obsessed with Mrs Sims. When she saw who was at the door she ran upstairs, followed by Carter, who shot her in the face (non-fatally) and then turned the gun on himself (fatally). Neighbours in Esmond Road all assured the journalist from the *Willesden Chronicle* that Carter's affections were unrequited.[3]

Other Crimes in the Area

There are numerous sad stories of babies who either died when they were born to mothers who had to conceal their pregnancies, or were killed or abandoned by mothers unable to look after them. In 1902, inquests were held into two babies who were found abandoned in the area – one in the open fields around Kensal Green and the other in Queen's Park itself. The latter baby had been discovered in bushes at the park by a park-keeper called John Hemstall, of 65 Kempe Road, where it appeared to have been for some time.[4]

In 1907 a baby's body was found abandoned in a field off Okehampton Road. It was traced to a 25-year-old servant girl, Louisa Day, who said she had been abandoned by her mother at the age of 7 and had been looking after herself since she was 15. A charge of murder was reduced to one of concealment and she received a three-month sentence. Kind people sent postal orders anonymously in her support.[5]

However, dramas of this kind were thankfully rare events for the Police of X Division based at Salusbury Road. A more typical event occurred in August 1901, when police interrupted a burglar at 40 Brooksville Avenue after the next-door neighbour heard strange noises. The 'tall, powerful' one-eyed perpetrator gave them the slip, but was seen disappearing down the alley that led to the backs of the houses on Montrose Avenue. Finding a window open at No. 39, they climbed in and searched the house (the occupants were not home). They were just about to give up the search

3 *Willesden Chronicle*, 9 November 1894.
4 *Kilburn Times*, 10 October 1902.
5 *Wells Journal*, 19 September 1907.

when one of the officers noticed a scratch on a banister rail just below a trap door to the loft. On investigating, they found the burglar crouched behind the water tank. He came quietly.[1]

That same month a man named William Robert Philpot was sentenced to a month's hard labour for attacking his housemate, Alice Lawson, with a screwdriver at the lodging house they both lived in at 49 Keslake Road.[2]

In April 1905, a carpenter called George Williams was sentenced to twelve months' hard labour for stealing fittings from houses in Hopefield and Kingswood. The owner of the properties, local developer Solomon Barnett, had become suspicious that something was wrong so he hired a watchman called Maurice Rothman who caught Williams in the act, loaded with brass taps, a bath plug and chain, a letterbox and sundry other items.[3] A similar crime happened in December 1908, when an 18-year-old man was caught stealing the brass doorknocker from No. 12 Kingswood (which was unoccupied at the time) by two passing police officers. He was sentenced to two months' hard labour.[4]

Some of the convictions handed out, though, seem fairly petty. In April 1910 Henry Nottingham, who lived at 24 Salusbury Road, was fined for parking his van on the street for 'longer than was necessary for loading or unloading' and fined 2s 6d.[5]

The number of people convicted for being drunk and disorderly is quite astonishing, given how few pubs there were in the area. On 13 May 1898 the 'stylishly dressed' Florence Pascal of 40 Harvist Road was arrested for being drunk and disorderly, and also for keeping two dogs without a licence. Apparently she and her husband had been drinking in the garden, and he locked her out of the house after an argument. Her defence – that she had taken brandy for purely medicinal purposes – was not successful, and she was fined 5s.[6]

In November 1911 Agnes Doris (also known as Margaret Romaine) of Victoria Road was charged with being drunk, disorderly and using obscene language in Brondesbury Villas (she had many previous convictions), and Rosetta Miles, of Maida Vale, was arrested after being found drunk on the pavement of Salusbury Road after celebrating her son's birthday rather too enthusiastically.[7]

1 *Kilburn Times*, 9 August 1901.
2 *Kilburn Times*, 23 August 1891.
3 *Kilburn Times*, 14 April 1905.
4 *Kilburn Times*, 18 December 1908.
5 *Kilburn Times*, 15 April 1910.
6 *Kilburn Times*, 27 May 1898.
7 *Kilburn Times*, 1 December 1911.

17

POLITICS

Ancient History

Watling Street was part of the boundary between King Alfred's Wessex and the Viking-ruled Danelaw in the ninth century, and it is often said that this section of Middlesex has been frontier-land ever since. Sadly, that second bit is a myth; Watling Street did form part of the border, but only from Bedfordshire northwards. In this area the border ran up the Lea Valley, skirting London well to the east before it met Watling Street, miles from here. But the myth became reality in 1851, when the architects of the national census of that year decided that the 'Metropolis' of London began south of Kilburn Lane and east of the Kilburn High Road. For the next 114 years, this area was at the extreme southern edge of Middlesex, in Willesden, while east Kilburn, St Peter's Park and the Queen's Park Estate were in London. This has not always made for joined-up government, or for Kilburn and the two Queen's Parks (the area regarded as Queen's Park today, in Brent, and the Queen's Park Estate designed for 'working men' in Westminster Borough) to get the focus they deserve.

As we've seen (in Chapter 2), until as late as 1900 the land south of the Euston Line was overseen by the Chelsea Vestry (a vestry being the room in a church where robes are kept, and historically where parish councils met), despite being wholly disconnected from the rest of 'Chelsea'. This does not seem to have made it any easier for local people to have unlocked funding from the parish. At the beginning of the last century, when the London boroughs were created, this anomaly was tidied up; the land between the Harrow Road and Kilburn Lane went to the new London Borough of Paddington, and Kensal Town; the 'Piggeries' and the 'Potteries' transferred to the Borough of Kensington.

The Start of Local Government

The oldest institutions of local government in the area were the parish and the manor courts.

The parish (essentially, a division within a Christian diocese) formed the basic unit of local government throughout the eighteenth century and was legally charged with responsibility for poor relief. The churchwarden, working under the direction of the vestry, was responsible for both the collection of the rates and their distribution. The rates (a form of tax) were levied on property owners and occupiers based on the yearly value of their property. The rates were mainly used to raise money for poor relief but also for other local services such as church expenses and education, as well as more prosaic needs such as creating and maintaining roads, drainage and sewer maintenance. The precise number of parish officers and employees and their duties varied from parish to parish, meaning that each community developed their own unique governance traditions.

The jurisdiction of the manor courts applied only to people who lived in or held lands within the manor's boundaries. The court generally met every few weeks and dealt with things like how the open fields were managed, local contracts and settling disputes. Part of the old feudal system, these courts became obsolete in the eighteenth century.

Willesden Local Board

Willesden's first recognisably democratic institution, the Willesden Local Board, was established in 1874. Local boards were set up as a result of the Public Health Act of 1848 to improve the sanitary conditions of urban areas. Their responsibilities included sewers, street cleaning, pavements, pleasure grounds, public lavatories and burials.

'Democratic' may be stretching it a bit. The fifteen members of the Willesden board were elected by local property owners and ratepayers; the more property you owned, the more votes you had, so board members tended to be wealthy locals who could command the confidence of the local elite. Women were only allowed to vote if they owned property or paid the rates *and* were single or widowed.

It seems there was often tension between the representatives from Kilburn – urban, fast growing, and in need of public works – and the rest of Willesden district, which was still largely rural and agricultural.[1] The board was peripatetic until 1891, when

---

1   www.british-history.ac.uk/vch/middx/vol7/pp228-232

it moved into permanent offices on Dyne Road in Kilburn; its first meeting places included White's Hotel on Shoot-up Hill.

Willesden District Council

In 1894, following the Local Government Act of the same year that aimed to reform local democracy, Willesden upgraded from a local board to a district council. All women now had the vote as long as they owned property in their own right or paid rates, regardless of their marital status, and they could stand for election for the first time. The first woman councillor in Willesden was co-opted in 1917.

At its outset, the council had a total of twenty-one councillors spread across seven wards, including North, Mid and South Kilburn, and Kensal Green. All of Queen's Park west of Salusbury Road (including the new park itself) was in Kensal Green ward, represented by Charles Pinkham (see below), Dr Crone and Albert Toley. East of Salusbury Road, the area between Lonsdale Road and Brondesbury Villas was part of Mid Kilburn ward, represented by councillors Coombes, Godson and Richards.

The new council assumed responsibility for a much wider range of services than its predecessor, including schools, hospitals, parks, libraries, and police and fire services: it was responsible for the opening of both Kilburn Library and Kilburn Fire Station on Salusbury Road in 1894, as well as the Kensal Rise and Salusbury Road schools.

In 1900, the Town Hall on Dyne Road was enlarged to create an impressive Gothic centre of municipal authority (sadly demolished in 1972). In 1909 the council expanded to eleven wards, including Brondesbury Park, which took over Queen's Park from Kingswood westwards (Mid Kilburn ward expanded to absorb everything between Salusbury Road and the park.)

To begin with, the council was not run on party-political lines: the first election to have overtly partisan candidates was 1910, when twenty Conservatives and thirteen Labour and Progressive councillors were elected. However, the political affiliations of many of the candidates who stood in earlier elections were clear to voters, even if they didn't use those labels in the council chamber; Charles Pinkham, who served as chairman of the board five times and sat on it from 1888 to 1919, was a leading light in the Conservative Party, for example (see p.151).

Labour were in opposition for much of the life of the district council, which was run first by the Conservatives and then by a 'ratepayers alliance'.

Suffragettes

Queen's Park was home to a significant figure in the Suffragette movement, Violet Mary Doudney. She was one of six children of a wealthy family from Leicestershire, whose mother treated the three boys and three girls equally. Violet went on to study at St Hilda's College in Oxford from 1908 to 1911, at a time when the university did not recognise women graduates. However, by the time she took her master's degree at Oxford the policy had changed, so she was able to collected her first and second degrees on the same day.

She joined the Women's Social and Political Union (WSPU) at Oxford, and became a passionate advocate of education as a key to enabling women's emancipation. This led her to enrol at the Maria Grey teacher training academy on Salusbury Road, where she boarded at Winkworth Hall (named after the female mountaineer and supporter of suffrage Emma Winkworth).

During this time, Violet became increasingly active in the militant Suffragette movement, and in June 1912 she was arrested for throwing a metal weight wrapped in paper saying Votes for Women through the window of the Home Secretary's residence. She was arrested and sentenced to two months' hard labour for the crime of breaking a piece of glass worth 2s. Research by her granddaughter – local resident and architect Maggie Toy – has found that a man who appeared in front of the same judge in the same court on the same day was sentenced to three months *without* hard labour for the crime of killing his wife 'because she nagged too much'.

In prison, Violet went on hunger strike and was subjected to forced feeding. She was released early in a frail state back into the care of Mrs Felkin, warden of Winkworth Hall, following exchanges between Violet's mother and the authorities. When she subsequently realised that she'd been released early, Violet wrote furiously to the Home Secretary demanding to go back and complete her sentence:

I understand that you ordered my release from H.M Prison Holloway on account of an undertaking given by my parents that I would do no more militant work. I wish you to understand that no pledge of any kind whatsoever has been even offered to me and that I have given no undertaking whatsoever. Moveover I am of age and I do not consider myself in any way bound by any pledge given without my knowledge or consent and [action] I certainly intend to take, 'militant' or otherwise which may appear necessary to me to be necessary and justifiable in advancing a cause which I have at heart … If upon receipt of this letter you think you have released me on false pretences and wish me to return to Holloway I am willing to do so.[1]

Willesden was home to another leading Suffragette, Eleanor Penn Gaskell, whose story has been told by local historian Dick Weindling.[2] Gaskell was secretary of the Willesden branch of the London Society for Women's Suffrage, and a regular speaker. She was arrested only once (in 1908, for obstruction) but she was very active in the movement. She nursed the militant suffragette Emily Wilding Davison (whose name appears on the same page as Violet Doudney's on the Suffragettes' roll of honour) at her home in Harlesden after Davison was released from prison in a weak state after being on hunger strike. This was a year before Davison was killed when she ran out in front of the King's horse at the 1913 Epsom Derby.

Suffragettes boycotted the 1911 census as a matter of principle. Eleanor's husband noted that:

A number of women suffragists spent the night of 2nd April (census night) in my house. As members of a disenfranchised sex they object to giving any particulars concerning themselves for the purpose of enumeration under a census act in the framing of which their sex has had no voice. They base their objection upon the principle that government should rest upon the consent of the governed, and as I myself uphold this democratic principle I do not feel justified in filling up any particulars concerning them against their will.

The census enumerator who collected the form wrote: 'I interviewed Mr Penn-Gaskell in order to obtain the necessary information, but was politely, but firmly, refused.'

Emily Wilding Davison also avoided the 1911 census, and made a statement in the process, by hiding in a broom cupboard for the night at the Houses of Parliament.

Eleanor Gaskell was also Honorary Secretary and Treasurer of the North-west London branch of the Women's Social and Political Union, which had a shop and office on Kilburn High Road from 1910 until 1917. The WSPU, led by Emmeline Pankhurst and her daughters, was the more militant wing of the campaign for votes for women; they were known as the Suffragettes, as opposed to the larger National Union of Women's Suffrage Societies (NUWSS), led by Millicent Fawcett, who advocated non-violent tactics and were known as Suffragists.

1   www.thescarboroughnews.co.uk/news/scarborough-man-tells-mothers-suffragette-story-710666
2   (http://kilburnandwillesdenhistory.blogspot.co.uk/2014/11/the-suffragettes-in-kilburn.html).

MPs

When Queen's Park first opened in 1887, the area was part of the old Harrow constituency, represented by a succession of Conservative and Liberal MPs including the wonderfully named Tory Harry Deeley Mallaby-Deeley (1910–18). None of them seem to have taken a great interest in the emerging district: the MPs for Paddington, Marylebone and Chelsea are the ones who keep cropping up in newspaper reports of the time.

In 1918, following major boundary changes, Willesden was split into two parliamentary constituencies. Willesden West included Kensal Green, Harlesden, Stonebridge and Willesden Green. It was Conservative from 1918 to 1923, represented for most of that time by Charles Pinkham, then held by Labour in every election until it was abolished in the 1970s. The one exception was the period 1931 to 1935, when it was held by the idiosyncratic Conservative campaigner for women's rights, Mavis Tate.

The new seat of Willesden East included Brondesbury Park (and therefore all of Queen's Park west of Kingswood), Mid-Kilburn (including all the rest of Queen's Park), Mapesbury, Cricklewood and Neasden. It was Conservative until 1945 apart from two years in the 1920s when it briefly went Liberal.

Charles Pinkham

Charles Pinkham was born near Plymouth in 1853, the son of an agricultural labourer. He left school at 14 to work in the building trade, and by 1891 he was married with three children (Archie, Annie and Charles junior), living in Hazel Road in Kensal Rise (opposite Kensal Green station) and working as a builder. He went into business with another builder from Devon – Charles Langler of College Road – and the two of them were responsible for building large parts of Kensal Rise including houses on Wrottesley Road and Clifford Gardens, and shops and houses on Chamberlayne Road.

By 1901 Pinkham was living in Purves Road, and in 1911 at 7 Winchester Avenue. He was a Willesden councillor from 1888 to 1919 and a Middlesex County Councillor from 1898 until the 1920s. He was also a magistrate, known for his dry sense of humour. Two homeless men were brought before his bench accused of begging in Walm Lane in May 1913; they had asked an off-duty police officer 'for a copper'. Pinkham quipped, 'They got what they asked for.'

When the First World War broke out he became a tireless advocate of enlistment, encouraging young men to volunteer and dealing harshly with many of those who tried to claim exemption on moral or practical grounds as chairman of the Willesden Tribunal (Chapter 21). He helped raise two battalions of the Middlesex Regiment and was made an honorary colonel in recognition of his work. He also raised money for military hospitals in Brondesbury.

When the war ended, Pinkham was elected to Parliament as the Conservative and Unionist MP for Willesden West, much to the delight of the *Kilburn Times*. He served just one term, retiring in 1922 for unspecified personal reasons.

Both his sons served in the First World War. Charles Junior went to Cambridge, where he represented his university at rugby and played cricket at a respectable level.

SECTION 4

THE FIRST
WORLD WAR

The First World War had a profound effect on the relatively new community of Queen's Park. It provoked tensions between different ethnic communities, it created great hardship, and it took the lives of hundreds of local men and irrevocably changed the lives of hundreds more Queen's Park people. [1]

Many local women were widowed and never remarried. There was another, more positive impact for women: the war accelerated their employment in occupations traditionally reserved only for men, and even though many were forced to give up their jobs when men returned from military service, the shortage of labour caused by the loss of 886,000 British soldiers meant that the gains made could not be fully rolled back.

Some of the attitudes of people at this time are shocking to us today: jingoism, xenophobia, casual racism and sexism, and a disregard for the values of people with different views, such as pacifists. It's particularly uncomfortable to read some of the comments made by clergymen in their pulpits. But these are the authentic voices of the time, and there are stories of courage and selflessness, and even humour, to be enjoyed along with the material that is jarring to a modern sensibility.

---

1 One local resident interviewed for this book remembered disabled veterans selling matches and shoestrings on Kilburn High Road in the 1930s.

18

BUILD-UP TO WAR

Few residents of Queen's Park in 1900 would have predicted that Britain would be at war with Germany in just a few years. France and Russia, not Germany, had been Britain's main competitors in the race to build empires for most of the nineteenth century. The British royal family were German, and every monarch from George I to Victoria herself married fellow Germans. For the first three years of her life Queen Victoria spoke only German. Many German traditions were brought to Britain in Victorian times. Having said that, there's an important German tradition that pre-dates the Victorian era: the Christmas tree. There's a widely held belief that Prince Albert, Queen Victoria's husband, introduced the tradition to England in 1840. However, the credit belongs to Queen Charlotte, the German wife of 'the mad king' George III, who set up the first known Christmas tree at Queen's Lodge, Windsor, in December 1800, after which they became popular with the aristocracy – thirty-six years before Victoria acceded to the throne.

Germany at the start of the twentieth century was seen as an economic competitor – 'Made in Germany' was the late Victorian equivalent of 'Made in Hong Kong' in the 1970s, a shorthand for 'low quality imitation'. But Germany was a latecomer to the 'Race for Empire' and therefore not a great political rival. Germans made up the larg-est minority population in Britain until the big wave of Russian Jewish immigration in the 1880s, often working as bakers, hairdressers and in hotels and restaurants. Both the German and Russian Jewish communities were well represented in Queen's Park in the 1900s. Solomon Barnett (who as we learned in Chapter 8 built most of Queen's Park) was a Jewish immigrant from Russia, and we can see from the 1901 census that there were nearly fifty Germans and Austrians living in the area at that point.

Attitudes to people of German origin living in Britain began to change in the early 1900s, partly because of the naval arms race between Britain and Germany. As Britain and France moved closer together, encouraged by the Francophile King Edward VII, the split with Germany deepened.[1]

Unlike the other major powers of Europe – France, Germany, Russia and the Austro-Hungarian Empire – Britain did not have a large army of conscripts doing 'national service' and a big reserve of older men with military training to call on. The British Army was a small, professional force, able to firefight around the globe but unsuited for major continental wars. This was underscored by the Boer War of 1899–1902, which gave the British establishment a major fright when a third of volunteers for the army proved unfit due to poor health, diet and living conditions.[2]

In response, the British government passed the Haldane Act in 1908, creating the Territorial Force – a forerunner of the Territorial Army designed to provide a reserve of soldiers able to be called up in the event of a major European land war. Initially intended for home defence only, its remit was soon changed to allow for overseas postings on a voluntary basis. It was immensely popular with the kind of young clerks that Queen's Park was full of in the 1900s and 1910s.

In his book *Londoners on the Western Front*, David Martin writes that, 'Those in the Territorials before the war were often in a job or profession but found a way of supplementing that income by spending their weekends at drill amongst friends. The highlight of the year was the annual camp in somewhere as idyllic as Devon or Sussex.'

The average young male civil servant in 1910 only received fourteen days' paid leave a year. If they were lucky (and not all departments of the Civil Service were as supportive of the Territorial Force) they could get another fifteen days' paid leave with their mates to go camping and practise soldiering, at a time when anything more than a day trip to the seaside was still an exotic luxury for most working people.

Many of the young men of Queen's Park who joined the Territorial Force found their way into the reserve battalions of the newly formed London Regiment. (Regiments were the basic organising unit of the British Army; they could be divided into as many battalions as they wanted or could fill up. In 1914 battalions were expected to be around 1,000 strong.) The 9th Battalion of the London Regiment (Queen Victoria's Rifles) had its headquarters in Davies Street, near Berkeley Square. The 13th Battalion (the Kensingtons) were based in Iverna Gardens, just off Kensington High Street. The 16th Battalion (Queen's Westminster Rifles) had headquarters at Buckingham Gate. The 19th Battalion (St Pancras) were located in Camden High Street. Another option for local

---

1   As Prince of Wales, Edward had been the royal sponsor of the 1879 Royal Agricultural Show in Queen's Park. His Germanophile mother, Victoria, blamed him for the early death of her (German) husband Albert and froze him out of important matters of state until he was well into his 50s. It's ironic that the iconic sketch of him arriving at the showground shows him riding on equipment that would later transport the allied armies on the Western Front.

2   The Germans, in contrast, had a welfare system from the 1880s onwards.

men on this side of the Middlesex/London border was to join the Middlesex Regiment instead of the London Regiment. The 9th Battalion of the Middlesex Regiment had their HQ in Pound Lane in Willesden. However, few local men seemed to have ended up in this unit, which spent the war in India and Iraq.

By 1910 around a quarter of a million British men had joined the Territorials, and a similar number belonged to the regular armed forces. It's hard to gauge how many professional soldiers lived in Queen's Park before the First World War, as any soldiers or sailors at their barracks or otherwise on duty on census night would have been recorded there rather than at their home address. In 1901, we know that two full-time sergeants were living in Harvist Road. Albert Grundy, who lived at 149, and Ebenezer Sanders, at 225, were both instructors in the 3rd Battalion of the London Regiment, one of the volunteer units that existed before the Territorial Force was founded. The battalion was based on the Harrow Road and nicknamed the Railway Rifles.

Meanwhile, the phenomenon known as 'spy fever' was gripping the country, reaching a peak in the first months of the war itself. Between the outbreak of war in August 1914 and November 1914, the Metropolitan Police received over 120,000 reports of espionage activity in London alone – a rate of over 1,000 a day, reported by suspicious members of the public. Most of them were completely false.

One of the drivers of 'spy fever' was the Edwardian spy novel, which became an immensely popular genre. This interest actually began in Victorian times, in 1894, when William Le Queux, an Anglo–French journalist and writer, published *The Great War in England in 1897,* in which French and Russian forces invade Britain thanks to the work of spies. Germany is not the villain in this story – the gallant Germans actually come to the aid of Britain in this book. The French were again the villains in the 1901 novel *Pro Patria* by Max Pemberton, in which they try to build a tunnel under the Channel to invade England.

In 1903 Erskine Childers published the first spy novel featuring German villains, and it was immensely successful. *The Riddle of the Sands* tells the story of two Englishmen on holiday in the Baltic who uncover secret German plans to invade Britain.

Some commentators have argued that the popularity of spy novels, in which the British often have to fight against great odds and a much better-organised enemy, reflects the shift from 'Victorian optimism to Edwardian pessimism' following the problems the British had winning the Boer War and the general anxiety over the arms race with Germany.

One of the most influential of all the great Edwardian spy novels was written by the man who started it all, William Le Queux. *The Invasion of 1910*, which first appeared in 1906, was commissioned by Alfred Harmsworth, owner of the *Daily Mail*, and published as a serial in that newspaper. It was a great success: when it came out as a book it sold more than a million copies. Le Queux described how the German invasion 'was preceded by a secret army of spies disguised as waiters, clerks, barbers, bakers and servants'. Apparently Harmsworth had paper sellers dressed as German soldiers when the story appeared in the *Daily Mail*, and he insisted that the story be rewritten so the invading German army passes through towns inhabited by large numbers of his paper's readers. The Germans rather improbably march from Chelmsford to Sheffield as a result.

Early in 1909 Le Queux returned to his theme with *Spies for the Kaiser: Plotting the Downfall of England*, which again featured German agents disguised as waiters, barbers and tourists. They were under orders to check out possible landing beaches and prepare to sabotage anything from telephone and railway lines to bridges and water supplies. As soon as the book came out, Le Queux began receiving letters from readers who reported apparently suspicious behaviour by German waiters, barbers and tourists around railway lines, bridges and telegraph stations, exactly as he described in his book. Le Queux passed these on to the head of military counter-intelligence, Lieutenant Colonel James Edmonds, who took them seriously although most of them were nonsense. Le Queux and Edmonds seem to have fed each other's belief in the scale of the German threat. When Edmonds was summoned to give evidence before a sub-committee of the Committee of Imperial Defence later in 1909, he repeated Le Queux's fantasies. The committee made four recommendations, one of which was to establish a standing secret service, which became MI5 and MI6.

Politicians like Lord Charles Beresford (an MP and navy admiral) used parliamentary privilege to claim knowledge of great spy rings across Britain, without offering any evidence, and the media also published inflammatory articles. One paper, *The Globe*, even published a letter from someone who claimed to be a German spy, who said he and his fellow Germans were just waiting for the order to start their sabotaging missions and described the authorities as 'so awfully stupid'.

Queen's Park was far from immune to this hysteria. Spy mania was accompanied by feverish speculation about a possible German invasion, which peaked in 1909. The *Kilburn Times* carried dozens of articles on the subject in 1909–10, including a report of a sermon given by a local vicar who argued that 'with the advance of science, invasion was quite possible', and urged his congregation to 'fight strenuously against some of those grosser evils which had long since invaded England's shores, and which ... threatened to destroy the very life-blood of the nation'. The report doesn't go into detail about what exactly these 'grosser evils' were.[1]

In 1912, two years before war broke out, the *Kilburn Times* lamented that the British government was unique among major Western powers in not taking German espionage seriously.[2]

---

1   *Kilburn Times*, 23 April 1909.
2   *Kilburn Times*, 9 February 1912.

Not all the media commentary was quite so po-faced. In 1908 the *Sketch* declared that, 'The German invasion scare is nothing compared to the scare which is being created in masculine circles by the present epidemic of hideous feminine hats.' The Edwardians also explored their invasion fears through entertainment. A variety show at the Willesden Hippodrome included a sketch dealing with a threatened invasion of England – 'The Beacon Ball', by Fred Ginnett's Company[3] – which was 'capitally acted throughout'.[4]

As well as emerging anti-German sentiment, anti-immigrant feeling had also been building in the years before the war, particularly towards poor immigrants fleeing persecution in Russia. Concern about the influx of 'pauper' immigrants into Britain led to the passing of the Aliens Act of 1905, which for the first time introduced immigration controls and registration in an effort to limit the entry of Jewish refugees from Eastern Europe. The sentiment of the Act is reflected in Walter Wood's 1906 novel *The Enemy in Our Midst*, in which one character says 'here you are, a bonny English lass, starving – an' for what? Because we've given a welcome to every bit of foreign scum that's too filthy to be kept in its own country!' E Phillips Oppenheim expressed similar sentiments in his book *The Great Secret* (1908), in which he wrote that 290,000 enemy aliens were living in London because it had become the 'asylum for all the foreign scum of the earth'. The spy fever of 1914–15 drew on some very deep-rooted public antagonism to immigration.

The one thing that spy fever was only loosely connected to was reality: a maximum of 120 German spies were at work in Britain during the First World War, eleven of whom were executed at the Tower of London. Very few sent back intelligence of any use.

Despite this, spy fever was a major driver behind the passing of the Aliens Registration Act of 1914, which led to the internment of 30,000 German and Austrian civilians living in Britain, as well as to anti-German rioting and acts of vandalism against German-run shops.

Community relations in Queen's Park seem to have weathered this turbulence quite well. There are no recorded incidents of vandalism of German or Jewish shops in the immediate area of Queen's Park either in the run-up to the war or after it started.

---

3   Ginnett was a film and stage actor, who starred in a short film called *Dick Turpin's Last Ride to York* (1908).

4   *Kilburn Times*, 21 February 1908.

19

THE HOME FRONT IN THE FIRST WORLD WAR

1914

War was declared on the bank holiday weekend at the beginning of August 1914. In its edition of 8 August, the *Kilburn Times* published the following report:

> Never since the institution of Bank Holiday have we witnessed one so remarkable as Monday last. The holiday crowds, the gaiety and life, were conspicuous by their absence. In our streets were to be seen only anxious people eagerly waiting for the various editions of the newspapers as they came to hand. Sunday last had been a day of tension and excitement, with the London papers shouted by Fleet Street vendors in our quietest thoroughfares.
>
> On Monday it was quite a rare event to see holiday-makers – the most that people appeared to be doing was going up to town to get the latest information. During that morning it was clear that Government officials were in charge of the large omnibus garages at Willesden and Cricklewood. A large number of buses were partially dismantled and taken away, apparently for transport purposes. Naval reservists, responding to the mobilisation order, were seen hurrying to the stations, many being loudly cheered as they went off.
>
> There was a good deal of excitement on Tuesday evening when notices were posted outside the post offices and public buildings calling up Army Reservists and Territorials. Crowds assembled in the streets and read the notices, which was the first intimation of general mobilisation.

The headquarters of the 14th Battalion Middlesex Territorial Regiment at Pound Lane, Willesden, presented an animated scene on Wednesday, and all day long the men were coming in to report themselves. Shortly before 8 o'clock they left the Drill Hall in full strength, and headed by the drum and fife band, marched down Harlesden Road to Willesden Junction station where special trains were in readiness to convey them to Sheerness. All along the route there were wild scenes of enthusiasm and an immense crowd awaited their arrival in the High Street, Harlesden. They were continually cheered, hats and handkerchiefs were waved in the air and good wishes were shouted from hundreds of windows as they passed by.

On 11 September, the *Kilburn Times* reported on the first general meeting of the newly formed Lonsdale Rifle Club, which already had fifty members. The club was based at Mr HK Wilkinson's garage at 10–12 Lonsdale Road, and it had already run a session for the local Scout group (based opposite). 'Already several members of this vigorous, though young, club show promise of becoming excellent shots, and thus forming a fine body of sharpshooters for defence if needed,' the paper advised. Mr Wilkinson was elected captain and promised prizes for the best shots, as did Solomon Barnett and a Mr Fay. The only cost was a small subscription of 2s 6d per year, with ammunition costing one farthing per shot. First-class and well-kept rifles were provided. A munitions factory opened on Salusbury Road, in the building next to Salusbury School where the Fitness First gym is today.

However, there was also a dark side to the war fervour.

On 21 August the *Kilburn Times* reported on a 'Startling Incident At Old Oak Common'. In the early hours of Monday morning two cleaners on their way to work were nearly killed by a nervous sentry guarding the railway line who fired three shots, just missing one and clipping the other on the ear.

On 25 September the paper reported that a painter called William Turner, aged 48 and from Paddington, had been called up in front of a magistrate for inciting a crowd to wreck a German baker's shop in Shirland Road on a Saturday night. Turner, who had been drinking, had just bought two loaves at the shop.

In the same issue there was a report of a raid on a dance at the Cricklewood Skating Rink during which five young Germans were arrested for travelling more than 5 miles from their homes without the necessary permits. The magistrate accepted that they did not intentionally break the laws and said 'the Bench did not want to exhibit any vindictive feelings against the defendants, because they assumed they had done nothing against the laws of this country except the offence which they had admitted'. They were each fined 5s.

On 23 October the *Kilburn Times* published a letter, signed 'A True Patriot', from someone urging locals in Brondesbury, Kilburn and Cricklewood to boycott bakeries run by Germans and Austrians:

These shops, for all we know, are probably more or less a hot-bed of spies ...
Moreover, much to my disgust, people are still to be seen buying from these day
by day; the persons offending are the female sex. I therefore make an earnest appeal
through the columns of your local paper to them to stop buying from these foreign
bakers and support their own kinsmen. While continuing to put money in the hands
of Germans and Austrians, we are acting falsely against our own country, and this, I
feel sure, will not be done by true and conscientious people. No matter if they have
been naturalised or been in residence many years, the fact of them being Germans
and Austrians, and the shameful and horrible way they have acted during this war, is
enough for us to look after ourselves and our own trade.

There are plenty of bakers of our own nationality who turn out bread and pastry
etc equally as good and probably better. I trust you will publish this letter in your
good paper to enlighten the minds of the public, who (perhaps thoughtlessly) are in
a way helping our foes.

On 30 October, the paper reported on another frightening incident involving a man
who was the worse for drink: a John Woods of Craven Park mistook a fellow railway
passenger for a German spy and restrained him from leaving the train by grabbing him
by the throat every time he tried to get up. The 'spy' was in fact a tailor from Devon.
Woods's solicitor accepted that his client had made a mistake but said 'at the same
time, he [does have] an accent ...'

1915

Judging by the *Kilburn Times*, the war had still not altered life in Queen's Park too
profoundly by the start of 1915. The first issues of the new year carried giant advertisements for the latest fashions in women's underwear, while Charles Baker & Co.
of the Edgware Road advertised school uniforms, illustrated with a drawing of a top-
hatted Eton schoolboy.

Local people were clearly determined to help the war effort any way they could.
On 8 January the Kilburn branch of the Soldiers' and Sailors' Families Association
announced that there would be 'a tea and concert' at Salusbury Road School for the
wives and mothers of servicemen.

A week later HJ Gandy, local secretary of the Stationers' Association, wrote to
the local paper to urge people to support a petition to Willesden Council, calling for
shops to close at 8 p.m. instead of the standard time of 9 p.m. This had been opposed
by the Kilburn Chamber of Trade on the grounds that shoppers would simply take

their trade elsewhere. *Nonsense!* thundered Mr Gandy. Would they go to the West End, where shops already close at 6.30?

In January the *Kilburn Times* also reported on the opening of clubs for soldiers' wives, 'who need cheering up in this depressing war time. They cannot be always singing as a tonic "It's a long, long way to Tipperary", and sometimes the real loneliness is very overpowering,' the paper reflected. One of these clubs was about to be opened at 3 Harvist Road by the Willesden Women's Local Government Association, in rooms lent by the Electric Railway Company. Donations of chairs, tables, floor coverings, curtains, teacups and saucers would be gladly accepted.

At the end of January, Willesden Council organised an army volunteer recruitment meeting at Harvist Road School. The government were looking for 92,000 volunteers a month at this time, but most months they fell far short. January 1915 was one of the few months when voluntary recruitment exceeded 100,000. Politically, however, conscription was not yet palatable. In fact, the chairman of the meeting at Harvist Road, in his opening remarks, said, 'The very word compulsion [is] abhorrent to every real Englishman,' although he went on to remind his audience that 'as a nation they were fighting for their very existence'. Alderman Pinkham reported that Willesden had so far supplied 5,000 recruits for the armed forces. He wanted to know whether the men present 'were going to answer the appeal from some of the Kensal Rise boys who were today in the trenches, and who were asking whether they were not going to help them'.

In March, it was announced that Father Vaughan's 'very commodious' house on the corner of Christchurch Avenue and Brondesbury Park (Solomon Barnett's former home, Restmorel) was being turned into a military hospital. 'Mission House', as it became known when it was acquired by the Catholic Church, was a large building with a conservatory at the back and 2 acres of grounds including a tennis court and a croquet lawn. Brondesbury Park Military Hospital eventually housed sixty beds and functioned as an auxiliary unit of the First London General Hospital in Camberwell.

Another military hospital opened the same month at 16 The Avenue. 'Beech House' was funded and run by the West Hampstead Division of the Red Cross. As the war progressed, the hospital expanded into No. 18 next door, eventually hosting eighty-one beds. Patients at Brondesbury Park and Beech House played cricket against each other.

The Bakerloo Line Arrives in Queen Park: 1915

The London and North Western Railway (LNWR) station at Queen's Park connected the new district with Euston, Kilburn High Road and Primrose Hill, as well as points north, but the company wasn't that interested in local traffic. In 1879, when the station opened, there was only an hourly service that stopped at stations between Euston and Watford – most trains were express services to Birmingham that passed by without stopping.

In 1906, in the face of increasing competition from other railway companies for commuter traffic, the LNWR announced plans to build a new electrified line between Watford and Euston, with sixteen stations on the route. In 1909, as part of this new strategy, the company suggested to the owners of the Bakerloo Line – already operating as a tube line between Waterloo and Paddington – that they extend the line from Paddington to Queen's Park and then run the service overground from there to Watford. The owners of the Bakerloo Line agreed, and in 1912 Parliament gave approval to the proposal. Construction was complete by 1915, despite the war. The new Bakerloo Line station at Queen's Park opened on 11 February 1915. (Maida Vale station, which opened on 6 June, was the first station in London to have an all-female staff.) There were twenty-four trains an hour in peak period and seventeen an hour at other times. Kensal Green station started operating Bakerloo Line services the following year.

Queen's Park station was rebuilt to accommodate the new service, including the present arrangement of two 'island' platforms, with the underground lines in the middle and the overground lines on the outside.

On weekdays and Saturdays the first train left at 5.16 a.m. and the last train at 12.43 a.m.. (Today it's 05.38 and 12.15.) On Sundays they started at 7.26 in the morning and ended at 11.43 at night.

May also saw a serious outbreak of anti-German rioting in Harlesden, Willesden Green and Kilburn following the sinking of the liner *Lusitania* by a German submarine. The shopfronts of many German-run shops were smashed by mobs including serving soldiers, and the police struggled to contain the violence. The first shop attacked belonged to a German-born man who was married to an Englishwoman and was a patriotic supporter of the British side in the war. In Kilburn three bakers and a hairdressers on the High Road and Willesden Lane were attacked. Many other foreign nationals were threatened in the mistaken belief that they were Germans, including a Russian furniture dealer called Mr Astrinsky, who had to display a copy of his passport in order to ward off hooligans intent on vandalising his business.

As 1915 progressed, the war seems to have weighed more heavily on local people. By September, Green & Edwards (the underwear retailers) were still advertising the latest fashions in corsetry, although the slightly salacious drawings of scantily clad women had now been replaced by a far more sober illustration of a fully clothed woman wearing the 'New Military Curve'. October 1915 saw the funeral of two men from Cricklewood who were killed in the latest Zeppelin raid, and November brought another great recruitment meeting, this time at the Kilburn Empire theatre. The guest speaker was Horatio Bottomley, the Liberal MP, who was a tireless advocate for army recruitment.

1916

The second full year of war opened on a much more sombre note than its predecessor. The full-page ads for corsets had disappeared, replaced by advertisements for hats and coats. Even Charles Baker & Co. had dropped the top-hatted Etonian in favour of a universal image of a schoolboy in an overcoat.

The pages weren't entirely free of comedy (although not necessarily intentional). In February, Mr SRF Freed wrote to the local paper to bemoan the failure of his campaign to persuade Willesden Council to rename Hanover Road, 'Willesden's only German Street Name'. As it is still there now, it seems Mr Freed was to remain disappointed. (Residents of Hanover Road tried twice to get the name changed, the first time to 'Louvain Road' in honour of the Belgian town where the invading Germans burnt a world-famous library and all its books.)

In January, the Military Service Act introduced compulsory conscription. In April, the *Kilburn Times* reported on the prosecution of three men who had failed to report for service, including Albert Bates, a 24-year-old chimney sweep of 13 Salusbury Road.

As the war progressed, women increasingly moved into traditionally male-dominated occupations to free up men to go to the front. There were women drivers, women police, and many women worked in munitions factories.

In April 1916, the *Kilburn Times* reported on the trial of a man accused of assaulting a 'lady tram conductor' in Cricklewood. The conductor – Dorothy Adams – was sworn at by the passenger, who objected to being told to move upstairs on the tram because there was no space downstairs. Adams told the man, 'You think yourself lucky you have not got a smack in the face.' The defendant replied, 'Go on, smack my face you xxxxx.' Adams did so, and was promptly punched back. The court held that it was perfectly reasonable for Adams to have struck the first blow since 'he had used insulting language, and the woman in her natural indignation attacked him'. He was fined £3 15s 6d and told that if the magistrates could have sent him to prison, they would have.

In June 1916 the paper reported the formation of a Middlesex Women's War Agricultural Committee, whose duty was to compile a list of every woman willing to work full or part-time for local farmers or other employers. Later that month the Suffragette leader Elinor Gaskell wrote to the *Kilburn Times* to urge local women to volunteer as fruit pickers on a farm in Wisbech, Cambridgeshire.

July passed with no mention of the Battle of the Somme, despite the first day of the battle being the costliest of the entire war in terms of British casualties. By mid-August, though, giant ads were appearing in local papers for a documentary film, *Somme Battle Pictures*, which contained apparently real footage of the battle. The advertisements promised that, 'This graphic and stirring official war film brings the heroism, the tragedy and the glory of the battlefield vividly before your eyes.' It put great emphasis on the numbers of German prisoners captured and the devastating impact of British shelling on German lines. There was no sense that the battle had not been a complete success.

In September, the *Kilburn Times* reported that the Rev. A Lindsay Skerry, assistant priest at St Anne's, had been recalled to active service. 'Mrs Skerry and myself greatly appreciate the many kindnesses shown us by many members of the congregation, and our stay here will always remain a bright and sunny spot in our memories,' Rev. Skerry wrote.

Later that month, the paper reported that Mrs Hewitt, of 49 Percy Road, Kilburn, had seven sons serving in the army.

The mood did not get any lighter as the year progressed. The Military Appeals Tribunal was now in full swing hearing men's cases for not getting sent to the front, and every issue of the paper contained at least a couple of reports from Alderman Pinkham's sessions (see Chapter 17).

There was a report in the autumn of the unfortunate death of a soldier's wife who lived on the Harrow Road. Annie Walter, aged 50, was killed when a live shell her husband brought home from France exploded. The coroner noted that it was 'quite ordinary' for servicemen to bring home souvenirs like this, and there had been a number of accidents as a result. The government was now clamping down on the practice.

Another war-related fatality was reported in November. Hilda Stranks, aged 33, of Malvern Road, died of heart failure as a result of her intense fear of Zeppelin raids. On the day in question there were no raids, but she became convinced she could hear banging, which signified that a raid was coming. Her brother-in-law found her lying comatose on her bed, and she died shortly afterwards.

All in all, 1916 was a grim year on the home front.

1917

The following year seems to have had a more optimistic feel than its predecessor, possibly a reflection of the fact that people had adjusted to living in a country at war. Advertisements for corsets reappeared in the *Kilburn Times* (although smaller than in 1915),[1] and Charles Baker was once more appealing to the parents of Etonians and Harrovians; ostentation was back in fashion.

At the same time, the German blockade of British trade was also having an effect – for the first time in the war, 1917 saw stories about adulterated milk (watered down with some of the fat removed) and short weight bread.

At the start of the year St Anne's reported that the Rev. HF Newton had replaced the Rev. Skerry as assistant priest, and a concert was held at the church that raised over £10 for the Brondesbury Park Military Hospital.

By January, women 'dustmen' were at work in Willesden, equipped with 'semi military costume'. Their appearance 'created quite a sensation', according to a newspaper report.

In April, a correspondent calling themselves 'Toleration' wrote a letter to the *Kilburn Times* headlined 'Beer Versus Tea'. The 1914 Defence of the Realm Act had limited pub opening hours to two hours at lunchtime and three in the evening (closing time was at 9.30). Temperance campaigners wanted to go further and ban alcohol altogether to aid the war effort, but 'Toleration' mounted a spirited (no pun intended) defence of 'the liberty to choose between one beverage and another'.

May 1917 saw the opening of the new wing of Brondesbury Park Military Hospital, with room for a further fifty patients. So far 1,150 men had been successfully treated at the hospital, the *Kilburn Times* reported.

In June an extraordinary flood hit west London: a huge amount of rain fell in a short amount of time, and the drains simply couldn't cope. This caused acute distress to many poorer people who saw their homes flooded, particularly in south Kilburn, where basements were flooded to a depth or 3 or 4ft and milk churns and other large items were seen floating down the streets. In addition, many major roads were paved with wooden blocks at the time, which rose up in arcs when water got underneath them. The Edgware Road, Bayswater Road, Shirland Road, Harrow Road and Great Western Road all suffered in this way.[2]

The Germans were gradually phasing out Zeppelin aircraft in 1917, due to the high losses they suffered. Taking their place were the huge Gotha bombers, aircraft capable of long-distance flights, manufactured by the Gotha Coach Factory owned

---

1   The advertisements, not the corsets.
2   www.ianvisits.co.uk/blog/2015/01/10/the-time-when-londons-streets-were-paved-with-wood

– ironically – by Charles Edward, Duke of Saxe-Coburg and Gotha, who was born in Esher and was the grandson of Queen Victoria, after whom Queen's Park is named.

On the morning of 13 June 1917 Gotha bombers set off from Germany to attack London. Fourteen reached London, while three dropped their bombs on Margate and Shoeburyness. The bombs they dropped were highly explosive and filled with shrapnel to cause maximum damage and injury. At about 11.25 a.m., bombs began to drop in the East End and the City, resulting in the highest casualties of any air raid on Britain in the war. Seventy-two bombs were dropped, killing 104 people and injuring another 423. The dead included eighteen children at a school in Poplar in London's East End, which suffered a direct hit.

The closest the Gotha bombers came to Queen's Park on that occasion was Hendon, but the local paper reported that there was great excitement over the raid and large amounts of shrapnel from British anti-aircraft guns fell in streets in the area.

In August 1917, an editorial in the *Kilburn Times* expressed the author's frustration with critics of the way the war was being managed:

When anyone asks me when this horrible war is going to end, I feel inclined to retort: 'When you put every ounce of energy into doing the duty that lies nearest to you to that end.' The question is often uttered by men and women who are not doing a single thing towards winning the war – some are even performing that most cowardly and criminal of actions, backbiting the Government and the Army and Navy and Air Service, and criticising the leaders and fighters and workers whose shoe latchets they are unworthy to unloose. Yet they would be woefully aggrieved if one told them that the guilt of the bloodshed of many of our gallant men is as truly on their heads as it is on the bestial Huns, from whose frightful domination of the free peoples of the earth the latter are struggling in this awful welter.

In the same edition it was reported that the Harrow Road, Willesden and Kilburn Association of Master Bakers had solemnly pledged never again to allow a German or Austrian, naturalised or not, to join their ranks. They also announced they would never again employ a German or Austrian member of staff.

August's papers reflected the increasing pressure on food supplies that was being experienced by people on the home front, with articles advising people on how to cook tough meat and how to find substitutes for potatoes.

In September, the Electric Theatre on Salusbury Road reopened under new management as the Paladeum Cinema. On Mondays, Tuesdays and Wednesdays they were showing *The Losing Game* (a drama in four parts), *Charlie At Work* (a comedy in three parts) and *Giddy, Gay and Ticklish*. On Thursday, Friday and Saturday their bill included *The Little Deceiver* and *Arcadian Maid*. They also offered a children's matinee on Saturdays at 2 p.m..

At the end of September, there was a memorial service at St Anne's for members of the congregation who had died in the war. By this stage over 200 men of the parish were at the front, and nineteen were known to have died. A Roll of Honour commemorating all nineteen was unveiled in the church. The choir sang Nare's anthem 'The Souls of the Righteous' and the hymns included 'Ten Thousand Times Ten Thousand' and 'On The Resurrection Morning'. The vicar paid tribute to the memory of the fallen and expressed the hope that in future, kings and their ministers would express only the will of their people, in which case there was little doubt that there would be an end to war.

On 19 October 1917, a German Zeppelin – the L45 – was sent to attack Sheffield but instead ended up over Northampton before flying south over London. It travelled down the A5, dropping a bomb near Cricklewood Station. It also dropped a number of bombs in the West End, where buildings in Piccadilly, Regent Street, Jermyn Street and Shaftesbury Avenue were damaged. This was known as 'the silent raid', because weather conditions and the altitude that the Zeppelin was flying at meant its engines could not be heard. It must have been terrifying to see a Zeppelin flying overhead. The L45, for example, was 650ft long. For comparison, the Gherkin building in the City of London is 590ft from top to bottom.

As a result of these attacks, it was announced that a number of public buildings had been designated as air raid shelters, including the police station on Salusbury Road and Kilburn Park underground station. Later the same month (October) a young man from West Hampstead was fined 20s for shouting 'all clear' in Warwick Avenue underground station in the middle of an air raid 'as a joke', while some 2,500 people were sheltering there.

December saw the annual meeting of the 13th Hampstead Boy Scouts at St Anne's Church. The troop was now 8 years old. It had been founded by Frank Hallett, who had died at the front in 1915 after only a few days in the trenches. All of the six original boy scouts who had been there at the start of the troop were now in the army, and one of those had been killed. By December 1917, fifteen past and present members of the troop were on active service.

1918

On New Year's Eve, as 1918 was ushered in, the vicar of St John's, Kilburn, gave a sermon warning against the 'insidious attempts which were being made by many disloyal people, known as pacifists, to bring about a premature peace'. He cautioned his congregation to, 'Set your face resolutely against the worst enemy that this country has – not the German, but the pacifist, the peacemonger, who would barter your birthright, your liberty and your honour, as well as your country's welfare, for the sake of a cheap and worthless peace. Better that the country should fight to the last until nothing is left than have that peace which would give Germany the power of renewing this terrible conflict a few years hence.' After the stroke of midnight the Rev. Martin wished everyone a happy new year.

The Gotha bombing raids continued in 1918 and this part of London was hit on at least two occasions. On 28–29 January 1918, a Gotha dropped three bombs along Belsize Road, killing two people and injuring two more. Some 118 houses were damaged. The Princess of Wales pub on the corner of Belsize Road and Abbey Road (now the Lillie Langtry) was destroyed. Three more bombs from Gothas landed in Priory Terrace, Mortimer Road and Greville Road, damaging seven houses.

February brought more evidence that the German blockade was causing serious problems with food supplies. One page alone of the *Kilburn Times* contained articles entitled 'Grocers and the Price of Coffee', 'Food Prosecutions', 'Willesden Food Control Committee', 'New Cricklewood Allotments' and 'Brondesbury Allotments'.

On the night of 19–20 May 1918, a 300kg bomb destroyed the Carlton Tavern in Carlton Vale, which was replaced after the war with the much more cottagey pub that we see today (thankfully entirely rebuilt now after developers destroyed much of it a few years ago).

Panther Patrol of the 13th Hampstead Boy Scouts cheered people up with a 'very successful' concert at St Anne's in April. Mr Bert Edwards had the audience in stitches with his jokes and comical dancing, and Miss M Lewis gave a whistling solo. During the interval the scoutmaster presented a 'Swastika' badge to Miss Hilda Jakeman in recognition of her courage in continuing to sing at their previous concert in February even though an air raid warning was being sounded.

In May, Alderman Pinkham was selected as the Unionist candidate for the seat of Willesden West. Later in the year the *Kilburn Times* urged its readers to vote for him, warning that a vote for the Liberals would see Ulster betrayed to the Irish republicans and markets opened to cheap imports from Austria and Germany. Worse would come if people voted Labour:

Bolshevik tyranny is a natural outcome of the tyrannical socialist 'expropriation' theory – the idea that to steal nationally is right. The anarchist, pro-Hun, anti-loyalist, pro-rebel groups that form the extremist parties in the Socialist ranks can always sway the more moderate of their fellow Socialists by the violence and forcefulness of their character. No mere disciples of co-operation and brotherhood would have a chance against the Bolshevik loud-voiced minority.

The paper got its way: Alderman Pinkham (who preferred to be known by his honorary title of Colonel Pinkham) was elected MP for Willesden West in December 1918, serving one term before standing down 'for domestic reasons'.

In July, the tireless Colonel Pinkham, chairman of Willesden District Council as well as the Military Tribunal and at this stage still the prospective parliamentary candidate for Willesden West, made an appeal at the Kilburn Empire on behalf of the 'Smokes for Sailors and Soldiers in Hospital Fund'. Thus far, he reported, the fund had provided 126 million cigarettes to servicemen in hospital, 276,000lb of tobacco, 268,000 cigars and 27,600 pipes. The paper ended its report by commenting that this 'will forge yet another link in the chain of affection which links together the wounded in our hospitals and the man who has so unsparingly devoted himself to their comfort and welfare since the outbreak of the war'.

Glamour came to the area in September, when the popular actress Miss Renee Kelly was reported to be moving to St Gabriel's Road, Mapesbury, proving that the area was a magnet for thespians even then. Miss Kelly was the star of a popular West End play entitled *Daddy Long Legs*. She went on to star in the 1919 film about the Spanish Armada, *Westward Ho!*

In October, it was announced that the home for Belgian refugees at 7 Harvist Road had now been returned to its landlord.

In the same month it was reported that rifleman Frank Webster, of 8 Montrose Avenue, was now a prisoner of war in Germany. His father, Mr WJ Webster, was a former warden of St Anne's. Frank wrote to say he was being treated well.

Meanwhile, reports of Spanish influenza were increasing in frequency.

Finally, in its edition of 15 November 1918, the *Kilburn Times* was able to report that the Great War was at an end. At 11 a.m. on Armistice Day, 11 November 1918, people in the streets 'cheered as they have never cheered before'. Factory sirens were sounded, flares set off and guns fired into the air. Factory workers from the munitions works on Salusbury Road rushed out into the street and began a procession up and down the road, drumming tin cans and singing popular songs like 'Good-bye-ee'. The schools on Salusbury Road were closed for the day and the children joined the impromptu march. 'A little boy, accompanied by a schoolmate about his own age, was overheard to remark to his companion on leaving the Salusbury Road council school "Well, I shall soon have my daddy home".'[1]

---

1 *Kilburn Times*, 15 November 1918.

As the day went on shopkeepers and residents dressed their properties with flags and bunting until every street was a blaze of colour. Groups came together to sing the national anthem on street corners, and people were still celebrating long after night fell, despite the fact that it was raining.

The *Kilburn Times* took the opportunity to remind readers of its pro-government editorial stance:

> We threw off the nightmare that had so long afflicted us and forgot the pessimist and the pacifist, the mischievous home Bolshevik and the cowardly 'conscientious' objector to military or citizen service, the grumblers at judicious and necessary restrictions of diet and fuel, and the pin-pricking critics of the men so whole-heartedly engaged in carrying the war to the splendidly successful issue that has been achieved. We only remembered with joyful thanksgiving the inspiring leadership of King George and Lloyd George, of the chiefs of the army and the navy and the air service, and of Foch, the great strategist.
>
> Let us trust that [our war heroes] have for ever prevented a recurrence of such a war as the one whose ruthless imbecility has tortured the world these four years.

Belgian Refugees

The German invasion – and occupation – of most of Belgium resulted in huge numbers of refugees, 250,000 of whom settled in Britain between the start of the war and May 1915. Over 360 settled in Willesden, many of them in Queen's Park: 7 Harvist Road housed three Belgian families, for example, and Belgian children were enrolled at Brondesbury and Kilburn High School and Kilburn Grammar.

There was enthusiastic fundraising for the Belgians in Queen's Park. In February 1915, Harvist Road School was the venue for a concert in aid of the Belgian War Refugees Relief Fund, featuring humorous songs performed by Mr Alf Morris, Miss Isabel Peachey and Mr Stanley Molland. Highlights included the song 'Cuthbert, Clarence and Claude', the tale of three clerks and their travel-related adventures.

In 1916, a Belgian School opened at Brondesbury Congregational Church (now the Maqam Centre) on the corner of Wrentham Avenue and Tiverton Road. It had spaces for sixty pupils and held lessons in English, French and Flemish. The school – named after the Belgian monarch, King Albert – closed in March 1919, once the majority of the Belgian visitors had returned home.[1]

---

1 MC Barres-Baker, 'Our Belgian Guests: Refugees in Brent 1914–19', *Local History*, July–August 2007.

20

SOLDIERS AND SAILORS OF THE FIRST WORLD WAR

The death toll of British men – particularly young men – in the First World War was horrific.

Around 6 per cent of the adult male population were killed in action or died as a result of injuries or illnesses they contracted while in uniform. We can't be sure of the exact number of men from Queen's Park who died in the war, as many of the Commonwealth War Grave Commission records don't carry addresses, but I estimate it to have been around 230. I have identified the names, and in most cases the addresses, of 191 of them in the wider Queen's Park area – the current QPARA boundaries plus Kilburn Lane, Allington, Claremont, Albert and Denmark Roads.

Many more served and came home again, often deeply traumatised by their experiences. I estimate that around 1,840 men from Queen's Park fought in the First World War in total, of whom more than 1,600 survived. Less is known about these men because, ironically, most of their service records were destroyed in the Second World War.

We get the occasional glimpse of the men who survived military service from newspapers. On 18 September 1914 the *Kilburn Times* reported that thirty-six members of the congregation of St Anne's were already serving or preparing to serve in the military. Six of them were killed in the war, including Frank Nolde, Albert Nason, Sidney Gabriel, Thomas Meech, Charles Meech and Charles Winter. The others were John Gilbert (of Linden Avenue), William Crawley (older brother of Ernest, who died in the war), Arthur Tozer (a medical student, of Donaldson Road), Allan Chidley,

Cecil Nason (Albert's brother), Frank and Harold Easton (of Windermere Avenue), Frederick, Arthur Sweetman and Frank Sweetman, George Cox (Clifford Gardens), Joseph Matson (Radnor Road), Jack Rilis, Arthur Rushbrooke (Wrentham Avenue), Richard Cust, Wilfrid Jervois, Walter Hawes, Walter Alfred Hawes, Harry Hawes (Dudley Road), Arthur Spittle (Hopefield Avenue), Edward Garside, Ernest Tanton, Reginald Vale Hadd, Rubin Moss, Robert Priest (Winchester Avenue), Henry Bolt, George and Arthur Taylor (Charteris Road), Alfred Taylor (Glengall Road), and Maurice Odell Tribe, the vicar's son. That's a mortality rate of 16 per cent – far higher than for the war overall but probably par for the course for those who were serving from the outset.

There are also at least 122 servicemen from Queen's Park listed on the national 'Roll of Honour' that was produced after the war.

In January 1918 the *Kilburn Times* announced that Sergeant Sherley, a long-standing resident of 85 Keslake Road, had been awarded a Military Medal and Bar. In July 1917 he had taken charge of his unit after all his officers had been killed or wounded and then single-handedly captured a German pillbox that had been pinning down his men. Under his command his men had captured over 100 German soldiers. In September, Sherley had again taken charge of his unit when all his officers had been incapacitated, despite being knocked out temporarily by a shell.

On the whole, though, we know far more about those who were killed in the war than those who survived.

Here are some of their stories.

1914: The Battle of Mons and the Great Retreat

When war was declared in August 1914, the British Expeditionary Force (as the relatively small British Army on the Western Front was known) headed to the Franco–Belgian border to meet the German advance through Belgium. They found themselves massively outnumbered, and after a defeat at the Battle of Mons over the border in Belgium (later creatively spun as a miraculous escape thanks to the intervention of angels and phantom bowmen), were forced into a gruelling march back to the River Marne outside Paris. By this time the German supply lines were over-extended, and it was their turn to retreat, to the River Aisne. The front line, once it finally settled down, stayed pretty much unchanged for the rest of the war.

Sydney Gray and George Edgecombe were the first soldiers from Queen's Park to die in the war: they were killed a day apart, on 15 and 16 September 1914, attempting to break through the German lines at the Aisne. They were both professional soldiers serving in the army when the war broke out. Sydney was born in Marylebone in

1876. When the war started he was with his unit in Belfast. He was 38, married to Anna Maria, and their home was at 87 Hartland Road. He served in the 1st Battalion, Dorsetshire Regiment – his father and his wife were both from Dorset. Sydney and Anna Maria were married in 1913; their only son, Sidney George, was born on 14 July 1914, just two short months before Sydney was killed in action.

George Edgecombe's home was in Albert Road (No. 19). He was 28 when he was killed, serving in the 4th Battalion of the Royal Fusiliers. Before sailing for France he spent time on service in India. Both men are commemorated on the memorial at La Ferté-sous-Jouarre in north-eastern France, for those soldiers who died in the area in the first year of the war and have no known graves.

1915: Ypres

Once the front line had settled down, both sides began building trenches and fortifying them along the whole of the Western Front from the English Channel to the Swiss Border. The British and Belgian armies held most of the section between the Channel and the valley of the River Somme.

In most places, the front lines followed natural strongpoints, which is why they were so hard to shift. But the town of Ypres in Flanders was different: the Allies managed to hold it during the first weeks of the war despite being surrounded by the Germans on three sides, often occupying higher ground. As one of the last towns in Belgium still in Allied hands, Ypres had enormous symbolic significance and had to be held, no matter what the cost.

Richard Henry Biddlecombe was another one of the professional soldiers from Queen's Park who were already serving when war broke out. He was born in the Devon village of Silverton, a few miles outside of Exeter, in 1891, and he enlisted in the 2nd battalion of the Duke of Cornwall's Light Infantry, who embarked for France on 14 December 1914. On 12 January 1915 they arrived at the front line in Flanders, taking over trenches at Dickebusch until they were relieved on 29 January. By this stage Richard had been promoted to lance sergeant.

Richard returned to the front line three more times in February and March. On the third occasion he was killed, on 14 March 1915. The battalion war diary for the day he was killed says:

The morning and afternoon were particularly quiet. At 5pm a terrific explosion took place under the mound, which collapsed, burying the machine gun team which was placed in it. At the same moment, trenches 17 and 18 were blown up by mines. The Germans at once swarmed out of their positions and proceeded to attack the blown-in trenches. They were headed by men who had no rifles but carried bombs and hand grenades. A and C companies were bombed out of their trenches and forced to retire after suffering very heavy casualties. D company on the right was not so severely attacked and was able to hold its trenches. B company remained in [trenches] 8 and 9. Officers killed 7, wounded 2. Other ranks killed 42, wounded 59, missing 35.

Richard is commemorated on the Menin Gate memorial to the missing in Ypres, indicating that his body was never found. He was 23 and unmarried when he died.

The small, professional British Expeditionary Force could not be expected to hold the line for long, so the Territorial Force was mobilised as soon as war was declared on the August Bank Holiday weekend of 1914. Territorial Force volunteers were on their way to that year's summer camps on the south coast that weekend. Some of them had already arrived and others were in transit when the order came to return home and get ready for war. The Territorials were not obliged to enlist in the regular army – conscription did not start until 1916, and some Territorials chose to join non-combatant units for religious or political reasons.

As we saw in the previous chapter, young men from Queen's Park joined a number of units of the Territorial Force before the war – many of them sections of the new London Regiment. Particularly popular battalions in Queen's Park included the Royal Fusiliers, the City of London Rifles, the Queen Victoria's Rifles and the Post Office Rifles. Three local youths joined the 13th Battalion, known as the Kensingtons as their HQ was in Iverna Gardens, just off Kensington High Street. They were Albert Nason, Charles Wilson and Alfred Dermott.

Albert was born at 22 Lynton Road in 1893. His father was a printer. After leaving school, Albert worked as a clerk for the Gas Light and Coke Company – what we now call British Gas. Charles Winter lived opposite Albert at 23 Lynton Road, and the third 'Kensington' was Alfred Dermott, of 36 Chevening Road. Service at the front in the event of a war wasn't compulsory for members of the Territorial Force – it was by definition a volunteer army – but most Territorials did sign up, and by 3 November Albert, Charles and Alfred were on their way to France. They landed at Le Havre on 4 November 1914.

On 9 May 1915 they were in the front line of a British counter-attack at the Second Battle of Ypres, which had begun the previous month with a major German offensive to take the town. The action started at 5 a.m. with heavy British shelling of the German lines – much of it inaccurate and some of it falling short or landing on British positions. The Kensingtons were ordered to move out into No Man's Land, at this point only 100 to 200 yards across. German bayonets could be seen in the trenches opposite.

At 5.40 a.m., following the detonation of two mines under the German trenches, the Kensingtons were ordered to rush forward and occupy the craters. They moved forward and captured ground behind the German lines and formed a defensive perimeter. However, by 8.30 in the morning, the rest of the British assault had fallen back and the three forward positions – including the Kensingtons' position – had been cut off from the rest of the front line.

For the rest of the day, the British tried to relieve the Kensingtons, but by 6 p.m. it was clear that all their attempts had failed and the effort was abandoned. Early the next morning the survivors were ordered to cross No Man's Land back to the British trenches. The three young men from Queen's Park were not among them.

Their bodies were never recovered. They are commemorated on the Ploegstreert Memorial to the missing of Ypres. Charles was 22 when he died, Albert was 21 and Alfred was 18.

The Kensingtons' War Diary for 9 May says:

2am Wire cut. Battalion ready for action.

5am Bombardment began. It appeared to lack the intensity of the Neuve Chapelle bombardment. A battery of 4.7 howitzers were understood to be bombarding Delangre Farm, our chief objective, apparently a strongly fortified position. No shell had struck it as yet.

5.40am Artillery lifted and two mines exploded. The brigade assaulted. The Kensingtons assaulted the enemy's trenches on a frontage 50 yards on either side of the right hand mine. Two companies in front line advanced in lines of platoons, remaining two companies advanced in lines of platoons.

Footing was obtained in the German trenches with heavy losses. Bombers worked down the lines 100 yards to the right and as far as 30 yards east of point 279.

6.30am by this time, a line had been established 50 yards east of points 878/879 and running back to track 50 yards north of Delangre Farm. Casualties were very heavy.

6.45am This line was extended to the south of Delangre Farm by two companies which had suffered very heavily in getting up.

Delangre Farm had been hardly touched by our guns and was held by the enemy with at least two machine guns and rifles. The machine guns of the West Riding Division were firing into us. There was no sign of any British troops on our right or behind us. Our right flank was completely in the air and the whole line was suffering from fire from Delangre Farm. Our machine gun on the right of the line was disabled.

7am The supply of bombs was running short, and a message was sent to Brigade HQ for reinforcements and bombs.

7.30am Captain Barnett and Lieutenant Sewell reported mortally wounded.

8.25am Message to Brigade HQ: 'Have exhausted every possible reinforcement.'

8.45am Lieutenant Sewell was brought into Battalion HQ.

9.05am Message from Brigade HQ: L '2nd Scottish Rifles moving to support you. You have done splendidly.'

9.10am One officer and two bombers of the 2nd Scottish Rifles with a small supply of bombs reached the left of the line at about point 879.

Casualties continued to be heavy.

9.20am The machine gun at about point 879 was disabled. Ammunition was running short. The machine gun belts were stripped and ammunition passed down the line.

10am Lieutenant Sewell died.

10.05am Captain Kimber reported 2nd Lieutenant Lawrie killed. 2nd Lieutenant Stern wounded, Lieutenant Burn slightly wounded.

10.45am Message to Brigade HQ: 'No sign of 2nd Scottish Rifles or ammunition. Please expedite both. Position is unchanged but casualties are increasing. Should Germans attack before support comes, fear I cannot hold on.'

11.30am Last grenade used. Ammunition very short.

11.45am Enemy broke through blocked trench and bombed us out of next traverse. Severe enfilade fire brought on our line. Casualties very heavy.

Enemy concentrating near point 872.

Enemy brought up a small trench mortar and drove us further down trench. Enemy also bombed our line.

12.30pm Enemy still checked but position desperate.

12.45pm Five men of the Royal Berkshire Regiment reached the left of our line with bandoliers.

1.15pm Our line between point 879 and Delangre Farm pushed slowly back.

Enemy worked further up the trenches and poured in a murderous enfilade fire.

A large concentration of the enemy was observed near point 831. Enemy had worked round to south of Delangre Farm. Our line suffering heavily was forced to draw back the right flank.

Enemy worked further round the right of our line. Our line was now enfiladed from both flanks and we were forced to retire.

2.45pm Brigadier General Pinney ordered the battalion to retire to the British breastwork.

3.55pm Message to Brigade HQ: 'Under the orders of Brigadier General Pinney, the remnants of the battalion, estimated at about 50 strong, are in process of rendezvous in the redoubts near Cellar Farm. A few more are in the crater and may be able to get out.'

5.30pm About 55 men reached Cellar Farm. Others dribbled in up to about 8.30pm.

Between 10.45am and 11.30am a signaller was trying to establish communication with British breastwork from German sap but could get no reply.

About 30 Germans were captured, four of whom were taken by the Colonel in a dug-out. Hardly 10 reached British lines.

1am After being behind Cellar Farm since 3.55pm on the previous day and after being shelled the whole time, the battalion was ordered to billet at Croix Blanche. 1.45am 2nd Lieutenant Robertson arrived with two more men. The battalion then numbered about 120.

[In total 95 officers and men were killed that day, another 222 were missing and 109 returned wounded.]

Not everyone died in big set-piece battles at Ypres. Frank William Marmaduke Hallett was born in 1889 in Paddington and baptised on 8 May of that year at St Augustine's, Maida Vale. His father was an accounts clerk for a firm of solicitors. Frank had one sibling – a brother called Herbert, who was three years older. The family seem to have been quite well off – until her death in 1900, the family were living in Maida Vale in the home of Frank's grandmother, Sophia, who was a widow with an independent income. They later moved to 122 Salusbury Road (now part of the Igar Hotel).

Frank went to a boarding school in Ealing called Castle Hill, and after school he got a job as an insurance clerk.

In 1909, Frank founded the 13th Hampstead Boy Scout Troop, with six founder members. They had their HQ in Lonsdale Road and were notable for the determined way they approached the start of the war, taking shooting lessons at the Lonsdale Rifle Club across the road and guarding an electricity sub-station in Neasden 'day and night' according to an article in Boy's Life magazine. By 1917 all six founder members were serving in the armed forces , and Frank and one other had been killed.

Frank was another Queen's Park local who joined the Territorial Force before the war, enlisting in the 9th Battalion of the London Regiment (the Queen Victoria's Rifles), which had its headquarters in Davies Street, near Berkeley Square. He was also on his way to summer camp when war broke out and his unit was recalled. His unit arrived in France on 5 November 1914 – one of the first territorial units to arrive.

Frank was killed on 27 May 1915 at Ypres. He is buried at a cemetery called Voormezeele, Enclosure No. 3, 4km south-west of Ypres. He was 26 when he died.

The war diary of the Queen Victoria's Rifles says that from 26 to 31 May three companies of the battalion were holding trenches at Voormezeele at any one time, and the fourth company was resting in support dugouts. During this period two soldiers were wounded and three were killed, one of whom was Frank Hallett.

It was common for sentries and other soldiers serving in the trenches to be shot in the head by snipers at this point in the war. Remarkably, steel helmets were not issued to British soldiers until September 1915. Up to then, they wore cloth caps. (The British weren't alone in this – none of the armies provided helmets for the first year of the war.)

The same thing is likely to have happened to Clement George le Sueur, of 155 Chevening Road, who was serving in France in 1915. Clement was born on

23 March 1893. He was an only child. His father was a clerk in the War Office. Clement attended Geneva House School on Shoot-up Hill, and Kilburn Grammar School. In 1910, age 17, he joined the Metropolitan Water Board as a clerk.

Clement joined the Seaforth Highlands on September 1914 at the outbreak of war. He was in the 5th Battalion (Sutherland and Caithness), which was yet another Territorial Force unit, based at Golspie, so he may well have been a 'Terrier' before the war. The unit went to France on 1st May 1915.

He was killed while on sentry duty in the trenches near Laventie on 17 July 1915, age 24. He was buried near Laventie in the Royal Irish Fusiliers Graveyard. He is also commemorated on the family gravestone in Jersey (his father came from a well-known Jersey family).

The family commissioned a stained glass window in his memory in (the old) St Anne's Church; when the church was demolished in 1995 the windows were stored in the Glass Depository run by the Worshipful Company of Glaziers.

His commanding officer commented: 'I hear from his comrades in the ranks that he was a fine soldier, and that his never failing good spirits helped others over the many depressing times we have here.'

Pals Battalions

It was clear from the start of the war that the regular army and the reserves, including the Territorial Force, wouldn't be sufficient to fight a land war against Germany and its allies. Conscription, at that stage, was a step too far for Asquith's Liberal Party:[1] Britain had never forced men to fight for their country. A recruitment campaign began as soon as war was declared, symbolised by the famous image of Lord Kitchener, the Secretary of State for War, with the slogan 'Your Country Needs You'.[2] The first of the 'pals battalions' – units where friends and colleagues served alongside each other – was formed in London in August 1914, when City stockbrokers formed the 10th battalion of the Royal Fusiliers.

Although most of the pals battalions were formed in the north of England and in Wales, there were a number in London, including the 17th Middlesex – the 'football pals'. Forty-one players, staff and supporters of Clapton Orient Football Club (now Leyton Orient FC) enlisted en masse in this unit. At least two men from Queen's Park joined them: Vernon Mann, an insurance clerk from 1 Brooksville Avenue,

1   Britain had a Liberal government from the start of the war until 1915, then a Liberal–Conservative coalition.
2   This image didn't actually appear in poster form until after voluntary enlistment had peaked.

and Thomas Earles, a married man from Donaldson Road. Both men died during the Somme campaign in 1916. Vernon was killed at the Battle of Delville Wood on 28 July, aged 22, and Thomas was killed at the Battle of the Ancre (the last major battle of the campaign) on 13 November 2016, aged 26.

1915: Gallipoli

The Western Front wasn't the only place where British soldiers were fighting in 1915. In April, Australian, New Zealand and British troops were sent to Gallipoli in Turkey with the aim of capturing Constantinople and knocking the Ottoman Empire out of the war. The campaign was a disastrous failure, with over 56,000 Allied servicemen dying for no particular gain. In most places the troops hardly managed to get off the landing beaches and had to dig trenches in stony ground on steep hillsides.

Three 'old boys' of Kensal Rise School fought at Gallipoli and never came back. Herbert Kempster of 17 Kempe Road was killed on 10 August 1915 during a British landing at Suvla Bay. The commander of the attack had forty-five years in the army but little experience of battle, and his dithering bought the other side time to reinforce their positions. Herbert was 18.

Edward Chipp of 112 Kempe died on 23 September, the same day that Australian journalist Keith Murdoch wrote a famous report to the British and Australian Prime Ministers that exposed the campaign as a mess. He described it as 'one of the most terrible chapters in our history' and 'a costly and bloody fiasco'. Edward was just 17, and like Herbert, his body was never recovered.

The third casualty in Gallipoli was Walter Kearey of Linden Avenue, who died on 28 November 1915, in the middle of fierce storms and blizzards that killed 280 men. He is buried at Hill 10 Cemetery, near the major battlefront of Suvla Bay. He was 28 when he died.

1916: Conscription

Although Asquith resisted the introduction of conscription, voluntary recruitment never produced the numbers of recruits the army needed to prosecute the war. Our impression of the First World War as a popular cause in which young men queued enthusiastically in vast numbers to sign up, shaped by films like *Oh What a Lovely War*, over-simplifies what happened. While many did sign up voluntarily, many more chose to wait until they were compelled to go.

In January 1916, the Liberal government finally gave in to pressure – including from its own Minister for Munitions, David Lloyd George – and introduced conscription for all single men aged between 18 and 41, with some exemptions for clergymen, teachers, men in reserved industrial occupations and those who were medically unfit. Over 200,000 people demonstrated against conscription in Trafalgar Square in April 1916, but in May, the Military Service Act was amended to include married men as well. In 1918 the Act was amended again to raise the conscription age to 51.

1916: The Somme

The first conscripts to finish their basic training and go to the front arrived during the Battle of the Somme, the Anglo–French campaign from July to November 1916 aimed at breaking through the German lines and ending the war. The first day of the battle – 1 July 1917 – was the deadliest day in British military history, with over 19,000 dead. It was also the deadliest day for soldiers from Queen's Park, with at least five men dying that day.

Four of them died in the same action. Captain James Richard Garland, aged 23, was another old boy of Kensal Rise School. He won a scholarship to Latymer School aged 11, and then did a degree at King's College, London University. As a graduate, he was a member of the Officers Training Corps (OTC) and was at camp with the 2nd battalion of the London Regiment (Royal Fusiliers) when war broke out.

Private Harry Mills, of 25 Summerfield Avenue, served in the same battalion as Captain Garland. He was the son of a schoolteacher and was 21 at the time of the battle. He had one sibling, a younger sister called Winifred.

Private Melvin Sims was a member of the 16th battalion of the London Regiment (Queen's Westminster Rifles), headquartered at Buckingham Gate. His family lived at 30 Kingswood. The family were prosperous enough to employ a live-in servant in 1901 – a 14-year-old girl called Minnie Plaster. Melvin had two younger brothers, Frank and Eric. We know Melvin left school by the time he was 15 – he worked as a 'lad clerk' at Paddington Station. He later followed his father into banking. Like James Garland, Melvin was 23.

The fourth soldier in this group was 20-year-old Lance Corporal Arthur Brook, of the 13th Battalion of the London Regiment (the Kensingtons). Like Garland, he was a former pupil of Kensal Rise School.

The four men died in a diversionary attack on the village of Gommecourt, intended to prevent the Germans switching troops and guns to face the main assault further south. By the end of the day, 28 officers and 475 other ranks were killed, wounded or missing. The commanding officer of that part of the front was later sacked by General Haig – almost inconceivably, the reason given was because British casualties were not high enough.

The attack on Gommecourt was described by journalist Philip Gibbs in his book *Now it Can be Told*:

> The Londoners of the 56th Division had no luck at all. Theirs was the worst luck because, by a desperate courage in assault, they did break through the German lines at Gommecourt. Their left was held by the London Rifle Brigade. The Rangers and the Queen Victoria Rifles — the old 'Vics' — formed their center. Their right was made up by the London Scottish, and behind came the Queen's Westminsters and the Kensingtons, who were to advance through their comrades to a farther objective. Across a wide No Man's Land they suffered from the bursting of heavy crumps [of shell fire], and many fell. But they escaped annihilation by machine-gun fire and stormed through the upheaved earth into Gommecourt Park, killing many Germans and sending back batches of prisoners. They had done what they had been asked to do, and started building up barricades of earth and sand-bags, and then found they were in a death-trap. There were no [British] troops on their right or left. They had thrust out into a salient, which presently the enemy saw. The German gunners, with deadly skill, boxed it round with shell-fire, so that the Londoners were enclosed by explosive walls, and then very slowly and carefully drew a line of bursting shells up and down, up and down that captured ground, ravaging its earth anew and smashing the life that crouched there — London life.

Harry, Melvin and James were buried in Gommecourt British Cemetery No. 2, at Hebuterne in the Pas de Calais. Melvin is also remembered on a memorial at the Private Banks Cricket and Athletic Club in Catford, and James on the memorial list of King's College. Arthur's body was never recovered; he is commemorated on the Thiepval Memorial to the missing soldiers of the Somme.

The fifth casualty of the first day of the Somme was William Horace Stanley Blake, another Kensal Rise School old boy. He fought with the 2nd Battalion of the Middlesex Regiment in another part of the line, about 10 miles south of Gommecourt. The battalion tried to force the German lines in a depression known as 'Mash Valley' (the other side of the hill was 'Sausage'). They had little success and suffered more than 650 casualties that day. William's body was never found and, like Arthur, he is commemorated on the Thiepval Memorial.

In total at least thirty men from Queen's Park died in the battles on the Somme between July and November 1916.

1917: Arras

The Battle of Arras, in April and May 1917, cost the lives of at least eight soldiers from Queen's Park, including 19-year-old Corporal Harry Preston and 18-year-old Private Charles Penny. Harry, who lived on Albert Road, was killed on the first day of the offensive.

Charles's father was a lady's tailor; he had two younger siblings, William and Emily. The family lived at 99 Hartland Road. Charles enlisted on 11 January 1915 at Pound Lane in the 7th Battalion of the Middlesex Regiment, aged 17 years and six months. He was dispatched to France on 30 November 1916, and was killed in action on 3 May 1917, aged 18. That day was the start of a fight known as The Third Battle of the Scarpe. Nearly 6,000 British soldiers died that day in an attack that was poorly planned, and faced German defensive positions that had recently been reinforced. Charles is commemorated on the Arras Memorial, indicating that his body was never recovered.

1917: Passchendaele

In July, a new offensive began in Flanders. The Third Battle of Ypres – also known as the Battle of Passchendaele – was yet another attempt by the Allies to break the deadlock and push through the German front line. It was a costly failure that left 70,000 dead and over 200,000 wounded on each side. At least a dozen local men lost their lives in this campaign, including George Saunders of 18 Summerfield Road.

George was a carpenter before the war, like his father. He served in the Royal Field Artillery, which specialised in providing close support for troops on the front line, using lightweight, highly mobile guns. He was killed on 18 August 1917 at Langemarck, and is buried at Mendinghem Military Cemetery in Flanders. Mendinghem, alongside Dozinghem and Bandaghem, were popular names given by the troops to groups of casualty-clearing stations posted to this area during the First World War.

Although the attack on Langemarck gained a lot of ground in the first hours, like most of the Passchendaele campaign, almost all of it was lost again and the assault achieved very little. George had been promoted to corporal by the time he was killed. He was 23.

1918: The German Spring Offensive

In March 1918, the German Army launched one last major offensive aimed at ending the war before the Americans could ship enough trained troops to the Western Front to make a decisive difference.[1] They were able to do so partly thanks to the soldiers freed up from the Eastern Front by the Russian withdrawal from the war following the revolution in October 1917. The offensive was initially very successful, gaining large amounts of ground from the British in Flanders and the Somme, although it failed to end the war the way the Germans hoped.

The offensive took a huge toll on soldiers from Queen's Park: at least twenty-four were killed in this campaign, many of them men conscripted under the 1916 Military Service Act. George Lewis, of 19 Charteris Road, was one of them. George, one of six children, was brought up by his widowed mother and left school early to work as a milk carrier. In 1916, when conscription came in, he was 36 and working as a furniture remover. When his call-up papers came he reported to the enlistment office at Mill Hill and asked to be allowed to serve in the Middlesex Regiment. He was assigned to the 2nd Battalion of the Sherwood Foresters (Notts and Derby Regiment) instead, and was killed on 23 March 1918, two days into the German Spring Offensive. He is named on the Arras Memorial, which commemorates nearly 35,000 British and Commonwealth soldiers with no known grave. He was 38 when he died.

Infantry sergeant Walter Wells is another soldier with a local connection who was killed in the Spring Offensive. Walter was a professional soldier before the war – a Yorkshireman, he was stationed out in India with the West Yorkshire Regiment before the war broke out. At some point in the war he met and fell in love with Edith Wells, a widowed domestic servant living at 119 Chevening Road. They were married at St Anne's, Salusbury Road, on 12 January 1918. Three months later, on 24 April, 27-year-old Walter was killed (like George) near Arras. He is commemorated on the Pozieres Memorial.

The March to Victory

Once the Spring Offensive had failed, German resolve to continue the war started to collapse and the Allies were able to advance. Nevertheless, the final phase of the war, known as the March to Victory, cost a great many lives as the retreating Germans put up a stiff resistance.

Eighteen-year-old William Lane, of 58 Charteris Road, was killed on 4 September 1918 near Ypres. William's unit was involved in an attack on strongly defended enemy positions along the Vierstraat–Wytschaete road, north-east of Kemmel. The attack began badly when the covering barrage fell behind, rather than in front of, their first objective, a railway line. The German machine guns,

---

1   The USA joined the war on the Allied side in April 1917.

which escaped being shelled, inflicted heavy casualties, while the British soldiers were also attacked with gas. Nevertheless, the soldiers pushed on and managed to reach the railway. They tried to hold on, but a strong German counter-attack forced them out with heavy casualties.

The battalion's war diary for September 1918, written by Major GO Searle, says:

Companies were reported in position for attack at 4am. C&D companies in front on the line of railway. The barrage for the attack commenced at 5.30am and by 6.15am C&D companies had reached their objectives – ie line of the road along the west end of Bois Quarante – and proceeded to consolidate. Casualties practically nil. As soon as covering barrage halted they were subject to heavy machine gun fire from [a trench] on their right rear and two large pill boxes in Grand Bois. In endeavouring to keep the men together all officers of the two companies with the exception of Second Lieutenant Reynolds became casualties.

A&B companies under Captain Rogers moved from railway and endeavoured to form a defensive flank and fill up the gap between C&D companies and 15th Hampshire Regiment. About 7.15am the enemy realised a lack of cohesion in the attack and counter-attacked C&D companies, at the same time filtering through small parties with light machine guns. D Company who had suffered severe casualties, were driven back to the railway and C [company] to a line immediately to the east of [a group of craters]. These positions were held until 1pm when A&B companies who had suffered heavy casualties from hostile shell fire fell back …

William is buried at Voormezeele Enclosure No. 3, the same cemetery as Frank Hallett of Salusbury Road, who died three and a half years before him.

One soldier from Queen's Park – Percy Barnes – died on Armistice Day, 11 November 1918; he died of TB at a hospital in London. Another, 22-year-old Fred Morgan of Kempe Road, died of his wounds in France the following day. Six more died of their wounds between January 1919 and June 1921, and one – Alfred Beak of Chamberlayne Road – died fighting the Bolshevik revolutionaries in Russia in 1919 and is buried at Archangel on the White Sea.

The Meech Brothers

No records were kept of how many brothers died fighting in the First World War, and there was no government policy to limit how many sons from one family would be allowed to die. There are many stories of families losing as many as five sons in the war.

In Queen's Park the hardest-hit family we know of was the Meeches, of 31 Honiton Road, who lost three sons. Henry (a Post Office worker) and Elizabeth Meech had six children in total, four boys and two girls. Their eldest son, Arthur, left school at 14 and worked first as a commercial clerk and then as a travelling salesman, specialising in hair products. In July 1911 he married Frances May Richardson, of College Road, at St Anne's, and in 1914 they had a daughter, Florence. It's not known whether he was a volunteer or a conscript, but by the time he was killed in the Arras offensive of May 1917, he had been promoted to company sergeant major, so either he had a long service history or he had great leadership qualities, or both. He was killed during the Second Battle of Bullecourt. The Australians took the brunt of the fighting in that battle, which only succeeded in taking 400 yards of ground at the cost of over 7,000 lives. Arthur was 31.

Arthur's brothers Thomas and Charles died within a few weeks of each other in the summer of 1918. Thomas – the youngest of the Meech brothers to die in the war – worked in a shop and then as a dental assistant. He joined the Territorial Force at 19 in 1912, and when the war started he served with the Royal Field Artillery from the outset. He was invalided home and died of pneumonia at the 3rd Southern General Hospital in Oxford on 8 June 1918 and is buried at Paddington Cemetery. He was 25.

Charles – the middle Meech brother – became a motor mechanic when he left school. He also joined the Territorials in 1912, aged 22. He was captured by the Germans in the Spring Offensive of 1918 and died in a prisoner of war camp in France on 27 July. He was 28.

They weren't the only local brothers to die in the war. The Prestons – Charles and Annie, of 54 Albert Road – lost their sons Ernest and Harry aged 23 and 19 respectively. Abraham and Charlotte Watson of 153 Kilburn Lane lost Thomas (19) and Leslie (20). Two members of the Bennett family of 112 Keslake Road also died in the war; according to the Commonwealth War Graves Commission they were brothers, although their dates of birth suggest they are more likely to have been father and son.

Edmund Bennett, at 46, was the oldest serviceman from Queen's Park who died in the war. The youngest was 16-year-old 'Boy Second Class' naval trainee Reginald Astlee, who died at the HMS Impregnable training base in Plymouth a month before the war ended.

Other Fronts

Although most soldiers from Queen's Park died on the Western Front and at Gallipoli, some died in other parts of the world. Twenty-year-old Reginald Bunn, of Kilburn Lane, is buried in a cemetery on the edge of the Negev Desert, south-west of

Jerusalem. He was killed on 31 October 1917 as part of Allenby's drive to capture the town of Beersheba. Fred Gidley, of Harvist Road, also died fighting in Palestine.

Percy Mann, of Chamberlayne Road, is buried at Amara Cemetery in southern Iraq. He was killed during the disastrous Mesopotamian campaign against the Ottoman Empire.

CWW Pavitt of Albert Road was serving with the South Wales Borderers in China in November 1914 when he was killed in an attack on the German base at Tsingtao.

Royal Marine Samuel Kelley, of 62 Chevening Road, is buried at Stanley Cemetery in the Falkland Islands. He was 45 when he died.

The Royal Navy

Most of the servicemen from Queen's Park who died in the war served in the army, but a few did serve in the navy. Oliver Newbon from Purves Road over in Kensal Rise, a former pupil of Kensal Rise School, was an officers' steward on board the cruiser HMS *Monmouth*, which was sent to the South Atlantic to search for a German squadron raiding merchant shipping off the coast of Brazil. The British ships found the raiders – the *Scharnhorst* and *Gneisenau* – but were outgunned by them. The badly damaged *Monmouth* was given the option of surrendering, but refused. The ship sank, with no survivors. Oliver was 22, and had been married to Winifred Jessie Burbridge Smith, from Second Avenue on the Queen's Park Estate, for just six months when he died.

Thomas Henry Pollington Stone also died at sea. Thomas left school at 14 to become an ironmonger's apprentice. When the war broke out he was living at 34 Carlisle Road, and married to Louisa, from Dundee. He served a stoker on a submarine, *D6*, which sank off the coast of Ireland after being hit by a torpedo from a German U-boat, *UB-73*. There were two survivors out of the crew of twenty-five.

It is worth noting that 'stoker' is a misleading title, as submarines were powered by diesel engines when they were on the surface and electric motors when submerged. The stoker's job on a submarine was to manage the fuel supply to the engines. The log of *UB-73* describes how they spotted *D6* on the surface and fired a torpedo that struck her in front of the conning tower. After the submarine sank, the *UB-73* rescued her commanding officer and watch officer from the sea.

The Air Force

A small number of men from Queen's Park also served in the air force – composed of the army's Royal Flying Corps and the Royal Naval Air Service until April 1918, and then the combined Royal Air Force – including air mechanics Ernest Ackroyd of Albert Road and Arthur Rodges of Salusbury Road.

Reginald Leach Johns was one of six children born to John and Hannah Maria Johns. He was born in Willesden in 1894, after which his family moved to 332 Kilburn Lane. By 1911, 17-year-old Reginald was working as a 'boy clerk' in the civil service and had moved with his family to 110 Chamberlayne Wood Road (today just called Chamberlayne Road) on the edge of Queen's Park. In early 1915 he left the civil service and joined the Royal Navy as an air mechanic, based in Scotland until June 1917, when he moved back to live with his family, who were now living at 77 Chevening Road, Queen's Park (which still stands today, having survived a bomb in the Second World War that took out the house next door). He then became a probationary flight officer with the Royal Naval Air Service, was quickly promoted to flight sub-lieutenant, and joined the RAF as a lieutenant on 1 April 1918.

Reginald downed nine enemy planes in his Sopwith Camel between 24 January and 2 June 1918. He was killed on 11 June 1918, aged 23, while trying to make a forced landing during a test flight in France.

A colleague described Johns as:

the greatest natural wit I have ever met. His comments on any unusual situation came as quickly as lightning, and were just as bright and penetrating. They were backed by a strong and humorous personality, and a power of comic grimaces and mimicry which have never been surpassed. One night he suddenly climbed up the iron pipe of our Canadian stove, which conducted the smoke straight up through the roof. The pipe was exceedingly hot where he embraced it, and he therefore had to scramble madly upwards to attain a cooler situation. When he had ascended about 6 feet and was clinging on with both arms and legs round the pipe, it gave way just where it entered the roof, and bent slowly in a graceful curve, with smoke pouring out of its open end. Johns was suspended in mid-air hanging on to it. He remained unperturbed, an extraordinary smile on his face. Then in a curious falsetto voice he made an impromptu speech, which started, I remember, as follows: 'Now lads, when I was aboard the French Frigate Flossie ...'[1]

His headstone in Aire Communal Cemetery, Pas de Calais, France, says: 'His loved ones honour him. He was the life & soul of the squadron. His C.O.'

---

1   www.naval8-208-association.com/1916-39PinkneyArmOffPage13.html]

21

THE APPEALS
TRIBUNAL

Over 8,000 men from Willesden appealed against being called up after the Military
Service Act of 1916 introduced compulsory conscription for all men aged 18 to 41.
Their cases were heard by the Military Service Appeal Tribunal, which was chaired
by Alderman Pinkham. The overwhelming majority were rejected. You can see their
stories at the National Archives, thanks to excellent work by a team from Birkbeck
College, University of London.[1]

Some appealed on the basis that their conscience did not allow them to take part
in military activities, but this was only one of seven grounds under which men could
appeal for an absolute, conditional or temporary exemption. The others were:

– doing a job that was in the national interest
– doing other work (eg volunteering) that was in the national interest
– being in education or training that was in the national interest
– serious hardship would result if the man were called up for Army service, owing
 to his exceptional financial or business obligations or domestic position
– ill health or infirmity
– working in one of the jobs exempted by the government.

---

1 www.nationalarchives.gov.uk/help-with-your-research/research-guides/middlesex-military-
 service-appeal-tribunal-1916-1918

Scores of men living between Chamberlayne Road and Donaldson Road (the boundaries of modern-day Queen's Park) appealed to the tribunal between 1916 and 1918.

Of these, relatively few appealed on the grounds of a conscientious objection. Nearly half did so on the grounds that being called up would leave their family in serious hardship, and almost a quarter said they couldn't serve due to ill-health or infirmity.

Charles Riches of 36 Chevening Road, aged 23, appealed on the grounds of 'being of a very nervous temperance and unfit for army life. Public building and mixing with people affects my nerves so much as to cause faintness.' His GP, a Dr Skene, confirmed that he suffered from 'neurasthenia', a common medical condition of the time that has fallen out of use and broadly equates to stress and anxiety today. He added that, 'He suffers from claustrophobia (fear of closed buildings, eg churches etc) and has had to avoid such places for two or three years now.' An army doctor couldn't find anything physically wrong with Charles, but confirmed that he had neurasthenia and recommended him for Field Service at home. Charles's employers, Carltona Ltd of Lonsdale Road, wrote to the tribunal to argue that their work making custard and blancmange powder was important to the war effort and therefore he should be allowed to continue working there. However, the tribunal ordered Charles to find work in a munitions factory, so an able-bodied man could be freed up to go to the front in his place.

Herbert Bramble, of 2 Hartland Road, was a 33-year-old married 'paperhanger' working for a firm of decorators called Halbrook and Co., of Cheapside. He appealed on the grounds of heart disease, poor eyesight and 'short-windedness' but did not provide any medical evidence. All of his appeals were rejected and he was forced to join up in 1917.

Some appealed on the basis that being called up would cause severe financial hardship to others. One example was Arthur Edington Rodges, who was managing the boot repair shop at 45 Salusbury Road set up by his father. Arthur's father wrote to the tribunal in the summer of 1916 to say that following an accident, he was unable to work and had to live quietly in the country. He therefore depended on Arthur to keep the business running, providing employment to three others ('all cripples'). The tribunal were unsympathetic, deciding that Arthur's father had had ample time to find another manager for the business, and rejected the appeal. Arthur's father appealed a second time, and this time was successful in getting an exemption for his son from being called up by the army. Instead, Arthur seems to have joined a local air force training unit, presumably running the boot shop at the same time.

A number of men from Queen's Park appealed on the grounds of conscience. Clement William Halliday, of 5 Creighton Road, argued that he was a missionary in Africa before the war and needed to return there to do 'work of national importance having for its object the uplifting and betterment of subject races, fitting them for true citizenship'. His appeal was rejected.

George Henry Dimond, of 169 Harvist Road, appealed saying 'regardless of consequences, I cannot and by the Grace of God will not assist in any way combative or non-combative in the prosecution of war or anything opposed to God's will'. The tribunal were unsympathetic, pointing out that he had spent most of the war working for firms that were connected with the war effort. George was arrested on 22 April 1916; the last record I can find of him is in prison at Mill Hill Barracks in February 1918 waiting for yet another court martial. He had already served three prison sentences for refusing to fight, two of them with hard labour.

George Arthur Burberry, an artist and designer of 108 Harvist Road, wrote to the tribunal to say:

> I cannot take part in destroying life in any way. I am a vegetarian, because I could not eat slaughtered flesh, I live such a clean life, and I have done so for years … I follow the Christian ideal, and claim that the only one who has the right to take life in any form is the maker of life … I shrink from militarism because I should become mad.

The tribunal argued that he was not a member of any religious denominations, had only joined anti-military groups a month before his appeal and had become a vegetarian to manage his rheumatism, not due to religious beliefs. His appeal was rejected and he was arrested and sentenced to four months in Lewes prison for continuing to refuse to fight.

His brother-in-law, John Soden, wrote to the Home Secretary on 26 July 1916 saying:

> I am an attested man awaiting my call to the colours, and shall be proud to serve my country when called upon, but I consider that no greater injustice can be done to any Englishman than the violation of that freedom of conscience which was handed down to us and purchased at so great a cost by our forefathers.
>
> I have known Arthur Burberry for quite nine years before the war and can testify to the absolute genuineness of his objection to any form of military service. I have disputed the point with him hotly on very many occasions. I know how very earnestly he holds his views, he is a vegetarian solely on the grounds of his objection to the taking of life, human or otherwise.
>
> I beg to apply for a revision of his case, knowing as I do of his tooted conscience and his firm determination to suffer any penalty the law can inflict on him, and as a plain, loyal Britisher, I ask only for a fair and British application of the exemption clause in the Military Service Act which in his case has been absolutely ignored by the tribunal as if it did not exist.

There is no record of any response from the Home Secretary.

Stanley Tennant, a clerk in the Colonies Office who lived at 37 Summerfield Avenue, was granted a six-month extension on the grounds of his conscientious objection. He was also offered a position at the Admiralty, which would have secured him a permanent exemption. He refused all of these offers. The tribunal commented that 'its endeavours to meet the appellant in a reasonable manner has failed and so eventually refused exemption by an unanimous vote'. A Reverend Clifford, from West Ealing, wrote a letter of support to the family, saying:

> I know … Stanley well, and have a very high regard for him and for his fidelity to his conscience. I recall a conversation with him early in the period of the war, and I should have been surprised if he had taken any course other than the one he has chosen. I sympathise with him completely although I do not interpret the attitude of the Christian to this war in the way he does.

SECTION 5

1918 TO 1945

The period between the end of the First World War and the end of the Second was a time of profound change in Queen's Park — and no little destruction. Some of this was caused by bombing during the war, some of it was accidental (usually the result of fires), and some of it was deliberate, carried out in the name of modernisation.
During these years Queen's Park attracted more Jewish and Welsh residents and settled down into a pattern of residency that would remain fixed until the 1980s: a mix of homes that were occupied by the same family for decades (often multiple generations of the same family), alongside houses that were converted into flats and bedsits.

22

THE INTERWAR YEARS

British people had an insatiable appetite for the cinema between the wars (and during and afterwards – cinema audiences continued to climb during the war and peaked in 1948), particularly after the advent of the 'talkies' with the release of the *The Jazz Singer* in 1927. Many local cinemas were either opened or renovated during this time to increase their capacity and appeal.

On Chamberlayne Road, the Palace cinema (down near the corner with Kilburn Lane) had a makeover in 1931 that increased its capacity to 2,000. The 'New Palace' even had its own in-house symphony orchestra, which would have played the national anthem at the end of every performance, as most cinemas did until the 1950s and often beyond.[1] The exterior was modernised, with new clean lines in place of the original Edwardian façade from 1913, which had featured a pair of towers topped with Indian-style domes with flagpoles on top, either side of a bold arch over the entrance.

Chamberlayne Road's Electric Pavilion (where NOKO is today), which boasted an organ from 1924, was modernised in 1935. Its original octagonal tower, with a dome on top, was removed, Edwardian detailing around the windows and doors erased, and the whole building got a stylish new awning to keep queuing cinema-goers dry when it rained.

Between June and December 1937, the Electric Theatre cinema on Salusbury Road was also the subject of major reconstruction. The tower on the corner of Lonsdale was removed and a plain, box-shaped frontage on Salusbury Road similar to what we see today was installed. The cinema was now called the 'Troc'.[2] According to Patricia Griffiths of Lynton Road, it was luxurious inside and more expensive than most local

---

1   Cliff Wadsworth, *Cinemas and Theatres of Willesden*, Willesden Historical Society, 2000.
2   Ibid.

cinemas. Children who attended the obligatory Saturday morning screenings, always accompanied by short serials with cliff-hanger endings every episode to ensure the children returned the following week, were given a complimentary bar of chocolate along with their ticket.

In December 1937, the grandest local cinema of them all opened on Kilburn High Road. The Gaumont State could accommodate more than 4,000 cinema-goers and was one of the largest in Europe when it opened. It had a fully equipped radio studio in its tower, which was supposedly modelled on the Empire State Building in New York. The opening night's performance was a live variety show featuring Gracie Fields and George Formby, and the first week's films included *Wee Willie Winkie*, starring Shirley Temple.

More destruction occurred in the name of modernisation in 1934, when Brondesbury Manor House was demolished and replaced with today's Manor House Drive. The manor, which had been used as a girls' school for fifty-two years, was described as being in a 'shabby' condition before it was knocked down.

Other losses were accidental. In May 1935, a serious fire on Salusbury Road destroyed multiple buildings between Salusbury School and Queen's Studios. More than a hundred fire fighters fought the blaze, which raged for five hours at night-time. Thousands of local residents left their beds to watch the conflagration on a windy night, which fanned the flames.

The fire is believed to have started in a print works, Samuel Sidders and Son, before spreading to neighbouring businesses including Delacour Brothers (manufacturers of briar pipes), Avery-Hardoll Ltd (petrol pump makers) and the Salusbury Road depository of Harvey Nichols. It also threatened Green and Edwards furniture depository (many valuable paintings and items of furniture were removed from there as a precaution) and the playground wall of Salusbury School started to bulge due to the heat; firefighters directed their hoses at the wall to cool it down, while others fought the flames from the top floor of the school. Nine families were made homeless by the fire, including the caretaker of one of the businesses, Mr Rabbitts, and his wife and daughter.

The following February, workshops on the opposite side of Salusbury Road nearly suffered the same fate when the Aaron Electricity Meter Works caught fire. The firefighters tackling the blaze were put in grave danger when they played their hoses over a 700V battery that had been left on when the workmen abandoned the building. FH Smith, the firm's electrical engineer, realised that there was a risk that either the firemen would be electrocuted or there would be a 'dead short' that would have blown the roof off the building. He rushed back into the burning workshop to turn off the battery, which was already starting to catch fire. Fortunately he succeeded and escaped unscathed. Although part of the roof fell in, and a number of rooms were badly damaged, the building was repairable. Fires were commonplace in a world where paraffin heaters and open fires were the most common forms of heating, and Queen's Park was fortunate to have its own fire station.

However, there were positive changes to the area between the wars. In 1924, the park acquired a second greenhouse. According to the City Corporation's history of the park, the greenhouses supplied all the park's bedding plants as well as sending flowers and other greenery to St Paul's Cathedral.

The lych-gate entrance to the park on the corner of Harvist Road and Kingswood Avenue was built in 1936, and six tennis courts were installed in the park the following year: they were erected by the wonderfully named firm of Grassphalte Ltd. During these years the park keepers wore brown uniforms with leather 'gaiters' and peaked caps, and carried sticks. They had a fearsome reputation. The perimeter of the park was ringed with shrubberies, which were a magnet for local children playing hide-and-seek or just building dens. Local residents who grew up in the area remember being chased out of the shrubberies by park-keepers known as 'Towser' and 'Long Tom'.[1] The shrubberies seem to have had a reputation for attracting paedophiles, so the park-keepers' zealous policing may not have been entirely mean-spirited.

In 1926 a government inquiry led to the Hadow Report, which recommended that children over the age of 11 should receive a tailored 'secondary' education. Schools would therefore need to split between 'infants' (age 5–7), 'juniors' (7–11) and 'seniors' (11–14). It took a while for these changes to filter through, and Salusbury Road School was one of the last in the borough to make the adjustments needed, in August 1935. They faced two choices in accommodating what was essentially a third school-within-a-school: purchase the vacant land next door where the warehouses had been destroyed by fire, or repurpose the existing buildings. The cost of buying the additional land was prohibitive, so the school literally 'raised the roof' and created a whole new floor on top. Jacks were used to lift the roof, and new walls and windows were built to meet it, including the dormer windows we see today.

Nos 105–109 Salusbury Road (the building now occupied by the Co-op, Sainsbury's and Fitness First) opened in 1938, replacing some of the workshops destroyed in the 1935 fire. Although the building isn't very imposing at street level, it is worth a closer look at the first and second storeys. The building was purpose-built for the Royal London Society for the Blind (later the Royal London Society for Blind People, and now part of the Royal Society for Blind Children).

---

1   Taken from 'I Remember …' by Margaret Chambers in the Queen's Park Centenary Brochure.

Politics

In a parliamentary by-election in 1923 caused by the resignation of sitting Conservative MP Sir Harry Deeley Mallaby-Deeley, the Liberal candidate Harcourt Johnstone sensationally won the seat. Mallaby-Deeley's resignation was ostensibly on the grounds of ill health, although it is suspected that this was a cover story to enable a more senior Tory politician to get back into Parliament. Johnstone held the seat in the General Election later in the year, but lost it in a further General Election in 1924.

In 1933, Willesden was finally successful in being upgraded from an 'urban district' council to a more prestigious (and powerful) 'borough' council. The new council had thirteen wards, thirty-nine councillors and a brand new coat of arms, featuring a royal orb (symbolising King Athelstan), crossed swords (representing the Diocese of London) and a pot of lilies (for St Mary, titular saint of the original parish). It also had a Labour majority for the first time. In fact, for the remaining thirty-two years of its existence, Labour was in control of Willesden Council for all but one year (1947). Queen's Park was still split between two wards at this point (and would continue to be until 1964). The dividing line ran down the side of the park, along Kingswood. Everything east of this point was in Mid Kilburn ward, everything west was in Brondesbury Park.

That same year (1933), on a Sunday night in May, 1,500 people gathered at Cricklewood Dance Hall for a protest meeting against the treatment of Jewish citizens in Germany. Mavis Tate, the Conservative MP for Willesden West (who had some rather unorthodox views on the subject), sent her apologies, as did Daniel Somerville, Conservative MP for Willesden East. Nevertheless, the meeting attracted a great many local luminaries who were united in condemning the Nazis' actions, with many calling for a trade boycott.

Demography

During the 1920s and '30s, the demographic make-up of Queen's Park began to shift, and also to stabilise. Where there was a huge degree of churn between the 1901 and 1911 censuses, a review of the *Kelly's Directories* for 1921, 1929 and 1938[1] shows a lot more continuity. In Carlisle Road, nineteen of the forty-two houses were occupied by the same families in at least two of these years (meaning that they were there for the best part of a decade), and eight of them were home to the same families for the whole seventeen years: the Israels at 4, the Bowyers at 8, the Smiths at 24, Kopps at 29,

---

1 I am grateful to Adrian Hindle-Biscall for his help with this research.

the Goughs at 33, the Walkers at 35, the Butlers at 37, and the Dows at 45. Over on Honiton Road, sixteen of the thirty-four houses were occupied by the same family in two of those years, and nine were occupied by the same family in all three years – over a quarter of all the properties.

At the same time, the number of Jewish and Welsh names in the area is notably higher in the 1920s and '30s. By this time, Willesden generally, and Queen's Park in particular, was an established part of the 'north-west passage' for Jewish people who settled in the East End when they first arrived in Britain and moved out when they could afford to. Willesden was also a magnet for Welsh people at this time, many of whom worked in the dairy industry. There were at least two London Welsh families on Lynton Road in the 1930s, including the Owen family (whose son Geoffrey was killed in the war), and another around the corner in Hartland.

23

THE SECOND WORLD WAR – THE HOME FRONT IN QUEEN'S PARK

The first year of the Second World War, between the declaration of war on 3 September 1939 and the beginning of mass bombing of London on 7 September 1940, was a time of great anxiety and intense preparation in Queen's Park, as it was throughout London.

Evacuation

Operation Pied Piper – the evacuation of vulnerable civilians from cities and other areas that were at high risk of being bombed or invaded – changed the lives of millions of children and their parents forever.

Every part of Britain was designated as either an evacuation area, a reception area where evacuees were sent (usually rural areas such as Wales and Kent), or a neutral area, which would be unaffected. Greater London, along with Birmingham and Glasgow, saw huge waves of evacuated children leaving behind everything they knew for unknown destinations; many stayed away for years. The experience of being separated from their families and homes, and of being plunged into a radically different world – sometimes for better, sometimes for worse – had a profound and lasting effect on the generation who experienced it.

On 31 August 1939 the evacuation order was given for the next day. Children assembled in their schools early the next morning – some as early as 5 a.m. – and the extraordinary logistical challenge that was Operation Pied Piper swung into action, two days before the war actually began.

London had 1,589 assembly points for departing evacuees, with trains carrying evacuees leaving the capital's larger stations every nine minutes that first day. A staggering 600,000 people – mostly children – were evacuated out of London in just three days. The queue of children from Salusbury Road School waiting to be evacuated on the first day stretched all the way from the school to the station.

Across the borough of Willesden, around 20,000 children, teachers and mothers of young children were evacuated during the first weekend of the war. Most of them were sent to Northamptonshire to be billeted with families across the county. Some got off their trains too early; half of the girls from Brondesbury and Kilburn High School alighted at Hemel Hempstead, less than halfway to their destination, but were quickly rerouted. Others overshot; around 100 boys from Kilburn Grammar School (out of 300 evacuated) stayed on the train all the way to Market Harborough in Leicestershire, and only re-joined their schoolmates six weeks later. The seniors and infants from Salusbury Road School were evacuated to Hemel Hempstead, and the juniors to Dunstable.

Some families made their own arrangements; 9-year-old Patricia Griffiths of Lynton Road went to Treorchy in South Wales with her mother and younger brothers to stay with relatives.

However, more than half of all children stayed put, including an estimated 6,000 children in Willesden, despite the fact that all the schools were closed. Many returned home from evacuation during the course of the so-called 'Phoney War' – the eight-month period at the start of the war when there was hardly any fighting (September 1939 to April 1940). This uneventful period of the war gave people a false sense of safety, with many believing that the danger of attacks on Britain had been overestimated. Despite a vigorous government propaganda campaign urging mothers to make sure their evacuated children stayed where they were, nearly half of them had returned to their homes by Christmas of 1939.

At the peak of the first evacuation, only around forty-five pupils of Kilburn Grammar School remained in London, but once the Blitz ended in 1941 the boys started returning home, and soon there were only 100 left in Northampton and more than 200 back in Salusbury Road.[1] As a result, the council was forced to reopen some of their schools as early as January 1940. As there weren't enough children to fill separate boys' and girls' schools, co-education of older children became the norm for the first time. Kilburn Grammar was briefly taken over by the army, so the boys who had

---

1   JAH Risbridger and DW Thomas, *Fifty Years of School Life, From 1898 to 1948* (history of Kilburn Grammar School).

stayed in London or returned joined the girls at Brondesbury and Kilburn across the road. They returned to their old school in 1943, only to be ejected again the following year after bomb damage.

Further waves of evacuation took place in June 1940, following the fall of France (when German aircraft had access to bases closer to the Channel and more cities came within range for longer) and September 1940, when the Blitz began. In the June round of evacuation, around 2,000 Willesden children signed up to be relocated, although the actual number that turned up was much smaller.[1] This time the children were relocated to Wales and the West Country – the children from Salusbury Road School were evacuated to Cirencester.

The renewed bombing of London in the summer of 1944, when Hitler's 'V' weapons began landing after three years of relative calm, triggered a final wave of evacuation. The first V1 landed in Willesden on 19 June, and by 10 July local children were being evacuated to Cheshire, Lancashire and West Yorkshire. Patricia Griffiths of Lynton Road – now 14 and a school-leaver – returned to Wales to stay with family. Patricia recalls that her two periods as an evacuee weren't particularly happy times; she felt that she was treated as a second-class citizen by the family members she stayed with, as well as by the wider community. However, she notes that many of her school friends and their families found life outside London preferable to living in the capital and never came back.

Civil Defence and the 'War Effort'

Even though the First World War was supposed to be 'the war to end all wars', after the bombing suffered by Britain (see Chapter 19), it was clear to successive governments that it would be foolish not to make plans to protect the civilian population in the event of another European war. Devastating bombing raids such as the one on Guernica in the Spanish Civil War in 1937 showed the stark horror of just how much damage could be done. As early as 1924, the government had established a sub-committee of the Committee of Imperial Defence to examine what Air Raid Precautions (ARP) should be put in place. The Home Office assumed responsibility for this planning in 1935 and created the Air Raid Precautions Department; by 1937 the mood was shifting significantly and things were moving up a gear. The Air Raid Precautions Act of 1937 meant that local government was required to start planning for air raid shelter-building programmes, blackout regulations and the issue of gas masks.

---

1   Kenneth J Valentine, *Willesden at War Vol. 1: The Impact on the Community*, 1994.

In April 1937 the government created the Air Raid Wardens' Service and over the next twelve months 200,000 volunteers, known as air raid prosecution wardens, were recruited. By September 1938, when it was clear that war was a real possibility, another 500,000 people had volunteered.

Willesden adopted an innovative approach to its air raid defences at the suggestion of Major General EM Steward, a former officer in the Indian Army who was appointed as the borough's Air Raid Precautions Officer. He suggested that Willesden organise around a hub-and-spoke model, with four semi-autonomous ARP districts, with control centres, ambulance stations and depots. The one for this area was called 'Queens' and was based in Salusbury School; the playground, which was one single space at the time, became a car park for ambulances and rescue vehicles. In his final report on the civil defence effort to Willesden Council in May 1945, Alderman WH Ryde noted that Willesden was one of only two local authorities to follow this approach at the start of the war, but by the end the government was urging everyone to follow suit. 'The Willesden conception of the problem has been almost universally admitted as right and no amendment has been rendered necessary by experience.' The central command point for the ARP service was in Willesden Town Hall on Dyne Road.

By 1939, the streets of Queen's Park were full of volunteers – and some full-time ARP employees, like George Charters at 22 Kingswood. In Windermere Avenue, next-door neighbours Harry Bunce (at No. 38) and Francis King (No. 40) were both ARP volunteers; Harry also served in the Auxiliary Fire Service (AFS) and Francis (whose day job was driving trains) volunteered as an ambulance driver. Their neighbour, Charles Sutton at No. 10, was also an auxiliary ambulance driver. In Hopefield, Leon Miesch at No. 33 was an ARP volunteer and Frances Carswell (No. 18) and Flora Cook (No. 28) were both volunteer air raid wardens. On Montrose, Dorothy Cook at No. 13 was a Red Cross auxiliary nurse and Charles Ogilvie at No. 17 was an ARP first-aider.

Another air raid warden, a schoolteacher – and later head teacher – at Salusbury Primary School, Mr Harris, would take to the roof of the school at night to watch out for incendiary bombs. One of the early lessons of the Blitz was that small incendiary bombs could be dealt with fairly easily by chucking them in a bucket of water or sand, or even removing them from roofs with a sweeping brush as long as you moved fast enough, but if they were left too long they would burn a hole in a roof and set light to the building below. St Paul's Cathedral had a couple of dozen men on its roof watching for bombs every night.

Inside Queen's Park itself, a barrage balloon was tethered near where the children's playground is today. Barrage balloons were about 19m long and 8m in diameter. Partly filled with hydrogen and capable of being deployed to altitudes of up to 5,000ft, these uncrewed tethered balloons played a crucial role in British air defences during the war by posing a dangerous collision risk to attacking aircraft. A thatched park-keeper's hut and a new purpose-built Nissen hut (a prefabricated steel structure for military use) were provided for the RAF personnel who managed the balloon.

Trenches were dug into the north field of the park to create air raid shelters with earth-covered roofs, able to shelter 500 people. These were only used for a short time as they quickly became waterlogged, and residents abandoned them in favour of Morrison shelters – metal crates that people would lie in during air raids, providing protection if the roof fell in. The Morrison shelters made putting together IKEA furniture look like a doddle – supplied flat-packed for DIY assembly, they had over 300 parts. Handily, they often doubled as a kitchen table. Anderson shelters were not commonly used in the gardens of Queen's Park for the same reason that the ones in the park had failed – the tendency for them to become waterlogged meant that they were often cold and very damp.

There was also an air raid shelter at the Royal London Society for the Blind on Salusbury Road, next to Salusbury School, able to take 500 people, and another at Kilburn Grammar School, with space for 200. Unlike in the First World War, Kilburn Police Station was not a designated air raid shelter, which was fortuitous as it took a direct hit.

Air raid wardens were given detailed instructions on what to do if a bomb landed, how to handle unexploded munitions, and even what to do if a woman gave birth in an air raid shelter (basically keep her warm, call an ambulance and contact the nearest midwife, which in this case was a Miss Furnival of Cavendish Road).

The southern part of the park was partitioned into allotments so locals could 'dig for victory'. The Dig for Victory campaign was an initiative of the British Ministry of Agriculture, encouraging people to grow their own food to supplement food available from shops, which was subject to strict rationing. Allotments became the order of the day everywhere – every available open space was transformed, from parks to gardens, and even the lawns outside the Tower of London. The shop on the corner of Salusbury Road and Harvist Road opposite the police station had weekly deliveries of meat pies, which were a vital part of people's diets during the hardest parts of the war, when enemy submarines threatened to cut off food supplies in the war on supply convoys known as the Battle of the Atlantic.

Victorian photos of the avenues to the east of the park show that many homes were built with iron railings on top of the garden walls, as well as tall iron gates. Most of these railings were sacrificed to the war effort, along with the decorative ironwork around the bandstand and the metal railings around the park itself. Government propaganda designed to boost morale and encourage people to accept hardship and sacrifice claimed that this iron would be melted down to make weapons and tanks. However, this is the subject of controversy, with multiple accounts of vast amounts of iron being dumped in the Thames Estuary, either because there was too much of it or because it was not of the right quality to be used in the war effort – or maybe both.

One of the biggest changes people had to cope with was the blackout – no lights were allowed after dark in order to confuse enemy planes, other than torches with filters to minimise the beam of light and safety lights near air raid shelters. At the start of January 1941, the daily blackout lasted for nearly fifteen hours, from 5.30 in the evening to 8.30 in the morning. By the end of March, there were still ten hours of darkness each day.

As well as rationing, the blackout and national service (for both men and women), local people had to cope with a greatly restricted social life, certainly to begin with: at the start of the war all the local cinemas closed, although by the summer of 1940 seven Willesden cinemas had reopened, including the Palace in Kensal Rise and the Envoy in Kilburn. All of them were heavily protected by sandbags. Dancing also resumed, particularly when large amounts of American troops arrived in Britain in the run-up to D-Day. Popular local venues including Mapesbury Hall on Willesden Lane and Wembley Town Hall.

The Blitz

After nearly a year of 'phoney' war, the bombing of London, the Blitz, started in September 1940 and lasted until May 1941. Up until then, the lead stories in local papers seem to have been mainly about tragic blackout fatalities, people being fined for stealing from the railways (for some reason there was a lot of that around here) and the competition with Lewisham to see who could raise the most money to pay for bombers.

The first fatal bombing in Queen's Park happened on 6 September 1940, the day before the London Blitz began in earnest. No. 3 Winchester Avenue was destroyed and at least two people died, including Mabel Stevens, wife of police sergeant Henry Stevens. Nos 5 and 7 were damaged and left unstable, so they subsequently had to be demolished too.

On 2 October there were fatalities at 49 Albert Street, and the next night a woman from Kempe Road was killed when a bomb hit Keslake Road – most likely where the more modern houses are now at 92–98.

Nos 71–75 Chevening Road were bombed on 14 October. Remarkably, the only recorded casualty was 25-year-old Gwendoline Watson, who lived at No. 75. Her mother, Winifred, and her three sisters were either not in the house at the time, or survived the bombing (her father was dead). She is buried in Willesden New Cemetery, where her inscription reads: 'In dearest memory of Gwen, killed by enemy action on Oct. 14th 1940, aged 25 years. "Until the dawn breaks".' Winifred died two years later at the age of 50 and is buried with her. The site of the three bombed houses remained untouched until 1950, at which point the council's Town Planning and Development Committee described it as 'an overgrown dump' surrounded by chain-link fencing. They recommended that the council acquire the land for housing purposes, and new flats were built there soon after.

There were multiple casualties on 15 October, when a bomb hit 216 Kilburn Lane, next door to where Ida's restaurant is today. A large block of flats has been built where the missing houses were.

The single worst bombing episode of the Blitz in Queen's Park was on the night of 6 November 1940, when Kilburn Police Station took a direct hit. At least fourteen people died that night, most of them police officers. There are a number of mysteries surrounding what happened at the station, including how many died, how they died and why they were there in the first place.

Taking the last one first, Kilburn Police Station was decommissioned in 1938: in theory, it should have been empty on the night the bomb hit it. As we have seen from Chapter 8, part of the station had been a 'section house' – accommodation for unmarried officers. In 1901 there were at least eighteen men living there, so there were plenty of beds. One account of what happened in 1940 says that the building was being used as a canteen and a section house for single officers, as well as temporary accommodation for officers whose homes had been bombed. According to this account, all the dead were asleep in the dorm when the bomb hit; others who were sheltering in the basement escaped unscathed. This seems unlikely; ten of the twelve police officers who died were married men who mostly lived nearby, and in at least two cases (20 Summerfield and 32 Creighton) their houses were intact.

Sadly, it seems more likely that the alternative version of events is correct: the men were simply sheltering from the bombing raid at the station when the bomb hit. This would explain the presence of a civilian cleaner among the dead. This account says that the men were in the basement when the bomb hit, severing a water main, which flooded the room.

The final mystery is over who died. A commemorative plaque at the new police station records thirteen names: twelve police officers and a civilian cleaner. The police officers were aged from 26 to 63. Eight of them were members of the Metropolitan Police Reserves – essentially volunteer police officers – and one (55-year-old Charles Summers of Kensal Rise) was a retired police officer who had re-joined the force at the start of the war. Most of them lived nearby – Kilburn Lane, Harrow Road, Paddington, Harlesden – although one came from Ruislip. The final name on the plaque at the station is Robert Vose (station cleaner). This doesn't match with any names on the official record of the war dead. The commemorative plaque at St Anne's Church agrees with the names of the twelve police officers who died, but also lists a 'Thomas Victor Boast' among the dead. The solution to this small mystery is that both plaques are half right – and both are misleading. The cleaner who died was called Robert Thomas Victor Boast (not Vose). He was 53, and lived in Lothrop Street on the Queen's Park Estate.

On 3 December 1940 at least seven people were killed or suffered injuries that proved fatal, including a number of staff, when a bomb hit Queen's Park Station.

During the Blitz, forty-six high-explosive bombs were dropped in this area (four of them landed in the park and at least two in Paddington Cemetery), plus one parachute mine and an unknown number of incendiary bombs.

Three high-explosive bombs landed on the stretch of Harvist Road between the police station and the park, destroying the first seven houses on the south side (including No. 7, which had housed Belgian refugees during the First World War), Nos 25 and 27 and Nos 39–43, and a fourth destroyed seven houses from Nos 229 to 241.

On 29 December, the heaviest night of bombing of the Blitz, a high-explosive bomb hit 764 Harrow Road, near the bottom of Kilburn Lane where The Case is Altered pub used to stand. Five people were trapped inside, and the only way to reach them was by tunnelling through the debris underneath a wall that was in imminent danger of collapsing. Edwin Povah, the deputy leader of an ARP rescue party, spent three hours digging his way through the ruins until all three were safely extracted. He won a British Empire Medal for his bravery.

Other high-explosive bombs destroyed Nos 7 and 9 Montrose and a pair of substantial semi-detached houses on Winchester Avenue where the Weston House flats stand today. One landed in the grounds of Kilburn Grammar School in the middle of a pile of coal, which was distributed liberally across the area.

Many of the bombs that landed were duds, including ones that landed in the middle of Summerfield Avenue, on the corner of Victoria and Salusbury roads and on the corner of Kingswood Road and Windermere Avenue.

In fact, it is estimated that one in ten of the bombs dropped in the Blitz didn't go off immediately. Some were on delayed timers and could be defused. Some suffered mechanical failure, like the one found on The Avenue in 2017. Others were deliberately sabotaged by munition workers in occupied Europe.

1944: The Flying Bombs

Queen's Park came under bombardment again in the later stages of the war, when Hitler's V1 and V2 weapons – the V stood for 'Vengeance' – were launched from bases on the other side of the channel.

The V1, or 'Doodlebug', was essentially a jet-propelled cruise missile that flew straight and level until it reached its target area, where it went into a dive. At this point the engine cut out, the sudden silence acting as a chilling warning to people that an explosion was imminent.

Fifteen V1s landed in the borough of Willesden between June and September 1944, and seven more landed on the other side of Kilburn High Road.

The first V1 to land in the Queen's Park area hit Paddington Cemetery 10ft from the boundary wall on the Salusbury Road side. It landed at 2.35 a.m. and left a crater 15ft wide and 6ft deep. Kilburn Grammar was badly damaged and St Anne's Church Hall – where the actual church stands today – was completely destroyed. The Maria Grey teacher training academy on the other side of Salusbury Road was also damaged in this incident, which happened on the night of 20–21 June 1944. Although the official account says that there were no fatalities, 76-year-old Catherine Crosby, who lived at 116 Salusbury Road directly opposite where the bomb landed, died in hospital eight days later as a result of the explosion.

Patricia Griffiths of Lynton Road was in her family's Anderson shelter when the flying bomb went over. The shelter was reinforced by her father, who had worked in the building trade; it was covered in bricks and had reinforced blast doors as well as its own electricity supply. 'We were taught to listen out for the engine of the V1s cutting out,' she recalls. 'After that there were three seconds to impact. When we heard the noise stop, we all braced ourselves for the worst.'

Mysteriously, the cemetery wall between the site of the explosion and the school, where most of the damage occurred, was largely intact. Kilburn Grammar lost its gymnasium, library, three classrooms (for geography, history and music) and its science laboratory. The official account of the explosion speculated that it might have been chemicals stored in the science lab that were responsible for a secondary explosion and subsequent fire, and recommended further investigation. The school had to move into temporary accommodation until the summer of 1945, with the fifth- and sixth-formers spending some of the time sharing space with the girls at Brondesbury and Kilburn High School across the road.

A week later, another V1 landed in the King Edward VII Park, damaging houses but producing few injuries.

At 1.30 in the morning on Wednesday, 19 July 1944, a V1 landed in the garden of a house on Hopefield Avenue, destroying a substantial number of homes on Hopefield, Montrose and Kingswood avenues. Miraculously no one was killed in this incident, although nine people were seriously injured and seventeen had minor wounds. According to the report in the *Willesden Chronicle*, one family had an amazing escape. Like the Griffiths family in Lynton, they were in a home-made shelter in their garden when the bomb landed almost on top of them, but they escaped with nothing worse than shock. The official reports of the bombing confirm that the couple escaped injury-free, although their shelter – made with 13 inch reinforced concrete walls – was 27ft away from the point of impact. There were nine Anderson shelters in total in neighbouring gardens.

On 24 July, a V1 landed on Denmark Road. Sixteen people were killed, including four members of one family and three of another, twenrtty-seven people were seriously injured and 119 suffered minor injuries.

On 15 August a V1 landed on Shoot-up Hill, near Kilburn underground station, killing thirteen people, and on the 21st a bomb landed on the junction of Mortimer Road and College Road, just up from Kensal Green station, at lunchtime. Fifteen people were killed, thirty-eight seriously injured and seventeen slightly hurt.

Dr John Beeston, the Borough of Willesden's assistant medical officer, was awarded a George Medal for his bravery in battling through the rubble of a V1 bomb blast in Ivy Road, Cricklewood, to give a blood transfusion that saved the life of a critically injured woman. According to the official notice of his medal in the *London Gazette*, Dr Beeston had to crawl through a tunnel dug out of the debris of the house to reach the trapped woman, who was in a pocket created by a couple of timbers resting on the arm of a chair. The whole time he was treating her, gas was escaping; other rescuers worked in shifts to try to free her because of the debilitating effect of the gas, but Beeston stayed the full hour and a half it took to get her out. During this time the remaining wall of the house was bowing under the pressure of the debris, and there was at least one fall of bricks while he was changing the plasma bottles.[1]

Frederick Rogers, a staff officer with the Willesden Borough Civil Defence Rescue Service, also received a George Medal for his bravery in rescuing two women from the basement of a burning building following a V1 attack. It took him half an hour to rescue them, while the building above him was in flames and in imminent danger of collapse.

Five residents of the borough were awarded George Medals for bravery during the war, and two received British Empire Medals.

In total there were more than 1,000 air raid alerts sounded in the Borough of Willesden over the course of the war; 572 high-explosive bombs and parachute mines were dropped on the area, fifteen V1s, four V2s and countless incendiary bombs. One hundred and twenty of them caused damage; the rest either landed on open spaces or failed to explode. Over 1,300 homes were destroyed or had to be demolished and 6,500 were severely damaged; 372 people were killed and 718 were seriously injured.

---

1 *The London Gazette*, 5 December 1944.

24

SERVICEMEN AND WOMEN IN THE SECOND WORLD WAR

We know less about the men and women from Queen's Park who served in the Second World War than we do about those of the First, for a number of reasons. First, censorship of local newspapers was far better in the Second World War than it was in the First. The vast amounts of information about troops at the front that can be found in local papers of the 1910s just aren't there in the 1940s. And secondly, the official records of service men and women who died in the Second World War don't give addresses, just districts (if that). Nevertheless, I have extracted enough information about soldiers, sailors and airmen who served in the war to know that the experiences of Queen's Park residents were a microcosm of Britain's war effort: every major theatre of war is represented there, from Dunkirk to D-Day and beyond.

1940: The Retreat to Dunkirk

The Second World War started in much the same way the First World War did, with a relatively small, professional British Expeditionary Force (BEF) being sent to northern France to head off a German invasion of France via Belgium. Unlike 1914, however, the German advance was not halted – the fast-moving, highly mechanised German forces punched through the Allied lines and succeeded in trapping large numbers of British, French and Belgian soldiers in a pocket on the north coast of France. The British counter-attacked at Arras – scene of so much fighting in the First World War

– and succeeded in pushing the advancing Germans back. During this battle 21-year-old Private George Pooler, of Lothrop Street on the Queen's Park Estate, was killed.

Despite this success, events elsewhere on the front were going badly, and the BEF's commander, General Gort, ordered his men to retreat to Dunkirk, where they could be evacuated back to Britain. Two more men from Queen's Park – 19-year-old Alfred Hawes and 34-year-old Patrick Ross – were killed during the evacuation, on 28 and 29 May. Although the Dunkirk evacuation (26 May to 4 June 1940) has been spun as a great success, it was in fact a major disaster for the British, who lost 68,000 soldiers and vast quantities of equipment and supplies, including nearly 2,500 guns, 20,000 motorcycles, 65,000 other vehicles including nearly 500 tanks, and 75,000 tons of ammunition.

It could have been a lot worse. The German land forces were poised to capture the town when Hitler gave the order to halt the advance so Hermann Goering's Luftwaffe could get the glory of finishing the job. They failed, and 338,000 Allied soldiers were successfully evacuated, thanks to the bravery of the sailors who rescued them from the beaches and the heroic actions of the French rear-guard who defended the town.

1940: The Battle of Britain

Conscription started much earlier in the Second World War than in the First: all men aged between 18 and 41 were required to register for military service from the day that war was declared. While the new conscript army was being trained and the survivors of the British Expeditionary Force were regrouping, war was raging in the air in the Battle of Britain (10 July to 31 October 1940). We know of at least one serviceman from Queen's Park who died in the battle – on 19 August 1940, Aircraftman Frederick Larkin was killed when German planes attacked RAF Honington, near Thetford on the border of Norfolk and Suffolk. He was one of six RAF personnel who died in the attack.

1941: The Japanese Enter the War

In December 1941, Japan joined the war on the side of the Axis Powers. They rapidly conquered the Malay Peninsula, Singapore and Burma (now called Myanmar), taking tens of thousands of British and Commonwealth troops prisoner in the process. Private Thomas Lee and Lance Corporal G W McReadie from Queen's Park were among the estimated 12,000 Allied prisoners of war who died during the construction of the Burma railway (in May and October 1943 respectively), along with 90,000 South-east Asian civilian forced labourers.

1941: Conscription Extended

In December, conscription was widened to all unmarried women and childless widows between 20 and 30, and men under 60. (Only those under 51 were required to fight.)

1942: War at Sea

Two men from Queen's Park who died in 1942 symbolise the critical battles for control of the sea that took place in this phase of the war. Able Seaman Albert Thorp was a Royal Navy gunner who was assigned to a Dutch merchant ship, the *Hobbema*. On 4 November 1942 the *Hobbema* was part of a convoy carrying essential supplies from the US to Britain as part of what became known as The Battle of the Atlantic. The convoy – SC107 – was intercepted by U-boat *U-132*. The *Hobbema* was torpedoed, and Albert was one of three Royal Navy gunners on board who were killed. The German submarine was destroyed when its last victim, an ammunition ship, blew up in a gigantic explosion.

Another local man, Sergeant Reginald Gladwish, died when the Lancaster bomber he was flying in was lost with all its crew. The plane had been laying mines in the Copenhagen Sound to prevent German ships from using the sea lanes. Although the Second World War lacked some of the more elaborate word play of the First (Mendingham, Sausage and Mash etc), Bomber Command's code names for mine-laying areas are wonderfully evocative: Copenhagen Sound was Daffodils, Oslo Harbour was Onions, Zeebrugge was Barnacles and the east section of the River Elms was Xerantheum.

1943: North Africa and Italy

By the end of 1942, the war was turning in the Allies' favour with victories in the Pacific and in the long-running campaign for control of North Africa. With American support, the British 8th Army had won the decisive Second Battle of El-Alamein against Erwin Rommel's Afrika Korps. Local men Lance Corporal Percy Reed and Driver Hugh Beard – both serving in the Royal Corps of Signals – were killed in February and March 1943 during the Allied advance through Tunisia. They were both 23.

In July 1943, the Allies crossed the Mediterranean and invaded Sicily, and on 3 September they landed on the Italian mainland at Salerno. On 11 September, 19-year-old James Blackwell was killed in fighting at the Salerno bridgehead. In

February 1944, 21-year-old Flying Officer Geoffrey Owen, from Lynton Road, was killed when his Wellington bomber crashed during a bombing mission in Italy. He is buried at Bari in the south of the peninsula. (A significant number of servicemen from Queen's Park were in the RAF in the Second World War – more than a quarter of all the service personnel from the area whom I have identified.)

The Allied drive north through Italy took far longer than expected, thanks to the difficult terrain and the exceptionally determined German resistance. The Allies were held up for four months (January to May 1944) at Monte Cassino, an ancient hilltop monastery dominating the only passes through the mountains in that part of Italy. American planes bombed the monastery to rubble, believing (probably incorrectly) that it was being used by the Germans. By doing this, they turned the ruins into a defensive strongpoint that German paratroopers held for months. Lance Sergeant Donald Riches, of 61 Kempe Road, was awarded a Military Medal in February 1944 for his bravery in the battle of Monte Cassino. He was killed on 31 May, shortly after the monastery ruins were captured. Donald was a butcher before the war, married to Doreen. He was 28.

1944: France and the Low Countries

On 6 June 1944, D-Day, the Allies stormed Normandy in the biggest amphibian invasion in history. Eighteen-year-old stoker Leslie Barnes, of 44 Hopefield Avenue, was killed on 15 June when a German submarine torpedoed the frigate he was serving on. HMS *Mourne* was on guard duty in the English Channel, screening the vulnerable invasion beaches and their temporary Mulberry harbours where huge amounts of men and equipment were being unloaded.

Two local men died on the same day – 19 August 1944 – during the fight to break out of Normandy. Twenty-one-year-old Lance Corporal Walter Batt and 29-year-old Corporal Frederick Bott were both killed during the fierce battle to capture Caen, the historic capital of Normandy.

Once the Allies broke out of Normandy, they swept through northern France and Belgium quickly, reaching the Netherlands in September. Operation Market Garden was an ambitious attempt to seize key bridges over the rivers of the Rhine Delta using lightly armed airborne troops, with ground forces relieving them as quickly as possible. The strategy came unstuck at Arnhem, where intelligence had failed to spot the presence of strong German forces. The main relief column could not break through to the city in time to link up with the airborne troops, who were forced to withdraw with heavy losses. The 2nd Battalion of the South Staffordshire Regiment were particularly badly hit. They landed in gliders on the outskirts of Arnhem on

Sunday, 17 September, and two days later, they were sent to try to relieve the small group of paratroopers who were holding the actual bridge over the Rhine. Out of 47,867 soldiers who went into the attack, only 145 returned. Thirty-year-old Kenneth Tarling, the commanding officer's driver, was killed during the retreat after the South Staffs failed to break through to the bridge.[1] The failure of Operation Market Garden ended hopes of a quick end to the war, as the Allies had to find alternative ways across the great natural barrier of the Rhine. The war in the Netherlands became a stalemate. In December 1944, when 27-year-old Private Alan Laundy of Queen's Park was killed at Maastricht, the Allies had still not found a way across.

Germany 1945

The Allies finally crossed the Rhine in March 1945 thanks to a series of amphibious operations and the seizure of a bridge at the town of Remagen, near Bonn, which the Germans failed to destroy in time. This gave the Allies access to the heartland of Germany, and they were able to advance rapidly during the remaining two months of the war in Europe. Nineteen-year-old Private Charles Ansell, of 60 Tennyson Road, was killed during this campaign on 3 March in western Germany. His unit, the Scottish Borderers, had fought in the Arnhem campaign the previous year.

It is estimated that 3 per cent of the world's population died in the Second World War. The Soviet Union (as was) lost the most people – around 24 million. China had the next highest number of losses at 20 million. Almost 500,000 people from the UK died, either in service or on the home front. Queen's Park, like every other part of the country, shared in this suffering.

---

1   Kenneth is commemorated on the Second World War memorial plaque at St Anne's Church.

SECTION 6

POST-WAR
QUEEN'S PARK

It's nearly eighty years since the end of the Second World War – a longer period of time than that between the end of the Royal Agricultural Show and Victory in Japan Day. My apologies for trying to cover such a long period, and so much history, in just one section of this book. It could easily have been split into two, called 'Decline' and 'Recovery', because the post-war history of Queen's Park is a story of two halves. It is hard to pinpoint the moment when the area's fortunes turned around, but there are a few contenders and they all centre on a few years in the 1970s when long-established residents took a stand to protect the area and there was an influx of new residents, intent on putting down roots in a family-friendly community. The rest, as they say, is history.

25

REBUILDING

Much of the bomb damage from the Second World War was repaired quite quickly. New houses on Montrose, Hopefield, Windermere, Brooksville and Kingswood avenues were erected between March 1947 and February 1949 by the West End firm of Frank, Batty and Smith. They were purpose-built as flats, and came with modern conveniences of which the occupants of older houses in the area could only dream. Verena Beane's mother was heavily pregnant when the family moved back into their newly rebuilt home at the park end of Montrose Avenue in April 1948, shortly after building work was completed. Their new home was still covered in dust from the construction work, and the garden was half Dig for Victory vegetable plot and half bomb shelter so deeply dug in that her father had to let it rust away rather than try to remove it.

Other damage took longer to put right: food rationing didn't completely end until 1954, and the police, fire and ambulance stations on Salusbury Road operated out of temporary buildings until the present, fortress-like police building was completed in 1980.[1]

Queen's Park's built environment suffered a lot less in the war than many other parts of London, but soon a new threat was looming. In 1950, Willesden Council published a comprehensive development plan for the borough, looking at its population, housing, retail, leisure and employment. The Willesden Survey announced that the houses in Queen's Park had limited life left in them – ten to twenty years at most – and the whole area was 'ripe for redevelopment'; in other words, being demolished and replaced by tower blocks.

---

1   Despite being one of the most secure police buildings in London, a 28-year-old man called Russell Grant, the son of former bank robber John McVicar, managed to escape from Kilburn Police Station in 1993.

South Kilburn showed what Queen's Park could expect to happen: between 1948 and the early 1970s, almost all the terraced houses of South Kilburn were destroyed and replaced with blocks of flats, initially four storeys high but increasingly tall as time went on.

Much of Queen's Park wasn't in great shape in the post-war period. As late as 1971, 4 per cent of homes had no hot water. Over a quarter of residents had to share a toilet and 43 per cent either shared a bathroom or didn't have one at all. Many houses were still lived in by families who had owned them for years (often multiple generations of the same family). Verena Beane remembers most of her neighbours on Montrose Avenue in the 1950s having been there for decades, if not (as was the case with her own family) owning the house since it was first built.

Like Patricia Griffiths, Verena's experience of Queen's Park in the 1950s was of a safe and friendly community. 'My mother used to let me take the washing to the laundrette around the corner in a pram,' she recalls. 'I can't have been much more than three at the time!'

Salusbury Road at that time literally had a butchers, a bakers and a candlestick maker (or at least a purveyor of candles). Milk was delivered twice a day by horse and cart (there were also horse-powered bakers' deliveries, rag-and-bone-men and coal merchants into the late 1950s), and the wine shop on the corner of Summerfield Avenue was a chemists and opticians with multi-coloured 'show globes'. Ration books were still needed to get meat and confectionery, but local children were allowed to play freely on the streets and in the park. One of Verena's best friends was the daughter of the vicar of St John's Church, whose vicarage, at 16 Kingswood, shared a fence with Verena's house. Verena's father even built a step so she could speak to her friend over the fence. Another neighbour was the granddaughter of Sir Rowland Hill, founder of the Royal Mail.

As well as depending on horse-power, 1950s Queen's Park was also driven by coal. While houses with gardens could arrange for coal deliveries to be taken around the back to the coal bunker, people who lived on the first floor of houses had no option but to have the coal merchant bring a sack through the house, leaving coal dust everywhere.

Although Queen's Park had a core of long-term residents, an increasing number of houses in the area were rented out as short-term lets in the 1950s and '60s, frequently as bedsits where every room was a bedroom and there was no sitting room or common space. The men who lived in these rooms, often sharing them, had few places to go when they weren't working apart from the pubs of Kilburn, and casual, drink-influenced violence was common. In 1971 only a quarter of homes in Queen's Park were owned by their occupants; 8 per cent were council housing and 67 per cent belonged to private landlords. Queen's Park in the 1970s was regarded as 'bedsit-land', with serious problems of vandalism and other low-level crime.

The area's last cinema closed in 1970, when the New Palace on Chamberlayne Road became a bingo hall, and later a nightclub. The Odeon (also on Chamberlayne Road) had closed in 1970, and the cinema on Salusbury Road didn't last much beyond the end of the Second World War; it's now the Salusbury Rooms (part of Salusbury School), where local craftspeople sell their wares on stalls on some Sundays, as an adjunct to the thriving farmers' market.

Some of the oldest houses in the area, on Willesden Lane, Lincoln Mews and Winchester Avenue, were demolished in the 1960s and replaced with blocks of flats, including Mapes House and Athelstan Gardens. The tower blocks of Kilburn Square also date from this time, having replaced a Georgian square of houses and a chapel built in 1835.

The threat of more widespread demolition ramped up in the mid-1960s, when the Greater London Council (GLC) announced plans for a new eight-lane motorway across north London, from Willesden Junction to Hackney. The 'North Cross Route', part of a 'box', or 'ringway', of motorways around central London, would have run along the top of Queen's Park, across Hampstead Heath and through the middle of Islington. There would have been a major interchange in West Hampstead, where the M1 would have terminated, that would have made Spaghetti Junction look tame. Some of it would have run below ground using the cut and cover method that was used to build the first underground railway in London – tear down all the buildings, dig a trench, put a roof on it and put new buildings above. Freud's House in Hampstead would have been demolished, along with most of Chalk Farm – only the Roundhouse would have been left standing. In Queen's Park, the motorway would have run through a cutting alongside the North London Line, involving a major loss of housing and of entire streets in the area.

The plans for the North Cross route were developed behind closed doors by the Greater London Council (remarkably, it was a Conservative administration that developed this idea). At the time, Queen's Park, Kilburn, West Hampstead and Islington were not fashionable areas and the GLC did not anticipate much resistance to widespread demolition. They did expect resistance from residents in wealthy Belsize Park, which resulted in a number of changes in the route and the proposal for a cut and cover section there. The districts that would have been ripped apart were described in the plans as 'Corridors of Opportunity'. The cost would have been £28.7 billion in today's money.

In the end, only a few hundred yards of the North Cross Route was completed in the East End. There was fierce public opposition – more than 100 groups sprang up to oppose it – and the Labour Party won the 1973 GLC elections on an anti-Ringway manifesto, which killed the idea once and for all. On Friday, 13 April, Labour's Sir Reg Goodwin returned to County Hall as the new leader of the

Council. His first act, having removed his hat and coat, was to direct the Planning and Transportation Department to abandon all plans for the North Cross Route. The Ringways were dead.

The announcement, later in 1973, that the new Labour administration at the GLC was making Queen's Park a General Improvement Area (GIA) using the powers of the 1969 Housing Act, was more good news for the area: GIAs were intended to bring investment to run-down areas to bring them up to a decent standard, rather than demolishing them and building high-rise blocks. The GIA brought millions of pounds of development funding into the area, and by November 1975, 182 homes had been upgraded. As the architect of this investment, the-then local MP Reg Freeson deserves huge credit for his role in preserving Queen's Park for future generations.

This era marked the beginning of a new chapter for Queen's Park. The early 1970s saw new waves of young families moving into the area, attracted by the park, the decent-sized houses, its proximity to central London and its transport links, and its relative affordability: Liz and David Till paid £6,600 for their house in Kempe Road in December 1971, the Hirani family paid £6,500 for their house in Carlisle Road a few months later. As demand increased in the high-inflation 1970s, so did house prices. By 1974, a house on Creighton Road cost £15,500 and a double-fronted house on Kingswood Avenue £29,500.

The Tills bought their house from a member of the local West Indian community – Purgy Dennis – and fairly typically for the time it was split into two flats when they bought it. They came to Queen's Park partly because the district was 'sold' to them by former neighbours in Goldhurst Terrace who had moved to Milman Road and were encouraging other friends to move in.

Their new house needed rewiring, a new roof at the back, work to address wood-worm and dry rot, a new central heating system and a new ceiling when one of them fell in. Also fairly typically for the time, they did this with a baby in tow, doing a lot of the decorating themselves. The whole renovation project cost £1,400.

Ruth and Christopher Kitching, of Creighton Road, also moved to Queen's Park in the 1970s, and like the Tills, faced a daunting job modernising the house: there was a single power point in the kitchen from which every electrical appliance on the ground floor was run.

Many of the new families who moved into Queen's Park at this time were from the Caribbean, India, Pakistan and other Commonwealth countries, joining others who first arrived in the area in the 1950s and '60s – people like Pearl Salmon, from Jamaica, who moved into Hartland Road in 1965, and the Hirani family from Gujarat, who bought their house on Carlisle Road in 1971 (see Chapter 30). By 1981, almost a quarter of households in Queen's Park were headed up by someone from a New Commonwealth country or Pakistan. In 1991, 21.5 per cent of the population of

Queen's Park were 'non-white', to use the white-centric census term in use at the time – although this was still the lowest proportion in Brent (the most ethnically diverse borough in England since the 1960s) by some way.[1]

The Irish community also grew strongly from the 1950s onwards. One of the Tills' neighbours, an Irishwoman called Mrs Peters, said that at one point she had forty-two first cousins living in 'the Rise'. The Roman Catholic Church of the Transfiguration on Chamberlayne Road wasn't just reconstructed to meet the needs of this community – they literally built it with their own hands (see Chapter 28).

Ironically, given the GLC's plan to build a motorway through the area, car ownership was low in Queen's Park in the 1970s. The 1971 census showed that 70 per cent of Queen's Park residents did not own cars. In some cases, this was a personal choice for environmental reasons or simply because of the ease of using public transport to get around. Poverty was also a big factor. This changed as the number of families living in the area increased; by 1981, 45 per cent of households owned at least one car, and in 1991 half the homes in Queen's Park had cars. Car ownership peaked in 2001 at 59 per cent, falling back to 53 per cent in 2011.

Geoffrey Stiff, of estate agents Cameron Stiff, says the Queen's Park housing market was very different when he joined the business set up by his late father in the 1980s. Side returns and basement extensions were unknown; the first loft extension in the area was so remarkable, it featured in an article in a national magazine! If people were intent on investing in property, they moved into larger houses on Kingswood or, more usually, out to the leafy roads of Mapesbury.

Meanwhile, property prices continued to rise, and the population fell as houses in multi-occupancy (HMOs) were converted into single-family dwellings. Between the 1971 and 1981 censuses the population of Queen's Park fell by 27 per cent, and it fell by another 13 per cent between 1981 and 1991 – a drop of more than a third in twenty years. By the end of 1981, houses on Keslake Road were selling for over £41,000 – more than six times what they were fetching a decade before and well ahead of inflation rates at the time. This fall in population went hand-in-hand with the rise in home ownership, which increased from 25 per cent in 1971 to 37 per cent in 1981 and again to 39 per cent in 1991.

In 1986 Brent Council, with the support of English Heritage, designated Queen's Park a conservation area, recognising that it was a place of 'special architectural and historic character with a collective quality worth preserving and enhancing'.[2] Initially this applied to the avenues between the park and Salusbury Road, and in 1993 it

1   By 2001, over 5 per cent of Queen's Park residents identified as African, 6.2 per cent as Irish, 7 per cent as Indian, and 10 per cent as Caribbean.
2   Brent Council, Queen's Park Conservation Area Design Guide, https://democracy.brent.gov.uk/documents/s14308/Queens

extended westwards up to, but not including, Chamberlayne Road. Parts of Queen's Park east of Salusbury Road were included in the new Kilburn Conservation Area in 1993, including Honiton, Lynton and Brondesbury Roads, and Brondesbury Villas.

The 1990s saw two significant developments in the area: the regeneration of the local high streets, and an explosion in property prices. Up to the mid-1990s, Salusbury Road was a practical but not very exciting retail and leisure hub. There was a green-grocer, a butcher, Bendev's hardware shop, Mount of Olives' Lebanese grocery shop, an antique shop and a lot of convenience stores and mini-cab offices. The Salusbury pub was run down and largely attracted an older clientele, and on the corner opposite Mr Fish was a wine bar, called La Folie. Lonsdale Road was entirely full of workshops. Received wisdom locally was that people from Queen's Park weren't interested in shopping or eating locally, so there was no point investing in new businesses.

Three things happened in quick succession: in 1995 Tris Murray opened a high-end gift shop, Worldly, Wicked and Wise, on Salusbury Road; Lonsdale Road was rezoned to permit bars and restaurants, not just light-industrial use; and Carol Charlton opened The Organic Cafe (later renamed Hugo's) on Lonsdale. Within months, a flood of new businesses had opened and Queen's Park was on its way to becoming a go-to destination.

This period also saw a huge increase in house prices. Between 1995 and 1997, houses on the avenues off Queen's Park rose in price from around £200,000 to over £300,000.

Since the 1990s, house prices have continued to grow strongly, and an increasing number of properties have had side extensions, basement excavations, or both. In some cases, properties stand empty for months while the building work is being done – a far cry from the 1970s, when renovations were often done with the whole family in situ, babies included.

Home ownership in the area actually fell back markedly between 2001 and 2011, almost certainly because of an increase in 'buy to let' investment, rather than any affordability issues; the proportion of home owners fell from 55 per cent to 44 per cent during that decade.

The 'noughties' also saw an increase in celebrity residents in Queen's Park. The area has always had its share of notable occupants; the novelist Barbara Pym lived on Brooksville Avenue, newscaster Richard Baker was an old boy of Kilburn Grammar and the model Twiggy attended Brondesbury and Kilburn High School. The director, DJ and musician Don Letts and the author Zadie Smith are long-term residents of the area. More recently, actors including Daniel Craig, Cillian Murphy, Sienna Miller, Thandiwe Newton and Mark Strong, and musicians Lily Allen and Dua Lipa, have lived locally.

Despite the increase in smart shops and restaurants, and the rise in house prices to levels unthinkable back in the 1970s, the essential character of Queen's Park remains remarkably unchanged over the past fifty years, and perhaps even longer; it is still a strongly family-friendly area with a diverse mix of residents, a determination to fight any change that doesn't have the consent of the local community, and a willingness to welcome and support refugees and those in need.

26

COMMUNITY ACTION AND THE QUEEN'S PARK AREA RESIDENTS' ASSOCIATION

A turning point for Queen's Park came in 1970, when high-handed behaviour by the City Corporation sparked a furious backlash from local residents and led to a campaign that gave the local community a sense of what collective action could achieve.

When it was originally built, the park had four entrances, one at each corner. By the late 1960s, there were also entrances in the middle of the park on Kingswood Avenue and Milman Road, but the most popular entrance was the one nearest to Queen's Park Station – the 'lych-gate', erected in 1936, on the corner of Kingswood and Harvist Road.[1]

Apparently driven by concern over crime, the City of London Corporation (which has managed the park since it opened in 1887) announced in February 1970 that it was planning to brick up the lych-gate and create new entrances on Harvist Road and on Kingswood Avenue opposite Montrose Avenue, large enough to take prams and wheelchairs. (The existing entrance on Kingswood was a narrow 'kissing gate'.) The Corporation also announced plans to dig up all the shrubberies in the park, in which children had played for decades, and their intention to take down a number of mature trees. There was limited consultation, and it's not clear what criminal behaviour was driving these changes. In a letter to *The Times* defending the

---

1 Local people have told me that the lych-gate – which you normally find at the entrance to churches – was connected in some way with St Laurence's Church on Chevening Road. That corner of the park was the south-easternmost point on St Laurence's parish boundary, so in a sense the gate was the entrance to the parish itself. I am still searching for evidence to stand this up!

plans, in March 1970, the chairman of the Corporation's Open Spaces Committee wrote that the park would be 'safer, because disturbances in the park can be spotted from surrounding roads'. At least one man was arrested for assaulting a child in the park in the 1960s, and a number of local residents have referred to problems of this type in the park in the past.

Local people, led by a Kingswood Avenue resident, GP and academic, Dr Elizabeth Wright, mounted a vigorous campaign against the proposals, but the City Corporation proceeded anyway, promising to review the changes and if necessary reverse them following a trial period. Seven acres of shrubberies around the outside of the park were grubbed up; it's hard to see how that could have been reversed. In the event, the Corporation decided it was right all along, and nothing changed.

To add insult to injury, the spoil generated by excavating soil to open the new entrance on Harvist Road was spread over the surface of the lower field, where children played football in winter and cricket in summer. The park authorities described this as 'top dressing' for the field, but the soil included rubble and bits of broken glass. Before they had a chance to clear the field, unexpected snow fell in March 1970 and the authorities erected a sign rather disingenuously saying 'No Games (Snowballs), Field Being Top Dressed'. The campaigners sprang back into action, and the Corporation eventually agreed to clear the mess that had been left by the builders.

Memories of the campaigns of 1970 were still fresh in people's minds three years later, when two potential developments caused concern: a proposal to build more houses in the park, and the Greater London Council's plans to turn Queen's Park into a General Improvement Area (GIA) under the 1969 Housing Act.[2] Fourteen local residents met around a kitchen table at 30 Montrose Avenue, and the result was the Queen's Park Area Residents' Association (QPARA).

The group agreed to organise a public meeting to test local opinion, and put 2,000 letters through people's letterboxes to advertise a meeting in the upper hall at Salusbury School on 24 May. Around 300 people came, and there was overwhelming support for the idea of setting up a residents' group. The first chair was an American, Bob Satin, who lived on Milman road, and the first secretary was Sadie Wright, who held the role for many years.

The GLC agreed to hold off on taking a decision on the GIA until local people had been able to express a view. In the end, there was strong support for the proposal, which had been championed by housing minister and local MP Reg Freeson and gave residents access to grants for home improvements. Many of the red concrete roofs in the area date from this period. It also led to proposals for traffic calming measures;

---

2   GIAs gave local authorities the power to invest in areas with lots of run-down or derelict properties rather than demolishing them and replacing them with modern buildings.

at one stage it was proposed to block off the end of every other one of the avenues between Salusbury Road and Kingswood Avenue, although the only remnant of these proposals is the 'pocket park' at the end of Keslake Road. The GLC set up a local office in Queen's Park to manage the GIA and administer its £2 million budget.

The GLC also bought up a number of properties in Queen's Park, although they often stood empty for extended periods of time after they were acquired. By 1981, the proportion of council and housing association properties in Queen's Park had increased to 15 per cent, up from 8 per cent in 1971.

The GIA wasn't the only issue for the new residents' association to tackle: in its first six months, agenda items included the building of the new police station on Salusbury Road, the redevelopment of the site of St Laurence's Church on Chevening, the installation of a toddlers' playground in the park, buses on Salusbury Road, commercial use of garages on Peploe Road and speeding traffic.[1] The City Corporation's proposal to build another two houses in the park withered away in the face of local opposition led by QPARA, and their hard-fought campaign to get a pedestrian crossing on Salusbury Road outside the school was also a success.

According to Robin Sharp, who succeeded Bob Satin as chair of QPARA in 1974, these kinds of local campaigning issues were the main focus of the residents' association in its early years. The park managers – including the much-loved Terry James and his superintendent, David James – were supportive from the start, but the councillors of the City Corporation were not used to ideas like 'engagement' and 'consultation'.

'They used to visit the park once a year,' says Robin Sharp. 'They would arrive in a big black Daimler, wander around inspecting their demesne, and then leave again without actually talking to any local people.' While the decision to block off the lych-gate entrance to the park was taken with relatively limited consultation, the creation of the pitch-and-putt area was decided on with no consultation at all.[2]

Community action began to snowball in Queen's Park in the early 1970s, much of it organised by the growing number of young mothers in the area. 'Mothers met by chance in the park,' remembers Liz Till. 'At that time many families could afford to live on one income when our children were small – we had a DIY mentality.' This burgeoning community often attended a pre-school playgroup in the Tiverton centre (now the Maqam Centre) where mothers were expected to volunteer on a rota to support the playgroup supervisor and, when not on duty, were welcome to stay with their toddlers as long as they wanted.

1   Sadie Wright, *In The Beginning ...* from the Official Souvenir Brochure of the Queen's Park Centenary, QPARA, 1987.
2   Until the pitch-and-putt course opened, people could walk the full figure-of-eight route that had been in place since the park opened in 1887; it only became possible to walk the route again when the Woodland Walk opened a few years ago.

As well as building an enduring friendship network, this group linked up with local activists called the Brent Campaign for the Under-Fives, who were fighting for more nursery classes attached to infant schools, more day nurseries, and better-trained childminders. The campaign was successful in persuading Brent Council to open a centre where unregistered childminders could be trained while the children in their care were supervised by qualified nursery staff. Bertie Road Nursery Centre allowed illegal, unregistered minders to become registered without any penalties. 'This was my first experience of voluntary community action, and it was an eye-opener,' says Till.

The group then lobbied the City Corporation for a 'One O'Clock Club' in the playground at the park, following the example of Holland Park. In classic 1970s campaigning style they drove a bus full of mothers and toddlers to the Guildhall, waving flags and accompanied by Reg Freeson MP. Although they didn't get their One O'Clock Club, which would have provided creative outdoor play, they did persuade the City Corporation to improve the playground.

Undeterred by the failure of their campaign to get the City Corporation to fund a One O'Clock Club, the local mothers and QPARA, led by Windermere resident Janet Cummins, Ann Sharp and others, lobbied the GLC's Area Improvement and Maintenance (AIM) team to provide facilities. Space was made available on the ground floor of the AIM's offices on Milman Road, run by a rota of local mothers – initially as a One O'Clock Club, and later one of the first After-School Clubs in the country.

The opening of Hopscotch Under-Fives nursery in 1983 at Winkworth Hall, the Suffragette hotbed of the 1910s, provided another focal point for local parents to build networks – and another cause to campaign for. Many of the early users of Hopscotch were involved in the community-led campaign to persuade more parents to send their children to Queen's Park Community School (QPCS) a decade later.

By the early 1980s, QPARA was running Queen's Park Days (and sometimes Queen's Park Sports Days) in the summer. These early Queen's Park Days were modest events, big on family activities but with only a handful of stalls.

A defining moment for the association came in 1987, with the centenary celebrations of the park's opening. This party in the park involved QPARA activists dressing up in period costumes. It was organised by Janet Cummins, whose husband Mark was QPARA chair during its formative years, edited the iconic centenary brochure and was a long-term Queen's Park councillor.

The success of the centenary celebrations gave a real kick to QPARA's social side, with increasingly ambitious Queen's Park Days being organised by Helen Durnford and others throughout the 1990s, 2000s and 2010s. The most successful was the pre-pandemic Queen's Park Day in 2019, when over 18,000 people attended. QPARA has also expanded into bi-annual Open Gardens events and helped facilitate open-air Shakespeare in the Park and the highly successful series of book festivals in Queen's Park.

QPARA, and the wider Queen's Park community, have built a reputation for effective campaigning over the fifty years since the lych-gate was bricked up. Queen's Park was one of the first areas in Brent to secure a Controlled Parking Zone (CPZ), as the area was plagued by commuters driving into the area and parking before taking the tube or overground into central London.

The building on Salusbury Road that opened as a music school in 2022 has also been a perennial subject of campaigns. In 1983, the GLC gave a grant to enable an organisation called the Brent Irish Cultural and Community Association to take over the old Aron Electricity Meter factory to convert it into an arts centre. For the best part of a decade the centre flourished, with Irish dancing classes, music and a hugely popular bar. By the early 1990s, concerns were being raised in Parliament about the financial management of the centre, and it was taken over by administrators. Half the property was converted into housing for older people in 1996, and the other half became the Corrib Rest pub.

Since hundreds of thousands of pounds of public money had been poured into the Irish Centre by the GLC and Brent, one of the conditions put on the Corrib was that it would provide function rooms for the use of the local community at affordable rents. For nearly twenty years this arrangement worked well for the most part (although residents of Hopefield in particular suffered from the effects of the private parties that went on until the early hours on a regular basis), with the Corrib offering a welcome for older residents in an increasingly young and affluent Queen's Park. In 2015, the pub was sold to developers who hoped to convert it into flats. QPARA, under its then chair Janis Denselow, campaigned hard to ensure function rooms continued to be available however the building was developed, and succeeded in getting it recognised as an 'Asset of Community Value' so local groups will be able to use it again in future.

Local campaigners Robert Budwig, Helen Durnford and Henrietta Green (the food writer and advocate of the local food movement) were among those involved in attracting a farmers' market to the area in September 2005. The market, which runs every Sunday, has been a huge success since the beginning and has won the accolade of best farmers' market in London. During the Covid-19 pandemic, queues stretched all the way down Lonsdale Road and halfway down Hartland Road at opening time as local residents waited to buy fresh ingredients directly from the producers.

27

POST-WAR POLITICS

From 1945 until 1965, Queen's Park was part of Willesden Borough Council, under Labour control for nineteen out of those twenty years. However, Queen's Park didn't get its own ward until 1964, when plans were already in place to wind up Willesden Council and fold it, along with Wembley Council, into the new London Borough of Brent. Queen's Park was finally becoming part of the capital city!

The marriage was not an easy one. Unlike many neighbouring boroughs, such as Ealing or Camden, Brent did not have a common centre of gravity. On the contrary, the valley of the River Brent, where the North Circular also runs, splits the borough in two. Willesden was industrial, urban, and increasingly diverse, while most of Wembley was the epitome of suburbia. The majority of the councillors elected in the first Brent Council elections in 1964 from the old Wembley wards were Conservatives, while the Willesden councillors were overwhelmingly Labour. Both Wembley MPs were Conservative; both Willesden MPs Labour.

The inaugural Mayor of Brent was John Hockey, councillor for Queen's Park, who lived on Montrose Avenue. He led the Willesden councillors elected in 1964 on the long walk up to the new Brent Town Hall (which was, in fact, the old Wembley Town Hall repurposed – Brent Council had the old Willesden Town Hall in Dyne Road demolished a few years later).

Labour held the two-councillor seat of Queen's Park from 1964 to 1990 with only one break, from 1968 to 1971, when it fell to the Conservatives. During that period notable Queen's Park councillors included Reg Freeson, MP for Willesden East and then Brent East for twenty-three years and a government minister, and Merle Amory, the first black woman council leader in Britain. Since 1990, Queen's Park ward has had a mixture of Labour and Liberal Democrat councillors. Notable Conservative Party candidates for the ward include Kwasi Kwarteng, appointed Secretary of State for Business, Energy and Industrial Strategy in 2021, and Richard Fuller, MP for Bedford and later North East Bedfordshire. The ward has expanded from its original boundaries – essentially the same as QPARA's today – to take in parts of Kensal Rise and Kensal Green.

MPs

Willesden East was Conservative from 1918 to 1945, apart from a brief period in 1923–24 when it went Liberal. It then elected Labour's Maurice Orbach (father of acclaimed psychoanalyst and author Susie) in 1945–59, Conservative Trevor Skeet (1959-64) and Reg Freeson (from 1964 until the abolition of the constituency in 1974).

Willesden East became Brent East in 1974. During its existence, the constituency was represented by three Labour MPs – Reg Freeson and Paul Daisley, who were both Queen's Park residents, and Ken Livingstone, Leader of the Greater London Council from 1981 until the council was abolished in 1986, and Mayor of London from the creation of the office in 2000 until 2008.

Livingstone was succeeded as Brent East MP by Liberal Democrat Sarah Teather, who represented the constituency for seven years and became Minister of State for Children and Families following the formation of the coalition government in May 2010, before the constituency was abolished later in 2010.

Queen's Park ward then became part of the newly created parliamentary constituency of Hampstead and Kilburn, represented first by the former actor Glenda Jackson and then by Tulip Siddiq, who campaigned tirelessly for the release (achieved in 2022) from an Iranian prison of her constituent, Nazanin Zaghari-Ratcliffe. Tulip has an impressive political heritage: her maternal grandfather is Sheikh Mujibur Rahman, founding father and the first President of Bangladesh, and her aunt is Prime Minister of Bangladesh Sheikh Hasina, the longest-serving female head of government in the world.

Reg Freeson

Reg Freeson, councillor for Queen's Park from 2002 to 2006 and then MP for this area from 1964 to 1987, had a stellar political career.

Freeson was born in St Pancras in 1926, the grandson of Jewish immigrants from Russia and Poland who had, like many local Jewish people, left because of the anti-Jewish *pogroms*. He volunteered to join the armed forces in 1942 at the age of 16, where he received training in journalism. After the war, this enabled him to pursue a career as a journalist, working for titles including the *Daily Mirror* and the *News Chronicle*, and later editing the anti-fascist magazine *Searchlight* from 1964 to 1967.

He first became a Labour councillor in the old Willesden borough council in 1952, becoming council leader in 1958. As leader of the borough, he was responsible for hugely increasing the stock of council housing and for ensuring that many of Willesden's Irish and African-Caribbean residents were rehoused in decent properties. He was a committed anti-racist who worked hard to build links between the borough's diverse communities, and a passionate campaigner against militarism. He was a founder member of CND in 1957 and participated in the anti-nuclear Aldermaston marches.

In 1964, Freeson was elected to parliament as MP for Willesden East. Despite his forthright criticism of the Wilson government for its failure to oppose apartheid in South Africa and the Vietnam War vigorously enough, and his obvious anger at Labour's immigration controls, Freeson was promoted through the ranks, becoming Minister for Housing from 1969 to 1970 and again from 1974 to 1979 – the longest-serving housing minister in history.

A bench in Queen's Park is dedicated to his memory.

Paul Daisley

Paul Daisley, MP for this area from 2001 to 2003 and a reforming leader of Brent Council for six years before that, was a Queen's Park resident (Montrose Avenue) and passionate supporter of local regeneration.

Born in West London in 1957, Daisley had a successful career as a business consultant. He was first elected to Brent Council in 1990, representing Harlesden ward. He became chief whip of Brent's Labour councillors in 1991 and group leader – and *de facto* leader of the whole council – in 1996. He worked endlessly to restore the council's reputation for probity and to build bridges between Brent's communities; he was a passionate anti-racist who tirelessly gave his time for the people he represented. Many local people in Queen's Park remember him for his enthusiasm, energy and love of life as well as for his political achievements.

Like Reg Freeson, Daisley was not afraid to take strong, principled stands – in Daisley's case, on issues including fox hunting and the Iraq War, both of which he strongly opposed.

28

FAITH IN POST-WAR QUEEN'S PARK

None of the places of worship that were established in Queen's Park in the 1900s are still standing in their original setting today; the post-war period has been one of retrenchment for the Protestant churches in particular. However, faith hasn't disappeared from Queen's Park during that time: new congregations have appeared, and old ones have adapted and innovated.

The first local church to disappear was Holy Trinity, on Brondesbury Road opposite where Algernon Road is today. It was destroyed by a fire at Easter of 1950 and never rebuilt. The part of its parish on this side of Kilburn High Road was transferred to St Anne's. Its name lives on in the parish of St Anne's and (see more in Chapter 11) Holy Trinity, Brondesbury.

In 1961, St Anne's new church hall, which replaced the old 'tin' structure destroyed by a flying bomb in 1944, was opened by Lady Pamela Hicks, daughter of Earl Mountbatten and a descendant of the royal who laid the foundation stone of St Anne's in 1904.

In 1965, Brondesbury Synagogue was gutted in a fire set by British Nazis (see Chapter 11). Although it was fully renovated after the fire, the congregation had been declining from the 1940s onwards and this effectively marked the end of the 'shul' in Queen's Park. At its peak in 1930, the synagogue had 540 seat-holders; by 1970 that had fallen to 250. Most of the congregation joined either the synagogue at the top of Brondesbury Park or one in Cricklewood.

The 1970s were a particularly tough time for local places of worship. In 1970, the ruins of Holy Trinity were finally demolished. In 1971, St Laurence's Church, on the corner of Chevening and Tiverton Roads, closed. It was merged back into its parent church, Christchurch on Willesden Lane, and Queen's Park west of Kingswood became part of the parish of Christchurch. The church was demolished and replaced with the present flats of St Laurence's Close. Two stained glass windows from the church by the artist Leonard Walker were donated to the Victoria and Albert Museum in South Kensington; a particularly fine one depicting a female saint is on display in the Sacred Silver and Stained Glass gallery.

Brondesbury Congregational Church, on the corner of Wrentham Avenue and Tiverton Road, also closed in 1971. It became a Brent Council youth and community centre, hosting a mothers-and-toddlers group (see Chapter 26) and a youth centre that was particularly popular with local African-Caribbean young people, and had a reputation for radicalism. Local resident Paul Sommerfeld, who was chair of the London Voluntary Services Council at the time, remembers telling a colleague where he lived and being told, 'Bro, you are on the front line!' Brent Council closed the whole centre overnight without warning, and it stood idle for years before being purchased by Yusuf Islam, to be reopened as an Islamic Cultural Centre. It currently hosts a swimming pool and a café.

The following year (1972) the Congregational Church in England and Wales merged with the Presbyterian Church of England to form the United Reformed Church (URC). St Andrew's Presbyterian Church therefore became the centre of worship in the area for both the former churches, as St Andrew's URC.

In 1974, Brondesbury Synagogue was sold to a Shia faith group, the Imam Al-Khoei Foundation, and became a mosque.

The Methodist Church on Chamberlayne Road, on the corner of Wrentham Avenue, was badly hit by fire on two occasions in the 1970s, both probably arson attacks. The second one gutted the church. The congregation found that the church hall building next door was adequate for the size of their congregation and their financial means, so they began holding services there.

Meanwhile, Kensal Rise's Roman Catholic parish acquired a new priest – Father William Dempsey – on 6 August 1977, the Feast of the Transfiguration. According to Susan Carberry, the former administrator of the church, Father Dempsey immediately decided that they needed to move to a church in a more central location, and set about buying the shell of the Methodist church on the rise, using every ounce of his charisma to secure the funds needed. He then persuaded the local Irish Catholic community – many of whom working in the building industry – to do the reconstruction. 'The men would come home from work, have their supper, and then put in a shift at the church while their wives, sisters and daughters made tea,' Susan remembers. 'Looking back, people had strict gender roles that wouldn't be acceptable today, but that's how it was then.' The Irish population of Queen's Park and Kensal Rise has fallen in numbers since the Church of the Transfiguration, as it was named, opened

– the community reduced by a third between 2001 and 2011 as many older residents passed away and many younger ones returned to Ireland – and the church now has one of the most diverse congregations in London.

St Anne's Church is also no longer in its original, Victorian building. The Rev. Fr Fergus Capie was parish priest and vicar of St Anne's Brondesbury, on Salusbury Road, from 1995 to 2012. During his period in office, the parish council of St Anne's Church on Salusbury Road decided that the subsidence damaging the Victorian church was irrecoverable. St Andrew's had also been considering its future for some time. Led by Father Fergus and St Andrew's Reverend Barrie Scopes, the two churches agreed to share a new, purpose-built church building on the site of St Anne's church hall. St Andrew's was sold to the New Life Bible Presbyterian Church, and the former St Anne's church was demolished and replaced with the St Anne's Court block of flats.

'The old St Anne's was a cavernous Edwardian building, slowly falling down,' remembers Father Fergus. However, it still had many good points, including its Willis pipe organ, which pre-dated the church and had been played by the composer and musician Felix Mendelssohn. The congregation had already seen St Anne's move from a very 'High Church' form of Anglicanism to a more liberal, Anglo–Catholic form better suited to the local community in living memory. The idea of basing services around an electronic (or strictly speaking, digital computer) Allen organ must have seemed like a very big step to take. The new organ was plugged in next to the Willis one Sunday by the church's organist, Peter Walter, who switched between the two instruments throughout the service – and it was generally agreed that no one could tell which was which.

While the new St Anne's and St Andrew's Church, which was to double as an inter-faith centre, was being constructed, the two congregations worshipped at first at St Andrew's and then at Salusbury Primary School. 'The one person who experienced most and constant change and inconvenience (apart from the priest, and it is our job to be inconvenienced) was the organist, Peter Walter,' remembers Father Fergus. 'He never once complained and always worked to accommodate change or something new. I once joked that we should change our name to "St Peter and St Anne".'

The foundation stone for the new building was laid on 1 July 1997 and the new ecumenical centre opened on 17 May 1998. The opening ceremony was performed by the then Bishop of London, Richard Chartres, and by Dr David Thompson, ex-Moderator of the General Assembly of the United Reformed Church. Queen's Park Singers sang at the dedication service.

The two churches shared the building until July 2020, when St Andrew's moved out.

Queen's Park Singers

Local choir the Queen's Park Singers is not a religious group; they are open to, and welcome, people of all faiths and religious beliefs, including agnostics and atheists. For many years St Anne's Church (old and new) was one of their main venues, and they frequently perform music that was first written for divine services. The choir's roots go back to 1974 when Liz Till, of Kempe Road, organised a concert to raise for funds for the new Under Fives Club she was involved in setting up. Encouraged by the success of this concert, Liz and her husband David organised a follow-up concert that December at Salusbury School, accompanied by a string quartet. This was the start of a series of concerts between 1975 and 1981.

Another local resident, Peter Burtt-Jones, proposed that the local musicians and singers involved in the concerts put together a choir. The new choir's debut was in December 1975, when they began the Queen's Park tradition of singing carols in the streets – a tradition that has continued in an unbroken chain ever since, except when Covid rules prevented it.

Queen's Park Singers was formally incorporated in 1998, and shortly afterwards became a registered charity. The singers performed three concerts a year under David Till's direction until 2009, and then under Peter Burtt-Jones's leadership until 2016. Oliver Till, a recent music graduate, was appointed musical director in 2016. The choir now has a professional conductor and accompanist, and uses professional orchestral players when they are required, but it maintains its charitable purpose of being a community resource, offering chances for local residents and their children to make music.

The young people's wing of the choir – the Queen's Park Junior Singers – began in 2001 when local resident Jane Cox decided the best way to create opportunities for her three sons to sing was to set up a local choir! David Till rehearsed them and included them in adult concerts, until Mary Phillips took over in 2004. Her major productions have included Britten's *Noyes Fludde* and an opera by Malcolm Williamson.

29

POST-WAR EDUCATION

Salusbury Road School

Salusbury Road School in the 1940s and '50s had high aspirations. Pupils were divided into four houses – Queen's, Park, Lonsdale and Grange – and the school's archives are full of photos of pupils practising gymnastics, boxing and other sports. The school had a choir, skilled enough to attempt Purcell's 'Nymphs and Shepherds' and Vaughan Williams's 'Linden Lea' at the Golden Jubilee celebrations in 1952. Prizes were given out for art, craft, history, hygiene, housecraft and penmanship, and for sports including swimming, tennis and athletics. From 1944 to 1967, the senior school on the top floor was a 'secondary modern' for girls aged 11 to 15.

At some point in the 1950s or '60s, things dipped. Helen Durnford first saw Salusbury School in 1971, and says it looked 'terrifying'. A newly qualified teacher and graduate of Goldsmiths College, Helen was on a tour of Brent on a borrowed bicycle because she had heard that the council was hiring 'pool' teachers. The first area she visited was Queen's Park, and she wasn't impressed. 'There was uncollected rubbish on the pavements in Harvist and Brondesbury Roads, and the school had metal grilles on its windows. It looked grim.'

She was successful in her application to Brent, and was assigned to her first school: Salusbury. Her second impressions were no better than her first.

I was one of a group of new teachers who arrived on the first day of school to cover for absent staff. The head wasn't particularly expecting me, and I was sent off to teach a class with no induction and no preparation. My training at Goldsmiths, where I was told never to correct a pupil's grammar or spelling in case it stunted their creativity, didn't equip me at all for what was coming. I was in charge of a vast class – more than forty pupils. The only learning materials we had were old Dick and Dora books (featuring Nip the dog and Fluff the cat) from the 1950s, many of them held together with string.

At that point, in the early 1970s, large numbers of pupils were joining the school from the Caribbean, South Asia, Africa and other parts of the Commonwealth. Many of them needed support that just wasn't available at the school – teachers like Helen had no teaching assistants or specialist staff; they had to design their own lessons from scratch and sink or swim on their own.

Things improved as the decade progressed and the recommendations of the Plowden Report into education were implemented; class sizes fell, money was invested in the school's infrastructure, creating new classrooms and even new mezzanine floors in the building, and providing much-needed resources. 'Our head teacher, Mr Harris, was terribly proud of his stockroom,' Helen remembers. 'Every Friday he would put on a brown work coat and ask us for our stock requests – notebooks, pencils, runners etc. He even gave tours of his stockroom to local dignitaries. No one else was allowed near it!'

By the late 1990s, under head teacher Carol Munro, Salusbury Primary School was a popular school that had no trouble attracting local children. It was regarded as progressive and inclusive. Ofsted inspectors noted that the school over-indexed in both children from very affluent backgrounds and those eligible for school meals, with a significantly high number of refugee children (at that time, mainly from Kosovo). In response, the school founded Salusbury WORLD, the only school-based refugee charity in the UK, dedicated to supporting refugee children and their families, many of whom had had traumatic experiences and travelled far from their homes in search of safety.

Although the school experienced problems after Munro left, it is once again popular, successful and well-led.

Kilburn Grammar, B&K and QPCS

In 1967, Brent Council abolished grammar schools. Kilburn Grammar became Kilburn Senior High School for Boys (KSH) and Brondesbury and Kilburn High School for Girls was renamed Brondesbury Senior High School. This arrangement lasted until 1973, when the two high schools were merged. The new co-educational school – Brondesbury and Kilburn High School (BKHS) – operated until 1989, when it merged with two other secondary schools in the area to form Queens Park Community School

(QPCS).[1] This radical reduction in secondary school places in the area reflected the fall in the population of the area during these years, but also the reluctance of many local families to send their children to Brent secondary schools, which were widely seen as underperforming. School numbers started to increase again in a few years after QPCS opened, driven by improving school performance and determined campaigning by local parents. The school is now one of the most over-subscribed in Brent.

The former school buildings were sold to two Islamic establishments. Kilburn Grammar School was sold to the Islamia Primary School, a Sunni Muslim school founded by Yusuf Islam (the former singer Cat Stevens). The school now has both a mixed primary and a girls' secondary school on the site, with a boys' secondary, Brondesbury College, nearby.

Brondesbury and Kilburn was sold to the Al-Khoei Foundation, which owned the former synagogue next door. The foundation, which follows the Shi'ite Twelver tradition of Islam, opened the Al-Sadiq and Al-Zahra Schools, for boys and girls aged 8 to 16.

---

1   The other schools were South Kilburn, which was on a site on Carlton Vale that has now been redeveloped, and Aylestone Community School. The new school was established on Aylestone's grounds in Brondesbury.

30

WINDRUSH AND THE NEW COMMONWEALTH

Queen's Park was never uniformly white, Anglo-Saxon and Protestant. In 1901, there were a small number of residents born in the Caribbean, India and what is now Malaysia (although it's very difficult to tell what their ethnicity was now), Japanese residents, Irish residents and Jewish residents from the Russian and Austro–Hungarian Empires and Romania. Between the wars, that diversity increased as more Jewish people in particular moved to the area. But it was only after the Second World War ended that Queen's Park – along with the rest of the heavily industrial Willesden borough – became a significantly multi-ethnic area, attracting large numbers of people from the Caribbean, India, Pakistan, Africa and Ireland.

On 22 June 1948, the *Windrush* arrived at Tilbury Docks in Essex, the first stop in the UK for 802 passengers who gave their last country of residence as somewhere in the Caribbean, of whom 693 planned to settle in the United Kingdom. The majority of them were from Jamaica (539 people), followed by Bermuda (139), England (119), Trinidad (73), British Guiana (44) and other Caribbean countries.

The Pathé news footage covering their arrival (even though this was not in fact the first ship bringing Jamaican people from the West Indies to post-war Britain) described it in terms intended to encourage goodwill from the country that had invited, and should have welcomed, them: 'They served this country well. In Jamaica they couldn't find work. Discouraged but full of hope, they sailed for Britain, citizens of the British Empire coming to the Mother Country with good intent.' All Caribbean people had been guaranteed UK citizenship by the 1948 Nationality Act.

However, the welcome these British Caribbean citizens received was not at all what they expected, or what it should have been. Openly racist attitudes and discriminatory practice were the norm, compounded by structural racism within social, economic, educational and political systems in Britain. Just two days after the *Windrush* docked, a group of eleven Labour MPs wrote to Prime Minister Clement Attlee decrying the 'influx of coloured people'.

Many of the people who came to Britain on the *Windrush* made their way from Tilbury Docks to London, as did further people from the Caribbean who came here in the 1950s and '60s, known as the 'Windrush generation'. Overall, around 500,000 people born in Commonwealth countries arrived in Britain before 1971. Today, Brent is the local authority with the fifth highest percentage of people with Black Caribbean ethnicity, after Birmingham, Croydon, Lewisham and Lambeth.

Pearl Salmon, of Hartland Road, is one of many Jamaicans who made their home in Queen's Park and helped shape the place it is today. Pearl – a trained dressmaker – came to the UK in 1960 at the invitation of the British government, which advertised for skilled professionals from Commonwealth countries to fill labour shortages. Men and women were needed to rebuild an economy weakened by the war years, especially in sectors vital to the rebuilding of Britain such as construction, public transport, iron, steel, coal and food production, and of course to work in the brand new NHS. Caribbean women in particular found jobs as nurses and nursing aides, and in manufacturing, especially in the white goods industries that started taking off in the 1950s.

Like many African-Caribbean and South Asian people who moved to Britain in the post-war period, Pearl was deeply shocked by the hostility towards them. 'We grew up waving the British flag and singing patriotic songs,' she says. 'We thought we were coming to help the country in a time of need. My husband's two uncles served in the RAF in the war. They arrived in Britain on the day their father died. That's the kind of service our families had given this country.'

In fact, it was almost impossible for professional people from Commonwealth countries to find jobs that matched their skills in Britain in the 1950s and '60s. Many gravitated to areas with industrial economies, like Willesden, because it was easier to get jobs in factories. Pearl rejected the offer of a job in a rag-trade sweatshop and got employment in a factory in Carlton Vale, making hairdryers and electrical grills.

'Children used to follow the Windrush men and women when they first arrived and ask to see their tails. They would ask the time, because they thought we couldn't read.' The irony was, Jamaicans' literacy skills were often better than people brought up in South Kilburn; many of the women Pearl worked with needed help from her filling in their timesheets.

If employment was a challenge for Caribbean people, accommodation was even worse. 'Everywhere you went you'd see signs in sweetshops advertising places to rent with the words "No Blacks, No Irish, No Dogs",' she recalls. Others specified 'No Children'. Buying a house was the only option for many people from the Caribbean, and Pearl and her late husband Patrick bought their house in Hartland Road in 1965.

'It was a tough life in the early '60s,' she says. 'There was a lot of anger among people who'd lived through the war and didn't get the rewards they thought they deserved, and they looked for someone to take it out on.'

She remembers the neo-Nazi leader Colin Jordan 'creating havoc' in the 1960s, as well as the flare up of far-right extremism and racism in the late 1970s when the National Front came to prominence.

Pearl is made of strong stuff: her stories of her life in Queen's Park with Patrick, bringing up their three daughters, are full of the stands that she has made against injustice (often inflicted by the bureaucracy of Brent Council), and the victories she has won. When the family were unhappy with the education one of their daughters was receiving, she successfully fought the council and her daughter, a talented musician, went on to study at Trinity College of Music.

She also has fond memories of Queen's Park in the past, from the chemists on the corner of Summerfield Avenue with its multi-coloured jars ('it was run by a lovely Jewish couple – you never left without a smile on your face') to Mr Abrahams's fabric shop and the grocers that always opened precisely at nine and closed on the dot of five.

Many people from India and Pakistan also settled in Queen's Park in the 1950s and '60s, particularly from Gujarat in India. In 2001, 6 per cent of Queen's Park's residents were Hindus, the second largest faith group in the ward. Although the number of Gujarati people locally has fallen slightly in recent years, it's still a strong part of Queen's Park's demographic make-up.

Mansuhklal Hirani's parents came to Britain from Gujarat in the 1960s. His father, who arrived in 1966, was a qualified accountant in India; in the UK he worked in factories in Park Royal, retraining as a carpenter. Mansuhklal's mother joined her husband in 1968, working as a dinner lady at Salusbury School, where her son now teaches. This was a standard pattern for Gujarati people in the area in the 1960s and '70s: they would come over singly, stay with family or friends for as long as it took to get established in a job, bring their partners over, borrow money from their community to buy a property, and then remortgage to pay the loan back. It was extremely hard for immigrants from India to get a mortgage without having collateral like an existing property at that time.

The Hiranis bought a house in Carlisle Road, where Mansuhklal and his siblings grew up. Like his elder brother and sister, Mansuhklal attended Salusbury Primary School in the 1980s, and then went to Aylestone School and Queen's Park Community School (QPCS).

Others followed in the Hiranis' footsteps, including Mansuhklal's uncle and aunt, who arrived in the 1970s. There are still Gujarati families on Carlisle, Dudley, Summerfield and Montrose roads, and many others in the area.

The Hindu Temple on Willesden Lane has been one of the focal points for the community since the 1970s (Mansuhklal's father was the secretary there for many years), but the park was also a popular meeting place. 'We spent all our time in the park when I was young, with our families. Someone always had food to share, and the kids would play while the adults caught up with each other.'

Like other communities before them, many Queen's Park Gujaratis moved out of the area into larger houses as soon as they could afford to, often moving out to Wembley. When Mansuhklal's uncle and aunt moved to London, though, his father cautioned his family to stay local and buy in Queen's Park – a wise move, in terms of how property values have changed.

Although Mansuhklal has fond memories of growing up in Queen's Park, he doesn't gloss over the racism he and his family suffered. 'There was quite a lot of open racism in the late 1970s and the '80s,' he says. 'We had excrement and fireworks pushed through our letterbox, and pro-National Front graffiti painted on local walls. The people doing it didn't try to conceal who they were; in some cases we went to school with their children.' When his father tried to buy another property (that was on sale) from a neighbour, he was refused.

Mansuhklal Hirani is now a teacher and the custodian of many of the records of Salusbury School that I used to research this book; he saved them from certain destruction during renovation works at the school.

31

THE JEWISH CONTRIBUTION TO QUEEN'S PARK

Jewish people have made an immense contribution to shaping Queen's Park from the very beginning, literally as well as figuratively: Solomon Barnett, who built half the district, was Jewish, and so were many of his workforce. In 1901, there were at least ten Jewish families in the area who had emigrated from Eastern Europe, and others who were born in Britain. Although the synagogue on Chevening Road, which opened in 1905, served a wider area than just Queen's Park and Brondesbury, many of its congregation came from this area. Its first minister, the Reverend Harris Myer Lazarus (who was born in Riga), lived at 1 Windermere Avenue. His wife, Ada, was born in Lancashire, but her mother, Bertha Cohen, was also from what was then Russia.

Reporting on the construction of the synagogue shortly before it opened, the *Willesden Chronicle* noted that 'The new Synagogue ... will supply long-felt want amongst the increasing Jewish community in the locality. Jewish inhabitants of other districts of London, recognising the healthy qualities and pleasant surroundings of the North-West, have moved up into the district of late years in great numbers.' The synagogue, which followed the orthodox Jewish tradition, had a reputation as an inclusive and forward-thinking establishment.

By 1911 the number of Jewish families in Queen's Park had increased. At 2 Summerfield, for example, was the Daiches family. Samuel, age 32, came from Vilna in Russian-occupied Poland; he had a PhD and was a lecturer in Bible and Talmud studies. His wife Nora, 22, came from Hamburg and they had a daughter, Ruth, aged 3. Many local businesses were Jewish-run. One of the main arguments used by Arthur Rodges's father to try to get him out of serving in the military in the First World War was that their boot shop on Salusbury Road was the 'only English shop in the road and near locality, the other one being a Russian Jew'.

By the 1920s, so many Jewish people had settled in the area, the synagogue could not accommodate them all so an attempt was made (unsuccessfully, in the end) to open a branch of the synagogue in Cricklewood. The 1920s and '30s saw the 'second wave' of Jewish immigration to north-west London, as Jewish people who settled first in the East End moved out.

In the 1930s, a new wave of Jewish immigrants moved into the area, fleeing Nazi persecution in Germany and Austria. Many arrived on the Kindertransport, the evacuation of nearly 10,000 mostly Jewish children from Germany, Austrian, Czechoslovakia and Poland organised by a team including Hampstead resident Nicholas Winton. Those who had foster parents already arranged for them were collected at Liverpool Street Station; others were sent to holiday camps like Dovercourt Bay in Essex before being housed in Jewish hostels, from which they were fostered out.

In 1939, twenty-three Jewish children enrolled in one class alone at Salusbury School – more than half of all the pupils in that form. Half of them were living in Jewish hostels in the area. Eight were living at The Home for Jewish Refugee Children at No. 5, The Avenue, including 11-year-old Henna Zajac and her 10-year-old brother Josef. Another three were living at a hostel at 39 Christchurch Avenue, including brothers Bernard and Walter Muhlgay, aged 10 and 8. There was at least one more Jewish hostel in the area, on Willesden Lane.

Others had been already been allocated to foster parents. Nine-year-old Traute Friedman was living with Erich and Hilda Wagner and their son Otto at 20 Brondesbury Road. Erich was a Viennese painter and graphic artist. Seven-year-old Eve Tolczyner was living with Max and Frederike Freimark at 89 Brondesbury Villas. Like the Wagners, the Freimarks were also refugees – Max was a Bavarian farmer.

A few were living with their parents. Ten-year-old Else Carow was living with her mother Alice, and George Lazarus and Ascher Wagner were accompanied by both their parents.

The German–Jewish sculptor Fred Kormis (whose original name was Fritz) also came to Britain in the 1930s as a refugee, settling in West Hampstead. He became friends with Reg Freeson – the grandson of Jewish refugees from Russia – who, as leader of Brent Council, commissioned Kormis to produce a memorial to the victims of the Holocaust, which sits in Gladstone Park. Freeson later donated another of Kormis's sculptures, 'Angel Wings', to Queen's Park. It is near the entrance to the Quiet Garden.[1]

---

1   For more on Fred Kormis's life and works, see Dick Weindling's blog, http://westhampsteadlife. com/2013/08/07/the-sculptor-fred-kormis/5075

As well as being leader of Brent Council and the MP for the area for twenty-three years, Freeson (a resident of Chevening Road), was also a local councillor for Queen's Park ward from 2002 to 2006. In the post-war period, Queen's Park was a centre for left-wing Jewish activists, and the Queen's Park ward has had several Jewish councillors since it was created in 1964. They include Barbara Eaton, one of the inaugural ward councillors, Bryan Stark, Reg Freeson and Neil Nerva.

In 1991, many local Jewish people campaigned for the release of the Palestinian writer and academic Abbas Shiblak, who was detained by the British government during the first Gulf War and threatened with deportation, despite his long-term opposition to Saddam Hussain's regime in Iraq. The campaign was successful, and Abbas continues to live and teach in Britain.

The Jewish community in Queen's Park has reduced in numbers since its peak in the inter-war years. The synagogue on Chevening Road closed in the 1970s, after a serious arson attack by British Nazis in 1965 (see Chapter 11) but also due to decreasing congregation numbers. However, the community remains strong in the area, and continues to grow; the most recent census, in 2011, found that 392 people, or 2.6 per cent of Queen's Park's population, identify as Jewish – twice the average for Brent as a whole, five times the average for England and significantly up on the total at the time of the previous census in 2001.

CONCLUSION

In many ways, Queen's Park has come full circle. The speculative builders who constructed it hoped they were building houses that would attract respectable, industrious, law-abiding families. It didn't quite happen like that: from the outset, Queen's Park has been a magnet for politically engaged, obstreperous people, happy to throw a metal weight through the Home Secretary's window and accept the consequences if the cause justified it.

However, the houses that Solomon Barnett and his contemporaries built are now mostly single-family homes, lovingly cared for by their owners and tenants. And I have no doubt that George Higgs would be thrilled to see the park, which he fought so hard for, being so well used and so well looked after (although I bet he'd still be arguing it should be bigger).

In the 1940s and '50s the area declined, and came close to being flattened and replaced by tower blocks. Disaster was averted by passionate, bloody-minded locals like MP Reg Freeson, and local people have been standing up for the community ever since.

Queen's Park today is often described as 'affluent'. That's by no means universal, any more than it was true to say that it was 'all bedsits' in the 1960s and '70s; the reality is of course more complex, nuanced and diverse than that. What is clear though is that people today in Queen's Park know where they live and are proud of their area and the vibrant, culturally thriving, cohesive community it has become.

SELECT
BIBLIOGRAPHY

Barres-Baker, MC, 'Our Belgian Guests: Refugees in Brent 1914–19', *Local History* magazine, July–August 2007.

Brock, Richard E, *A History of the Kilburn Grammar School, 1897–1967*. (RE Brock, 1967)

City of London Corporation, 'A History of Queen's Park', www.yumpu.com/en/document/view/11961755/a-history-of-queens-park-the-city-of-london-corporation

Cummins (ed.), Mark, Official Souvenir Brochure of the Queen's Park Centenary, QPARA 1987.

Colloms, Marianne, and Weindling, Dick, 'The Sculptor Fred Kormis', http://westhamp-steadlife.com/2013/08/07/the-sculptor-fred-kormis/5075

Kirby, Dick, *Scotland Yard's Gangbuster: Bert Wickstead's Most Celebrated Cases*, Pen and Sword True Crime, 2018

Lazarus, Dayan Harris, History of Brondesbury Synagogue, https://jewishmiscellanies.com/2020/04/27/brondesbury-synagogue-semi-jubilee-celebration-record-compiled-by-dayan-harris-lazarus-1930

McDonald, Erica, and Smith, David, *Artizans and Avenues: A History of the Queen's Park Estate*. City of Westminster Libraries, 1990

Risbridger, JAH, and Thomas, DW, Fifty Years of School Life, From 1898 to 1948, https://kgsoba.org.uk/archive

Snow, Len, *Willesden Past*, Philimore, 1994.

Valentine, Kenneth J, *Willesden at War Vol. 1: The Impact on the Community*, KJ Valentine, 1994.

Wadsworth, Cliff, Cinemas and Theatres of Willesden, Willesden Historical Society, 2000.

APPENDIX:
HOW THE STREETS OF QUEEN'S PARK GOT THEIR NAMES (WHERE KNOWN)

Brondesbury Road	After the manor of Brondesbury
Brondesbury Villas	Ditto
Chamberlayne Road	After the manor of Chamberlain Wood
Chevening Road	After the estate in Kent, home of Lord Stanhope, chair of the Ecclesiastical Commissioners
Creighton Road	After the Bishop of London, Mandell Creighton, who dedicated Kilburn Grammar School. Old Boys of Kilburn Grammar are known as Old Creightonians. Originally called Sinclair Road after the Dean of London
Donaldson Road	After John Donaldson, Solomon Barnett's solicitor[1]
Hartland Road	After Hartland in Devon
Harvist Road	After Edward Harvist. Originally called Mortimer Road
Honiton Road	After Honiton in Devon

1   Dewe and Sansom, *Brent Street Names*, London Borough of Brent Library Service, 1975.

Kempe Road	After John Edward Kempe, prebendary of St Paul's[1]
Keslake Road	After a local builder called Thomas Keslake[2]
Kimberley Road	After the Seige of Kimberley during the Boer War
Lonsdale Road	Probably after the fifth Earl of Lonsdale, who introduced the rules of modern boxing
Lynton Road	After Lynton in Devon
Milman Road	After Henry Hart Milman (1791–1868), poet, historian and Dean of St Paul's Cathedral
Peploe Road	After Hanmer Webb-Peploe, prebendary of St Paul's
Salusbury Road	After the Salusbury family, owners of Brondesbury Manor
St Laurence's Close	After St Laurence's Church, which stood on the site
Sinclair Road	The original name of Creighton Road. Named after William MacDonald Sinclair, Archdeacon of London (1850–1917)
Tiverton Road	After Tiverton in Devon
Victoria Road	After the Victoria Rifle Corps, whose shooting range occupied the land behind Kilburn Square

1 Ibid.
2 Ibid.

ABOUT THE AUTHOR

Steve Crabb is an author, consultant and non-executive director, and a former award-winning journalist. His life-long love of history led him to study the subject at Oxford University, where he gained a first-class degree and met his wife, Natasha Finlayson (OBE). They have lived in Queen's Park since the 1990s; their children, Ellie and Rhydian, grew up there, as did their whippet, Xander. Steve is currently serving his second term representing Queen's Park as a councillor.

INDEX